Isabelle Harbrecht

Entering Society

Isabelle Harbrecht

Entering Society

The Adolescence, Identity and Development
of Vocational Education Students in Shanghai

Würzburg
University Press

Dissertation, Julius-Maximilians-Universität Würzburg
Philosophische Fakultät, 2018
Gutachter: Prof. Dr. Björn Alpermann, Prof. Dr. Doris Fischer

Impressum

Julius-Maximilians-Universität Würzburg
Würzburg University Press
Universitätsbibliothek Würzburg
Am Hubland
D-97074 Würzburg
www.wup.uni-wuerzburg.de

© 2019 Würzburg University Press
Print on Demand

Coverdesign: Jule Petzold
Foto: Lu Kai

ISBN: 978-3-95826-096-2 (print)
ISBN: 978-3-95826-097-9 (online)
URN: urn:nbn:de:bvb:20-opus-168626

Preface

Against the rapid development of China's economy, its educational system is also increasingly attracting international attention – it has inspired both awe and criticism. For instance, the country has seen a tremendous increase in the number of students engaged in higher education since around the start of this century. Enrolment in undergraduate and graduate programs of regular higher education institutions stands at 29 million in 2016, compared to just 3.2 million in 1999 – a nine-fold rise. When China first participated in the Programme for International Student Assessment (PISA) organized by the OECD (Organisation for Economic Co-operation and Development) its top scores in science, mathematics and reading abilities of 15-year-olds generated headlines. Part of that surprise was unjustified since only students from China's most advanced metropolis, Shanghai, participated who are hardly representative for the whole country. As the scope was widened to also include Beijing, Jiangsu and Guangdong, China's PISA ranking dropped accordingly. But in 2015 it still outperformed Germany in science and mathematics (the latter by a large margin) and was only slightly behind in reading. This makes it hard to dismiss China's educational achievements.

However, at the same time reports on these developments are also quick to point out that they are gained at great personal and social costs: The higher education expansion has devalued college degrees so that these are no longer seen as an entry ticket into the expanding middle classes anymore. They are a necessary but far from sufficient condition to climb the social ladder. Students at Chinese schools scramble even harder to score high on the national college entrance exams (gaokao) in order to get into elite universities that still offer the best chances of social advancement. Yet those who fail to get into higher education, or even worse, are sorted out already at the level of senior middle school entrance exams (zhongkao) are seen as losers in the intensified educational arms race. For them, the only option for further educational advancement in an increasingly knowledge-based economy is vocational education. In fact, this need not be a bad choice, since many experts argue that China's economy will need better-trained workers if the country is to succeed in shifting its development model from low-cost manufacturing to higher value-added business activities. Therefore, Chinese local governments have opened more vocational schools and enrolment in secondary vocational schools rose from five million in 1999 to 16 million in 2016. But despite all efforts to raise the standing of this form of education, mainstream public opinion still accords it a low prestige. So, students entering this form of schooling generally face a sort of social stigma.

Isabelle Harbrecht's study is devoted to this particular group of Chinese students. In a growing field of research on China's educational system, this is the first study to use an innovative mixed-methods approach and panel design to follow cohorts of students throughout their educational career at vocational schools. Through her unique data Harbrecht produces some surprising insights into the social worlds of vocational schools, in particular from the perspective of the students themselves. For example, we learn that the label of "losers" in the educational rat race is oversimplified and does not adequately express their own sense of self-worth. Moreover, she traces the trajectories of student attitudes throughout the process of vocational education and demonstrates how these change over time – a key contribution going beyond earlier works on the subject.

The author not only uses cutting-edge methodologies, but also relevant sociological theories to analyze her findings, while also contextualizing them by drawing on empirical studies on China and beyond conducted by other scholars. This makes the book a rewarding read not only for those interested in Chinese education or even the China specialist. It provides a lens to study Chinese society more broadly through the specific prism of vocational education. This should be of interest for sociologists as well as education specialists who want to see whether their own models of explanation hold in a quite different society such as the Chinese one.

Björn Alpermann
Würzburg, November 2018

For the vocational students,
who shared their thoughts and dreams with me,

and

for Bernhard and Doris Harbrecht, and Madeleine Marx-Bentley,
whose support allowed me to share students' thoughts and dreams
with you.

I also want to express my deepest gratitude to Ms. J., Ms. L., Ms. Y. and Mr. Z. for their unconditional trust throughout the years of my research, and to all the teachers who allowed me into their classrooms, assisted me with my surveys and shared their valuable opinions and experiences with me, and lastly to Mr. K. who played a vital role in the beginning of this project and helped me starting my research.

Table of Contents

List of Abbreviations

CCP	Chinese Communist Party
EI	Engineering Index
GDP	Gross Domestic Product
IQ	Intelligence Quotient
KFC	Kentucky Fried Chicken
MOE	Ministry of Education
MOHRSS	Ministry of Human Resources and Social Securities
OECD	Organisation for Economic Co-operation and Development
PISA	Programme for International Student Assessment
RMB	Renminbi
UK	United Kingdom
USA	United States of America

List of Tables

7 Experiencing Work

8 Values and Responsibility

1 Introduction

Rapid economic development, the abolition of the 'iron rice bowl' and a transition towards a competition based market economy are three of the factors which have caused profound changes not only in the Chinese economy but also in Chinese society. Before labour market reforms in the 1990s, the individual in urban China was assigned a work unit (*danwei* 单位) in which accommodation and food was provided along with guaranteed income. Today, Chinese citizens can no longer rely on the state and instead have become responsible for their own livelihood. Work, housing and retirement, which used to be a given for the older generations, need to be attained through the individuals' own efforts. This has led to heightened rivalry for jobs, and academic credentials have become an important asset in the labour market (Hanser 2002a, 2002b). The birth-control policy which drastically reduced the number of children born since the early 1980s has also increased the pressure many young Chinese feel to succeed. Parents rely on their children for old-age support and therefore invest all their resources in their children's education to make sure they enter the competitive Chinese labour market in a good position. In urban areas, where the birth-control policy was effectively a one-child policy, all hopes and expectations are placed on the one offspring (Fong 2004).

With the end of the *danwei* era, the Chinese individual has been disembedded from traditional institutions. Young Chinese still face several constraints which are beyond their control, but they also seem to have more freedom than their parents or grandparents had, and the choices to shape their futures. Their situation has come to resemble what Ulrich Beck (1986) describes in his theory of individualization in second modernity – a theory which he himself suggested could be adapted from its original basis in liberal democracies to appropriately explain social phenomena in modern China (Beck, Grande 2010). Through analyzing the empirical data on which the present study is based, it can be seen that the general assumptions of Beck's individualization thesis are indeed an adequate framework for explaining vocational education students' realities in 21st century Shanghai.

The rising importance and popularity of university degrees have led to so-called 'diploma inflation', meaning that university degrees have become increasingly common and can no longer guarantee a stable, well-paid job with good working conditions. Instead, even poorly paid jobs with simple tasks might require a tertiary education. Higher education is therefore not just a sufficient but also a necessary condition for good employment (Liu 2008a). The flipside of this rapid expansion of academic education in recent years is a short-age of skilled workers. Despite the government's efforts to strengthen vocation-al education, it is still considered a bad choice and its students are stigmatized as 'dumb' and 'difficult' (Hansen, Woronov 2013). Via an exam and a quota system, the government channels just fewer than 50% of all students entering upper secondary education into vocational schools. This measure enforces the general opinion that only poor performing students enter vocational education. On top of that, this is a one-way street. Once students have left academic educa-tion, they cannot return. If they want a tertiary education degree, they need to pass another exam and then can only enroll in vocational courses. Due to these policies, a considerable proportion of each generation is thus forced to 'fail' in the academic school system and has to learn to live with the consequences.

Therefore, vocational education needs to satisfy the educational desires of millions of young Chinese and their parents. It needs to provide young people with skills which enable them to make a living for themselves and their families because for them, vocational education has become the only educational path left open. Hence, the significance of this education in regard to poverty preven-tion and the promotion of social stability cannot be overestimated.

In addition, vocational education is an important factor when it comes to China's economic development and international competitiveness. Skilled workers are needed to modernize industrial production and to improve the quality of products 'Made in China' (Zhang 2013a; Ministry of Education, Min-istry of Development and Reform, Ministry of Finance, Ministry of Human Resources and Social Securities, Ministry of Agriculture, State Council Depart-ment for Aid-the-poor 2014).

When it comes to social research in China, common subjects explored are migrants, members of a new urban middle class, singletons, university students, and similar subjects. Although they are by no means a negligible minority, vocational education students have very rarely been the focus of sociological studies and, if they are, scholars have usually turned to rural schools or sub-standard schools in urban areas. Contrary to this, the present study focuses on very good vocational schools in Shanghai, where the question arises whether the belief that vocational education equals failure is as uncontested as it seems. Migrant workers' children in Shanghai might consider it as a success as it would raise their education level above their parents', let them experience better edu-cation quality compared to their peers in the provinces, and lead to easy em-ployment. Similarly, Shanghainese parents with nine years of schooling or fewer might be content if their children graduate from upper secondary level with a technical degree which immediately makes their children more qualified than the parents have ever been.

As a result, the present study focuses on students' attitudes towards their education and how these attitudes change throughout their years in vocational education. Drawing on Morrissey (2016: 8–9), attitudes are understood as a construct consisting of feelings, beliefs and behaviors. Consequently, the study at hand presents a comprehensive analysis of students' lives, personalities, beliefs, values and feelings in relation to vocational education. It specifically highlights how students manage their stigma after entering their new, undesirable schools. Central questions are: What kinds of identities do they develop? What motivates them? What are the values they internalize? The study follows students when they enter society and asks how they see themselves as vocational education students in Chinese society. Do they see themselves as winners – sought after in the labour market – or losers – who dropped out of the academic education system? Finally, the present study draws attention to how individualization creates an environment in which students feel responsible for their own future, and perceive chances and opportunities while navigating risks. It shows if and how vocational education enables them to survive in society.

This study is based on quantitative and qualitative data collected over three years in two of Shanghai's key vocational schools. A panel design and mixed method approach allow an in-depth insight into students' worlds. Semi-structured interviews have been conducted with 21 electrical engineering students from different cohorts. Each student has been interviewed up to three times. In addition, all first and third year students in both schools filled in questionnaires and first year students filled in a follow-up questionnaire after they had entered their second year in vocational school.

1.1 Outline of the Thesis

Chapters Two to Four belong to the first part of the thesis, which provides important background information, while the second part, Chapter Five to Nine, is based on the empirical data and contributes to the existing body of research. Chapter Ten provides a final discussion and summary of the research results.

Chapter Two gives an overview of existing related studies and literature, and subsequently introduces the three most important theoretical frameworks of this thesis. Namely, these are the above mentioned theory of individualization and, closely connected, the theory of risk society, both of which have been put forward by Ulrich Beck, as well as Anthony Giddens, Zygmunt Bauman and others. The analysis of students' identities and their stigma management is based on Erwin Goffman's ideas about the stigmatized individual. Chapter Two

Section Two introduces Goffman's theory and gives a brief overview of how definitions of identity have changed, while pointing out underlying similarities and putting Goffman's oeuvre into perspective. The last part of the chapter summarizes Edward Deci and Richard Ryan's conclusions on motivation formation which are based on numerous empirical studies in different settings.

Chapter Three introduces the Chinese education system and explains culturally specific characteristics such as high competition and the link of a person's worth to their academic performance. The second part of this chapter introduces the vocational system and its deficits, which are mutually dependent and lead to a vicious cycle causing and reinforcing the deeply rooted bad reputation of vocational education in Chinese society. Finally, attention is drawn to Shanghai as the research setting because it is important to acknowledge that Shanghai is a special case in China, which has significant implications for the research results. Looking at key vocational schools in Shanghai means looking at best practice models which might be transferred to other provinces in the future. It also means that deficits existing in these schools would also exist and probably be more severe in other places.

Chapter Four describes the research process and the empirical data which consists of questionnaires, interviews with students, teachers and tutors, as well as classroom observations and factory visits.

The main part of the study is divided into five chapters all based on the empirical data and each concerning a different aspect of students' lives. The chapters proceed from the environment, i.e. family background and social circles, through students' opinions on vocational education and their experiences with work and finishes with students' inner perspectives, highlighting their value systems and providing insights into their identities and self-perceptions.

Chapter Five, the first empirical chapter, portrays students' families pointing out differences and similarities between Shanghainese and migrant parents. While parents' education level is generally low, migrants have fewer years of schooling compared to Shanghainese. Some students have siblings and the overwhelming majority lives in nuclear families. In school, most students are able to make friends with their peers and also have what they characterize as 'good relationships' with their teachers.

Some of the central research questions, such as students' opinions on vocational education and their changes over time, will be discussed in Chapter Six. Combining the results of questionnaires and interviews, common attitudes as well as exceptions to these are elaborated. It becomes clear that vocational education was not a free choice for the majority of students but their experiences are nonetheless positive once they enter their new schools. Subsequently, students form more critical and differentiated opinions throughout their education.

Chapter Seven follows students into the labour market. During their internships, which are part of vocational education, students have their first experiences with work. Often these lead to more negative attitudes towards vocational education and an adjustment of future plans. The second part of the chapter focusses on graduated students and their employment situation. It becomes clear that finding a job is not difficult but finding what students consider a 'good' job is a much bigger challenge. Also, working in a training-related field is not a priority for the students. Hence, vocational education cannot, or only to a limited degree, satisfy the economy's need for skilled workers.

In Chapter Eight the thesis turns to students' value systems which are characterized by a mix of collective/family-related and individualistic/independence-focused values. The argument of the present study is that these are not antagonistic but functionally dependent: individualistic values support overarching collective ones. This chapter subsequently elaborates how students have a strong sense of responsibility which relates directly to Beck's individualization thesis.

Chapter Nine gives a detailed insight into students' self-assessments and thereby answers several of the core research questions. The chapter describes their personal development and analyzes their motivation. A brief subsection highlights the differences between genders and portrays the difficulties female students face in a technical training course. Later, students voice their opinions on their generation and their ideas of growing up. Finally, their social identities and ways of dealing with their stigma are evaluated. The last part of this chapter lets students themselves answer the question of whether they are winners or losers in Chinese society.

Last, Chapter Ten discusses and summarizes the results of the empirical chapters and thereby answers the question of whether vocational education succeeds in providing its students with the skills necessary to compete in the Chinese labour market and to make a living in an individualized Chinese society.

2 State of Research and Theoretical Framework

2.1 Related Studies and Literature

Several empirical studies in Germany proved the long-lasting effect of schools, and failure in school, on a person's biography (Kramer 2014: 428). Since 1954, attitudes, expectations and the values of youth are collected through the Shell Youth Studies. Roughly every four years a representative sample of German youth aged between 12 and 25 provide the data. Social scientist Klaus Hurrelmann has been part of the organizing team since 2002. His focus is the influence of school on the socialization of youth (Hurrelmann, Neubauer 1986). As early as the 1980s he succeeded in proving with a longitudinal study the influence of failure in school on students' lives and attitudes. Students project poor performance in school on themselves and lose their self-esteem (Kramer 2014: 425–426).

In the 1990s, Dieter Nittel (1992) employed qualitative interviews in order to gain insights into how schools influence students' identities. He pointed out that the first teacher has an important role, but also that schools already influence students before enrolment by creating certain expectations. Nittel developed his theories with the concept of an adaptation trajectory (*Anpassungsverlaufskurve*) and a failure trajectory (*Schulversagensverlaufskurve*), and he, as well as Hurrelmann, pointed out that failure in school has a long-lasting negative effect on students' self-concepts, interests and feelings of belonging.

Nittel focused on the *Gymnasium*, the high school level which ends with the *Abitur* exam which allows students to enter a university in Germany. Ulrike Schaupp (2014), on the other hand, looked at students who had already dropped out of this preferred school form and had to attend a high school level which does not qualify for university. She pointed out that after what she termed 'negative selection' students underwent a positive development as their grades improved and so did their self-esteem. This raises the question of whether Schaupp's findings are valid in China as well, and if students who had to enter a vocational school due to poor results in the lower middle school experience a similar positive development and gain self-esteem despite being looked down on by society.

Carsten Rohlfs (2011) used a longitudinal study design to research schools in disadvantaged areas in the city of Bremen, along with their students' attitudes towards education. He concluded that students' performances in school not only influenced their self-esteem but also their attitudes towards education

– which in return influenced their later performances in school. He proved that positive attitudes towards education can be fostered by giving students some autonomy and a feeling of self-effectiveness, as well as by supporting their feeling of belonging in their social environment. Additionally, teachers can support students' positive attitudes by taking care of their needs and interests (Rohlfs 2011: 342–348).

Since the influence of school and failure in school are undisputed, these kinds of studies are common also in other countries. Differently from Germany, where sociologists and education experts focus on this matter, in China we mainly find scholars in the field of Chinese Studies doing education and society related research. With its bad reputation, vocational education is the most suitable educational form when analyzing students' handling of failure in school and the resulting long-lasting effects.

In Germany, the most common methods employed in this field of study are quantitative. Studies are designed to be representative of all of Germany. In China, on the other hand, it is much more complicated to administer broad quantitative studies due to political restrictions. At the same time, huge regional differences make it difficult, if not impossible, to design a quantitative study which is able to capture all of China. As a result, qualitative studies which rely mainly on interviews with students, teachers and parents are the most common method. The qualitative datasets are sometimes complemented with questionnaires. These studies commonly provide a portrait of the situation for a certain region in China.

T.E. Woronov is an urban anthropologist who conducted several studies in vocational education in an urban environment in China. Most notably are two related studies she published in 2011 and 2015 drawing on data she gathered during a year-long field study in Nanjing between 2007 and 2008. Woronov argues that vocational education graduates form a new class in urban China's society between the new middle-class and uneducated migrant workers. Woronov is one of the few scientists who researches how vocational education students deal with their label as 'failures'. Comparing her work with the results of the present study allows us to see the similarities and the differences between vocational education students in poor schools in a second-tier city and top schools in a first-tier city. Since Woronov did not compare different age groups in her study and was not able to do a quantitative survey or analyze real panel data, the development and changes of attitudes among the students, which the present study was able to bring to the fore, will add further valuable insights to Woronov's findings.

Mette Halskov Hansen has done numerous anthropological studies in rural China, including provinces of Zhejiang, Fujian, and Yunnan. One of her focuses is the growing individualization in China and its consequences for the individual and society as a whole. Hansen found that many of her subjects share a strong sense of responsibility concerning their lives and interpreted this with reference to Ulrich Beck as a proof of individualization within Chinese society (Hansen, Svarverud 2010; Hansen 2015). Taking rural middle schools as an example, Hansen elaborated how socialist values are taught and how, at the same time, individualism develops within China's younger generation (Hansen 2013a: 15, 2012b: 135). Hansen and Woronov (2013) conducted a study on vocational education in urban and rural areas in Nanjing. After several weeks in the field, they concluded that despite the expansion of vocational education, the bad reputation persists and influences teachers, students and parents. In a separate publication, Hansen (2013) also observed that qualified teachers and good students are drawn to good schools, leaving poor students in substandard schools and thereby cementing a status quo of student performance and school quality.

Between 2008 and 2011, Ling Minhua (2015) conducted several months of empirical research with a focus on migrant students in vocational schools in Shanghai. She described the consequences students are facing when they have to leave the academic education system and how the bad reputation of vocational education stigmatizes the students. Like the present study, Ling found that the differences between migrants and local students in these schools are minimal because they have similar financial backgrounds and living environments. She also found that the state policies which channel certain students into vocational schools result in a reproduction of society – a conclusion which is again affirmed by the results of the present study.

Amy Hanser (2002) and Lisa Hoffman (2008) focus on the Chinese labour market and how young job seekers are coping with the recent changes. Both scientists analyze techniques which are commonly used by young people to secure jobs, and both found that young people are becoming increasingly enterprising, meaning that they seek self-development through their work. Hoffman introduced the idea of 'patriotic professionals' to describe how young people seek jobs which help them improve while also being concerned with the development of the nation. With this notion she argued against Stanley Rosen (2004) who proclaimed the "victory of materialism" and wrote that money has become the most important factor of success in every aspect of life, including employment. Hanser maintained that *guanxi* (关系), personal relationships, are still relevant, especially for people with a low education level, when competing for jobs. Several other authors have discussed the relevance of *guanxi* in modern China, most of them relying on their own qualitative fieldwork. These are

Bian Yanjie (2002), Scott Wilson (2002), Reza Hasmath (2011), and Millissa F.Y. Cheung, et al. (2009), to name a few.

Yunxiang Yan (2009, 2010b, 2011) conducts anthropological studies in North-Eastern China. In several of his publications he focuses on the rise of the individual especially within the younger generation in China. Yan argues that the individualization processes in China are substantially different from the same in the west because of Party control. Chinese individualization is limited to economic and private lives but does not include political rights or a liberal democracy. As Yan regularly concludes: China demonstrates pre-modern, modern and post-modern conditions at the same time. This leads to a moral crisis which includes diminishing social trust, cynicism and the changing of collective to individual values.

Andrew Kipnis (2001, 2011a, 2011b, 2012) is another anthropologist worth mentioning. He gathers his data in Shandong province. Several of his publications focus on education in China and the new so-called education for quality (*suzhi jiaoyu* 素质教育). Kipnis (1997, 2002) also researched the use of *guanxi* – personal relationships – in modern China and, its related customs, such as gift giving.

Vanessa Fong (2004, 2007) focusses on the generation of children born without siblings during the 1980s. Since 1992, based on a longitudinal design, she followed a group of only-children and their families, and discussed their value systems, their goals, their consumption patterns, their attitudes towards filial piety, and other relevant topics.

Lin Yi (2005, 2007) is concerned with education opportunities for ethnic minorities. He shows in his work how the political discourses on minorities and *suzhi* influence minority children's identities and ultimately lead to a reproduction of society.

Scott Rozelle and Shi Yaojiang have done several studies with bigger research teams focusing on education in rural areas, unequal education opportunities for poor rural students and the effects of nutrition on educational attainment (Wang et al. 2011; Yue et al. 2016). Noteworthy in relation to the present study is the mixed-methods analysis on reasons for the high drop-out rates in rural secondary schools. Using statistical data as well as data from interviews, the authors found that drop-out rates in rural vocational schools were especially high because the education quality was deemed so inferior that it was not considered worth the time. There were also considerable short-term benefits of dropping out: an unskilled worker can earn in one month more than the annual per capita income in poor rural areas according to a third-party study quoted in the publication (Shi et al. 2015).

Most of the above-mentioned authors conduct their research in the field of anthropology and mainly or exclusively employ qualitative methods. Few of them use real panel data for their research and, apart from Scott and Rozelle, none has combined a real panel with qualitative and quantitative data. Also, unless they focus on migrants, most scholars choose to conduct their research not in first-tier cities but in urban or rural environments of other more 'average' or poor places. Therefore, the present study on vocational education students not only focuses on a less-seen subject but it is also unique due to its location and its study design. By providing an in-depth view of the process of growing-up for vocational education students in Shanghai, the present study adds to the existing body of studies on Chinese society and youth in particular, as well as to the studies concerning the question of school influence on students' lives and identities.

When it comes to studies published in the Chinese language, only very few turned out to be relevant as resources. Most studies are based on quantitative research. Tan Lilian et al. (2007) conducted a study on students' personalities in a vocational school in Guangxi, and concluded that close to half (48.12%) of the 929 participating students had 'difficult personalities' – meaning they lacked self-esteem, the ability to learn and understand, or communication skills. Zhang Qingxia et al. (2007) did another survey on the psychological wellbeing of 362 students in a vocational school in Qingdao. The results showed that male students experience more pressure compared to female students, and students in the countryside are disadvantaged compared to urban students because they have fewer material resources and less family support, which results in poor psychological wellbeing and poor communication skills. Tang Tuhong et al. (2013) wrote about the values and characteristics of the so-called 1990s Generation which is supposed to be increasingly materialistic and influenced by media. Yang Weili (2013) gave an overview of youth research in China and pointed out that research has been overly focused on theory and guided by politics instead of problems. Current youth research neglects migrants, peasants and working youth, according to Yang. The Ministry of Education and the Shanghai Education Commission regularly publish articles about employment rates, income, field of employment and mutual satisfaction of employers and employees, which contain official statistics (Ministry of Education 2016; Shanghai Education Commission 2015). Overall, Chinese studies often focus on representativeness and quantitative information.

Filial piety is an important concept which is also a common topic for Chinese social scientists. Jiang Xia and Tang Peng (2007) discussed what they experience as a decline of filial piety in Chinese youth, and Kong Runnian (2012) gave a brief overview of the history of filial piety. English language publications are by the above-mentioned Vanessa Fong, Yunxiang Yan, and Andrew Kipnis, as well as by Liu Fengshu (2008b), Cheung Chau-Kiu et al. (2009), H.J. Zhan et al. (2008), and Hu Yang and Jacqueline Scott (2016). In Chapter Eight the on-going debate about the continuing or diminishing importance of filial values among the younger generations will be outlined in further detail, and the present study proposes a new framework of values with filial piety at the core.

Aris Chan (2009) wrote about children of migrant workers in the country-side as well as in cities, and the education-related difficulties they encounter. The All-China Women's Federation (2013) has done research on the same issue, and numerous authors have conducted empirical studies on migrant's lives in Chinese cities, e.g. Zhang (2002), Lan (2014), Goodburn (2015), Griffiths (2010) and Sun (2008). Since roughly half of the students in the sample are not local Shanghainese, the present study adds new insights to this body of publications as well.

Finally, for more information on the vocational education system, see the Chinese publication by Xu Xiaozhou (2009); and Schulte (2012, 2013), Wang (2010) and UNESCO-UNEVOC (2013) for English language publications.

2.2 Risk Society and Individualization

In reaction to substantial changes in modern German society triggered by tech-nological development, globalization and new threats such as environmental pollution and terror, Ulrich Beck (1986, 1994) developed his theories of risk society and individualization as parts of his theory of second modernity in or-der to explain and understand the new developments. People in second moder-nity – which has also been labeled late or reflexive – face different risks which are unevenly spread and perceived differently. Some risks occur globally such as climate change or contagious diseases, while others are restricted to certain nations or locations and often caused by politics and/or unbalanced develop-ment such as corruption, pollution or infrastructure-related accidents (Han, Shim 2010: 471). In consequence, some locations face higher risks than others. Although occurring risks harm all people in the same way, the means to escape these risks depend on available resources, like access to education, financial assets, or mobility. Therefore, social differences are still relevant in second mo-dernity but the social classes cease to be the defining feature of a society (Beck 1986: 31–35). Biographies are no longer pre-defined and standardized. Children do not necessarily pick up their parents' occupation but choose one by them-selves. People often have to change occupation during their lives and, in consequence, professions lose their identity-creating feature. This is what Beck calls individualization: the breaking down of existing social structures, loss of stability and traditional securities, and new control over the course of life (Beck 1986: 206–207). Success and failure are attributed to the individual and individuals need to make their own life choices. Whereas in the past, unemployment, for example, was usually experienced by whole groups of workers together, nowadays it has become a risk which threatens individuals throughout their working lives. Everybody can become unemployed at any time during their career and it is up to the skilled individual to avoid it (Beck 1986: 143–151). This leads to a heightened sense of responsibility and with that, new risks of psychological distress, low self-esteem, or sense of failure occur. Individualization does not mean that each life is becoming individual and unique, but it means that the individual constantly needs to make choices and actively create their own biography. Ronald Hitzler described this new way of living as 'do-it-yourself biography' (*Bastelbiographie*) (Beck-Gernsheim 1994: 120; Hitzler, Honer 1994: 311). Yet throughout his works, Beck stressed the fact that individualization and choice cannot be misunderstood as freedom. Not every choice is a desired one, the individual is exposed to unavoidable risks and lives with institutional, economic and personal restrictions (Beck 1986: 211; Beck, Beck-Gernsheim 1993: 181–182).

Beck also elaborated the consequences for the education system. Due to technological advancement, more time is spent in school – which heightens the relevance of school as an influential factor in the individual's life – and with the loss of set biographies and class stratification, competition arises and education becomes the most relevant factor for career advancement (Beck 1994: 47–48). Higher education degrees are sought after and become more widely spread until they lose the power to guarantee good employment and instead become a necessity for many positions which used to be open to lower qualified people (Beck 1986: 242–246).

Anthony Giddens expressed in his own holistic theory on modern society, some similar views with Beck. He agreed that people are living in a risk society where nothing is predestined (Giddens 1991: 28) and where the individual is constantly forced to make choices (Giddens 1991: 80–81). Crises appear frequently in second modernity, whenever life-goal-related activities suddenly become inadequate. This adds to existing uncertainties (Giddens 1991: 184–185). Old authorities such as family, community, etc. have disappeared. The individual is disembedded (Giddens 1991: 194–196). While people used to live in small communities, they nowadays have to deal with the outside world from an early age when children are handed over to institutional care (Giddens 1991: 30, 33). In order to be able to live surrounded by risk, the individual needs to have set routines and basic trust, which is developed during childhood (Giddens 1991: 38–40). Choosing a traditional lifestyle and/or relying on religion can help making decisions or finding answers to uncertainties (Giddens 1991: 142). Although Beck does not mention the option of returning to tradition, Giddens and Beck agree in principle: the individuals are forced to work on their own biographies (Furlong, Cartmel 1997: 8).

Nicolas Rose is another sociologist who is concerned with how people organize and live their lives in post-modern societies. Following Michel Foucault's approach on governmentality – the conduct of conduct – he described the appearance of an enterprising self. In modern liberal democracies, the state retreats from private lives and individuals are urged to become responsible and make a living by themselves (Rose 1992: 149). Every aspect of life – such as work, relationships or living situation – becomes a project which needs to be drafted, worked on and completed successfully. The enterprising self is a striving individual who seeks to actively shape their future (Rose 1992: 146).

The similarities between individualization in second modernity and the enterprising self under neoliberal governmentality are that human beings are forced to become active and work on themselves in order to reach their own self-defined goals in life, and both theories have been developed for Western, democratic societies. However, there is also a substantial difference as Rose (1996: 130, 134) pointed out. According to him, the emergence of an enterprising self is caused by a specific mode of government, in which free individuals are governed in a way which will make them act and live in the way desired and defined by the authorities. In contrast, the development of risk society and individualization as described by Beck and Giddens is caused by historical events such as development of new technologies, demographic changes, etc. Rose, however considered it unlikely that these changes could have such a profound influence on how human beings live their lives. Yet, Beck suggested that individualization in the Chinese case is simultaneously forced and restricted by the state, who pushes economic growth by requiring people to become active, striving individuals while at the same time curbing individual rights (Beck, Beck-Gernsheim 2010a: 203–205). With this adjustment of the original individualization theory a bridge towards Rose's postulate has been created: while individualization in China still depends on technological, demographical and other developments, it is ultimately controlled by the state – which employs neoliberal and socialist modes of government, which themselves fall under the catch-all phrase 'socialism with Chinese characteristics' (Liu 2008a: 196). Therefore, the present study will analyze the emergence of an 'enterprising self' as a result of government induced individualization in China.

As has just been pointed out: Beck, Rose and other authors have developed the idea of a second modernity and all the related consequences for Western societies, meaning liberal democracies, and the issue about the transferability of these concepts to other, non-Western societies, is widely debated. Jack Barbalet (2016) and Yunxiang Yan (2010b) warned against transferring Beck's theories directly to China because sociohistorical and political backgrounds are too different and the party state is still the dominating authority regulating all aspects of life in China. What appears to be individualistic might in fact be collectivistic, wrote Barbalet, drawing on the example of migrant workers in cities who face many risks of an individualized society and appear to be free of traditional social structures while in fact being deeply rooted in their families for whom they also care financially (Barbalet 2016: 16, 19–20). Nonetheless, these authors still agree with other authors such as Hansen (2010) and Alpermann (2011) that the theories of risk society and individualization can be, when applied in a differentiated way, very valuable approaches to gain deeper insights into certain aspects of Chinese society.

Beck himself suggested that his theory is not only applicable for Western societies. Instead, the development of second modernity in Europe is just one specific example of how individualization can appear (Beck, Beck-Gernsheim 2010b: xiii; Beck, Grande 2010: 415–416). According to him, China is taking its own path to individualization (Beck, Beck-Gernsheim 2002: 1). With the ongoing opening reforms which have led to rapid development since the end of the 1970s and changes towards a market economy, the argument that currently in China modernity and second modernity overlap has been brought forward (Yan 2010b: 510; Han, Shim 2010: 467). With the de-collectivization and the privatization of economy, housing and medical care, people are no longer assigned jobs and apartments. Instead they have to compete in an unregulated labour market and make their own living. University degrees can no longer guarantee good employment but are often required even for simple jobs, and the Chinese state does no longer shoulder the responsibility for its people. Instead young Chinese people are told that they have to be self-responsible. Rural-urban and inter-city migration has become possible and therefore mobility is more and more required of job-seekers. Also, with the liberalization of the marriage law and new living arrangements apart from the traditional family, social norms are more diverse in modern China (Yan 2010b: 495–505). Yet, there are no welfare state, no democracy and no basic individual rights. The Chinese state limits political participation and keeps a tight control over the individuals. Therefore, individualization is allowed and forced by the state in limited spheres of lives (Beck, Grande 2010: 421).

Also, the rise of a Chinese enterprising self has been detected by different researchers. The individual is still under the direct control of the state, yet this state is urging people to become more self-reliant and competitive, thereby fostering the development of enterprising individuals. Young Chinese are found to accept a high level of personal responsibility and self-development is becoming more and more important (Kleinman et al. 2011: 4; Yan 2011: 69–70).

The situation of vocational education students in Shanghai can indeed be explained in light of the above described theories. With relatively low education degrees in a highly competitive labour market, often far away from their hometowns and sometimes away from their parents, the students face all the uncertainties of the risk society and they are forced to make choices and learn how to make a living by themselves while at the same time having very limited opportunities – especially compared to graduates from academic higher middle schools who continue on to university. The aim of the present study is to find out if these theories can also explain students' own perceptions. This is done by asking the following questions: Which kind of risks do students sense in their lives? Do they experience freedom and necessity of choice? What kind of opportunities and restrictions are they identifying in their own lives? With which strategies are they preparing for the competition in the labour market?

2.3 Identity Formation and Stigma

Identity is a common topic in psychology and sociology and different understandings have been developed over time. The most prominent identity theory has been formulated by Erik Erikson (Keupp 2014: 169), who described identity as the sameness with one's self and continuity, and the perceived acknowledgement of this sameness and continuity by others (Erikson 1998: 47). Identity develops during childhood and adolescence and is not static (Erikson 1998: 19–20). Erikson described several development phases with each phase (ideally) resulting in the development of certain strengths such as hope, willpower, love, etc. (Noack 2008: 44–45).

George Herbert Mead (2013), a psychologist and a philosopher, was, at the beginning of the 20th century, concerned with the question of how human identity develops. Differently from Erikson, who understood identity as a unity, Mead distinguishes an 'I' as the acting part of the self from a 'me' which is the reacting and reflecting part (Jörissen 2008: 99–100; Rohlfs 2011: 95). The self develops during childhood when the child takes over different roles while playing alone, and later when the young person learns to put themselve in different roles while interacting with peers (Garz 2006: 45–46). Mead and Erikson agree that the social environment has a decisive influence and that childhood and adolescence are important stages during the development of identity and the self respectively.

Sociologist Erwin Goffman (2003) advanced certain aspects of Erikson's and Mead's theories (Engelhardt 2008: 124, 126). Goffman also recognized the duality of a person's identity, which he described as incorporating a social and a personal part. Social identity is made up of all the roles a person has in their work place, their family, among their friends, and so on. Personal identity is the individuality, the unique experiences of a person. Following Erikson's definition, Goffman describes an ego identity which reflects social situations and regulates personal and social identity (Goffman 2003: 74–76, 2003: 132–133; Engelhardt 2008: 126–128).

In the 1960s, Lothar Krappmann (1982) continued to analyze identity in the context of social interactions. Identity was understood as the condition and the product of social interactions. In every social interaction the role- and situation-related expectations are interpreted in the light of one's own background and experiences. This enables the involved individual to participate in the interaction and to develop an identity. In consequence, identity depends on the social situation and can change accordingly (Veith 2008: 179–180). Following Goffmann and Mead, Krappmann distinguished two parts of identity: personal and social identity. The social identity is conditioned by the role expectations encountered by the individual; the personal identity is what makes the individual and its biography unique. Both parts need to be balanced (Veith 2008: 188–191). Krappmann's theory was taken up, among others, by pedagogics and resulted in the request for a better incorporation of social expectations and opportunities to train social interaction in schools (Veith 2008: 198–199).

Social psychologist Heiner Keupp (2014) also acknowledged the ambiguous requirements placed on identities which need to be unique and socially acceptable to place a person within society. Modern society requires individuals to construct and reconstruct their own identities. The influence of society makes identity culturally dependent. Former existing identities, such as worker or housewife, lose their relevance in second modernity. Since identity is no longer a given at birth, individuals have to create a coherent identity by themselves. Trust and acceptance are necessary for identity formation (Keupp et al. 2004: 237). Within the identity, the self-perception has to be harmonized with society's perception, meaning that inner and outer dimensions of identity need to be aligned – a task which requires the ability to reflect. In addition, Keupp stresses the relevance of material resources for this task. They enable the individual to participate in society, and prevent exclusion. Also, individuals need to create their own value systems and social circles. Without the pre-formed identities, values and social circles are, as well, no longer a given.

In summary, there are two dimensions to one's identity: the inner dimension that is the self-perception and the unique definition of one's self, and the outer dimension involving the roles the individual has in its social surroundings and the views of these surroundings on the self. A successful identity construction needs to align these two dimensions and solve contradictions that might exist between the self-perception and the roles and views the individual is confronted with in society. Under the circumstances of second modernity, identity formation becomes an even bigger challenge. Whereas, in traditional societies the individual was able to take on an identity which was linked to class and profession, identity formation in second modernity comes down to individual efforts. The necessity to create one's own identity, to set and reach one's own goals, emphasizes individualization in modern society as Ulrich Beck, Anthony Giddens and others argue (Renn 2008: 206–207).

When entering a new school, students' identity formation is at a critical stage. They need to harmonize their identity, which has been defined by their own personality and their role in the family so far, with the roles and expectations school challenges them with (Kramer 2014: 424). Their identity as a student comes to the fore, while other identities such as son or daughter are still relevant but not dominant. Student identity can be a positive or negative experience for the students (Engelhardt 2014: 99–103), and failing in school has a long lasting effect on students' identities (Ecarius et al. 2011: 94). Erikson highlights the fact that adolescents can switch to negative identities if their social surroundings expect negative identities (Erikson 1998: 88–89) and that, generally, negative images are accepted by the affected individuals, which is a way to bring self-perceptions into accordance with external views (Erikson 1998: 57). Adolescence is described by Erikson as the final stage of identity development and a state of confusion of role and identity (Noack 2008: 44–45). The present study poses the question: What kind of identities do students form and how do they incorporate the negative reputation vocational education students have in Chinese society?

In order to analyze how the students deal with their image, we need to return to Erwin Goffman and take a look at his stigma theory. A stigma is a discrepancy between virtual and actual social identity, meaning that social norms are not met. Whether a certain trait is considered to be a stigma depends on the social surroundings and the situation of the individual and it can also change over time. A person of color, for example, might be stigmatized in one country but not in another (Goffman 2003: 11). Goffman lists different kinds of stigma such as physical (e.g. a disability), in character (e.g. being a criminal) or phylogenetic (e.g. race or religion) and he describes different ways of dealing with a stigma – stigma management (Goffman 2003: 12–13). This includes trying to hide the stigma, to get rid of the stigma (e.g. through an operation), to counterbalance the stigma with other positive traits, to fight for normalization of the stigma or to stay among the stigmatized (Goffman 2003: 18–19, 140-152). Following Goffman's approach and building on the insight that vocational education is stigmatized in China (Ling 2015), this study will analyze what kind of stigma management students employ.

2.4 Motivation and Self-Determination Theory

Edward Deci and Richard Ryan have done numerous empirical studies on factors increasing and decreasing motivation. They distinguish between intrinsic motivation, which refers to doing an activity simply because it gives pleasure or satisfaction, versus extrinsic motivation when an activity is done in order to gain or get something else, e.g. rewards of some sort, or achieve something else indirectly related to the activity (Ryan, Deci 2000: 71). While intrinsic motivation is the most stable one, which does not depend on external factors, Deci and Ryan further describe four different kinds of extrinsic motivation which differ in stability, ranging from integrated regulation, when the activity has become part of the self; identified regulation, when the activity is considered of personal importance; introjected regulation, when the activity is done with self-control or because of internal rewards; and external regulation, when the activity is done because of external rewards and punishments. For example: When a person is aware that studying in school ultimately leads to the ability to find a good and satisfying job, the person is extrinsically motivated because they do not enjoy the process of studying, yet this kind of motivation is stable and unlikely to change over time. A person who studies well in order to get a reward from teachers or parents has a much more unreliable extrinsic motivation. When teachers or parents stop giving rewards for good grades, it is likely that this person will stop studying (Ryan, Deci 2000: 72). Obviously, many tasks in school are not very enjoyable in day to day life and most students have no intrinsic motivations to do these tasks. The goal for educators thus needs to be the development of stable extrinsic motivations.

Through several quantitative studies, Deci and Ryan developed a self-determination theory which says that competence, autonomy and relatedness are three universal psychological needs which support a stable motivation. In relation to students this means that they need to be able to succeed at tasks (competence), they need to be able to make a choice (autonomy), and they need a sense of reliance and respect in their environment (relatedness) (Deci et al. 2001b: 931). Students who have a strong feeling of belonging, who believe in their own competence and in their ability to make a choice are better equipped to understand and internalize educational values (Ryan, Deci 2000: 74). This self-determination theory has been developed in the US and tested in other countries, for example with workers in a state-owned company in Bulgaria (Deci et al. 2001b: 930–931). One of Deci and Ryan's most debated conclusions is that tangible rewards will diminish intrinsic motivation. Students who study in a controlling environment will lose their initiative (Ryan, Deci 2000: 70–71). Yet, Deci and Ryan do not forget to admit that tangible rewards are not harmful if the task itself is boring and if there was no motivation to begin with (Deci et al. 2001a: 14). In this context, the present study analyzes what kinds of motivations students display.

3 The Chinese Education System

3.1 Education in China

The modern Chinese education system with six years of primary school and three years each on the lower and higher secondary level was created in 1922 by a group of American-influenced education reformers (Schulte 2014: 502). Today, it is divided into five stages. Pre-school, the first stage, can be attended voluntarily for one to three years. At the age of six, children enter primary school and after six years, they proceed to the lower secondary level, lower middle school, which lasts three years. These two stages are compulsory for all children in China. After lower middle school, students can either enter the upper secondary level, higher middle schools and vocational schools, or start working. An exam at the end of lower middle school (*zhongkao* 中考) determines which options are available for each student. Higher middle school ends with another exam (*gaokao* 高考) which is also known as the University entrance exam. The fifth stage is the tertiary education level, with vocational colleges offering a two year higher education degree called *dazhuan* (大专). Universities offer four year Bachelor and two to three year Master degrees, as well as Doctorates of at least three years duration. Schools charge for all non-compulsory stages of education. In 2014, gross enrollment for primary school and lower middle school reached 103%[1] and 94% respectively. 95% of lower middle school graduates enrolled in a higher middle school or a vocational school and the gross enrollment in tertiary education reached 39% according to the National Bureau of Statistics (OECD 2016b: 10–11).

Several laws and regulations which have been passed during the last 30 years control rights and responsibilities in the education system. These are most notably the *Law on Compulsory Education* (*Yiwu Jiaoyu Fa* 义务教育法) (1986), the *Teachers Law* (*Jiaoshi Fa* 教师法) (1994), the *Regulation on Qualifications of Teachers* (*Jiaoshi Zige Tiaoli* 教师资格条例) (1995), the *Education Law* (*Jiaoyu Fa* 教育法) (1995), the *Vocational Education Law* (*Zhiye Jiaoyu Fa* 职业教育法) (1996), and the *Higher Education Law* (*Gaodeng Jiaoyu Fa* 高等教育法) (1998) (UNESCO-UNEVOC 2011).

---

[1] The gross enrollment rate is defined as the number of children enrolled in a school level, regardless of age, divided by the population of the age group that officially corresponds to the same level. 103% indicates that 3% of children enrolled in primary school do not belong to the primary school age group (UNICEF).

According to the *Education Law*, State Council and local governments are responsible for the management and supervision of educational work. Primary and middle school education is managed by the local governments "under the leadership of the State Council", whereas higher education is under the supervision of the State Council and administered by the Provincial (Autonomous Regions, Municipalities) governments under the central government (Ministry of Education 1995 §14). As the highest educational administrative institution, the Ministry of Education (MOE) is responsible for defining policies, implementing laws, regulations and policies, as well as overall coordination (UNESCO-UNEVOC 2011).

Table 3.1: The Chinese Education System.

Age 18+, min. 2 years	University (Bachelor 4 years, Master 2 years, Doctorate 3+ years)	Vocational college (2 years)
University entrance exam (*gaokao*)		
Age 15–18, 3 years	Higher middle school	Vocational school
Higher middle school entrance exam (*zhongkao*)		
Age 12–15, 3 years	Lower middle school (compulsory education)	Vocational school (largely abolished)
Age 6–12, 6 years	Primary school (compulsory education)	
Age 3–6, 1–3 years	Kindergarten	

Source: Author's own illustration

Other institutions include the National Education Examinations Authority which coordinates and supervises national examinations; the Basic Education Curriculum Research Center; the China Scholarship Council, which is a public non-profit organization supporting Chinese students financially; the China Academic Degrees and Graduate Education Development Center; the China

National Institute for Educational Research; the National Center for School Curriculum and Textbook Development, which is affiliated to the MOE and does research on the evaluation of education, defines standards for assessment of learning results and teaching material, and assesses textbooks and curricula, and so forth; and the State Education Inspectorate which monitors, and examines, educational activities and schools and the implementation of laws (UNESCO-UNEVOC 2011).

Curricula in Chinese schools consist of three levels: a national curriculum, a regional curriculum and a school-specific curriculum. Consequently, the central government, local authorities and schools all develop curricula. Recent reforms stress the importance of students' overall development (instead of cramming knowledge) and a focus on basic skills (OECD 2016b: 23). With the definition of key competencies, output control started to replace input control in curriculum development. Also, different disciplines are placed in relation to each other so that the ability to judge and discuss has become more important for students. Under the heading of 'education for quality' (*suzhi jiaoyu* 素质教育) the new curricula aim to train students' creativity and innovative skills. Yet, as shall be explained below, China's assessment system is still exam-oriented (*yingshi jiaoyu* 应试教育) since exams ultimately decide which students are allowed to enter the next education level and which education institutions will be open to them (Schulte 2014: 525).

The employment of adequately qualified teachers is one of the current priorities for the MOE (OECD 2016b: 16). Although teaching is historically a very respected profession which still offers stable working conditions, becoming a teacher lost its attraction to many young people because of the relatively high qualification requirements and the comparably low income (OECD 2016b: 17). Rights, responsibilities and qualification requirements are regulated by the *Teachers Law* and the *Regulation on Qualifications of Teachers*. After the recent reform of the qualification system, teachers in public schools on primary and middle school level are examined nationally and they need to renew their qualifications every five years. They also have to complete at least 360 further training classes in five years (OECD 2016b: 18–19).

One of the biggest challenges is recruiting qualified teachers in rural areas where salaries and standards of living are considerably lower than in the cities. Through different measures the government tries to attract teachers to less developed places. The *Special Teaching Post Plan* of 2006 recruits new graduates for rural schools in central and western China for three years and teachers in large and medium cities are required to work shorter periods in rural schools (OECD 2016b: 28–29). Since 2007, six universities under the MOE offer tuition-free teaching degrees to attract more students. Once they graduate, students are obliged to spend at least two years in rural schools before being allowed to work in a city, and the government pledges students to work at least ten years as teachers after their graduation (Ministry of Education 2007). Yet, as Barbara Schulte (2014) pointed out, it is questionable if newly graduated teachers are able to improve the quality of education in the countryside during their two year postings. Other tested measures to keep teachers in rural schools and less attractive areas have included charging Shanghainese schools transfer fees when hiring a rural teacher or rotating teachers between different districts in Beijing in order to even out the quality (Schulte 2014: 523).

Education in China is financed by the central government, as well as by local governments. Donations from individuals or other non-state organizations are encouraged (Ministry of Education 1995 §60). Government appropriations are the main source of funding, providing 80.5% of the education budget. They are supplemented by taxes and fees, business funds, money raised from private schools, and donations. The education law requires the government to increase investment in education at all levels proportional to the growth of the national economy, and in the last ten years, education investment increased at an average rate of 19%. In 2011, China's average spending per student from primary to tertiary level was still the lowest among the countries surveyed by the Organisation for Economic Co-operation and Development (OECD), although the annual spending per student represented 27% of the GDP per capita – equal to the OECD average (OECD 2011). In 2012, the Chinese government finally reached its goal of investing 4% of the country's GDP in education – a goal which was first mentioned in 1993. By 2015, investment in education had risen to 3.6 trillion RMB, which was 4.3% of China's GDP according to official sources. Compared to the OECD average of 5.2% in 2013 however, China's 4% goal looks unambitious (China Daily 2012; Zhou 2016; OECD 2016a: 205; OECD 2016b: 14–16). China is still lagging behind Korea and Japan, who in 2014 invested 5.9% and 4.5% of their GDP respectively in education, and it is also well behind the USA and the UK who invested 6.2% and 6.7% (OECD 2016a: 205).

However, the Chinese government does put a lot of effort into guaranteeing a free compulsory education for all students and providing subsidies for students from poor families. Starting in 2017 not only tuition fees but also textbook fees for students shall be waived (Xinhua News Agency 2015). At the upper secondary level vocational education in rural areas and agriculture-related vocational courses in urban areas are tuition free and students from rural areas as well as students from poor families receive an annual subsidy (Wang 2010b: 13–14). National grants are also available for higher middle school students (OECD 2016b: 23). The empirical study conducted in 2011 by Yi et al., which was based on empirical research in 105 schools in the provinces of Zhejiang and Shaanxi, would suggest though, that a considerable percentage of poor students do not receive any money from the government.

Since the enforcement of nine years' compulsory education, China has managed to eliminate illiteracy among the younger generation with literacy rates of 99.7% for the male and female population aged 15 to 24 (Ministry of Education of Taiwan 2016: 19–20). School-life expectancy for students at the age six or older was 13.78 years in 2014, which already exceeds the compulsory education period but is still lower than in developed Asian and Western countries. The enrollment rate at tertiary level was with 2.5% of the overall population in 2013, also comparatively low (Ministry of Education of Taiwan 2016: 46, 92).

All of these comparisons show that China's education system has not yet reached the level of other developed Asian and Western countries but it is catching up and can already compete in certain aspects. Yet these international comparisons do not account for the huge regional differences within China, where Shanghai, with the highest regional per capita GDP, comes closest to Saudi Arabia, and Guizhou, the province with the lowest regional per capita GDP, resembles India (The Economist).[2] There are also huge income gaps between provinces, and between rural and urban households. In Shanghai the annual per capita disposable income of urban households reached 43,851 RMB in 2013, and the per capita net income of rural households reached 19,595 RMB. In Gansu, the province with the lowest annual per capita income, urban households had 18,964 RMB on average and rural households 5,108 RMB. The urban-rural income ratio was as high as 3.8 in Guizhou. Tianjin and Heilongjiang had the lowest ratio with 2.0.[3] Also, life expectancies range from 68.2 years in Tibet to 80.3 years in Shanghai (National Bureau of Statistics of China 2014).

It is clear that resources are not evenly spread across China, and with the decentralization reform in the 1990s, local governments have become responsible for financing education in their jurisdictions. Between 1979 and 2008, education expenditure rose from 50% to almost 80% of local governments' overall expenditures. Schools' finances and general conditions depend on the financial situation and priorities of their local governments, and education investments per students can be up to 60 times higher in cities compared to certain areas in the countryside (Schulte 2014: 513–514). Consequently, there are not only huge qualitative differences between different regions but also between schools, since

---

[2]   The PPP conversation rate as for whole China was used. Since in poorer provinces the cost of things will be lower than in richer provinces the differences are somewhat reduced.

[3]   Ratio of urban residents per capita disposable income to rural residents net income, rural income as 1.

the central government concentrates resources only in certain educational institutions.

The government grants special financial support to selected schools on the upper secondary level, and to universities. These key schools need to fulfill certain criteria concerning student-teacher ratios, teacher qualifications, school facilities, etc. In return they receive special funds from the government and can charge higher fees from their students (Kuczera, Field 2010: 31). This system is controversial since the government selects schools which are already doing well and, since enrollment is based on exams and conditioned by fees, the best students enroll in these schools. Students who performed poorly in lower middle school or who come from poor families usually do not have the chance to enroll in a key school or key university. Therefore, the system not only cements the quality of a school by leaving poor schools underfinanced while sponsoring good schools, it also enforces the disadvantages students with learning difficulties or students who come from poor families have (Li 2016). The system is additionally rigid because the best teachers choose to work for the best schools (Hansen 2013b: 175). Teachers' performance is usually assessed by the exam results of their students which is one of the reasons why teachers prefer to teach good students. This tendency also strengthens the exam orientation of the education (Fong 2004: 119; Murphy 1999: 12–14).

To build equity during compulsory education, the Chinese government decided that students must enroll in primary and lower secondary schools close to their place of residence, but many well-off families in cities like Shanghai and Beijing get around this rule by purchasing apartments close to prestigious schools or by paying illegal fees (Schulte 2014: 515–516; OECD 2016b: 22).

To facilitate enrollment in lower middle schools, Beijing matched some of these schools with primary schools and encouraged the establishment of schools which offer both primary and lower middle school education (OECD 2016b: 38).

3.1.1 Exams and Discrimination

Exams play a vital role in the Chinese education system. As mentioned earlier, compulsory education ends with a final exam in lower middle school, the *zhongkao*. The exam results decide if students are allowed to enroll in an academic higher middle school which requires a higher result, or in a vocational school. Although this exam receives far less public attention than the *gaokao* – the University entrance exam at the end of higher middle school – it is arguably more important since a good higher middle school raises students' chances of being admitted to one of the key universities (Hansen, Woronov 2013: 244; Ling 2015: 119). Therefore, students' academic future is not only decided at the end of higher middle school by the *gaokao* but actually three years earlier by the *zhongkao*.

Despite the fact that educational resources are allocated according to *zhongkao* results, government, media, educators and society focus solely on the *gaokao*. Since the exam was reinstated in 1977 after the Cultural Revolution, it has been reformed numerous times. Generally, students can choose between a focus on humanities or on natural sciences, and all students need to complete tests in Chinese, Mathematics and a foreign language (usually English).

In the early years, the exam was the same nationwide. In 1985, Shanghai was granted the right to draft its own exam followed by Beijing, Tianjin, Chongqing, Guangdong and others. Today, about half of the provinces and municipalities have the right to administer their own *gaokao*. Admission rates for universities have been rising since the first *gaokao* in 1977, when only 5% of the candidates were admitted to tertiary education. Since 2010 roughly three quarters of all candidates have been admitted each year (Yuan 2015).

In Chinese society, a university degree has become one of the most important measures of a person's worth, and it is portrayed as the ideal educational career, something to which everyone needs to aspire (Kipnis 2012: 198; Chen 2016: 175–176; Xu 2017b: 114). The *gaokao* results decide in which kind of university a student is allowed to enroll. Differences in quality and prestige among the higher education institutions are vast and range from internationally recognized top-tier universities to vocational colleges offering two to three year courses and a tertiary degree below a Bachelor – a *dazhuan*. All students would like to go to a good university, teachers are evaluated by their students' exam results and schools are judged by their graduating students' higher education admissions. This creates a highly competitive education system in which the focus is solely on exams (*yingshi jiaoyu* 应试教育).

In order to provide a more holistic education, which not only imparts knowledge but also develops students' potential and creativity, the government has started to reform the *gaokao*, with Zhejiang and Shanghai as test regions implementing a 3+3 system. Students write exams in Chinese, a foreign language (usually English) and mathematics and then choose three subjects from among physics, chemistry, biology, politics, history, geography and technology.[4] In Zhejiang, the elective subject exams can be taken twice. For each subject, students can receive up to 150 points and the final results are given in A, B, C,

---

[4]   Technology is only an option in Zhejiang.

and D levels. In Shanghai, students can be admitted to two universities (OECD 2016b: 32). Additionally, since 2003 some MOE approved universities can conduct their own entrance exam and recruit 5% of their new Bachelor students through this direct channel. By 2014, over 90 universities had been granted this right (Yuan 2015). This direct enrollment option was supposed to reduce the exam pressure students are facing in their last year of higher middle school but instead it increased stress levels because students prepare for interviews and tests with universities while still cramming *gaokao* content. It is also controversial because of the risk of corruption and discrimination (OECD 2016b: 43).

The *gaokao* is not only criticized because it leads to high stress for students and a teacher-centered cramming education style, but also because it favors students from big cities – especially Shanghai and Beijing, where most of the top-universities are located. Western media especially point out that top-tier universities in Beijing and Shanghai admit local students with lower exam scores, while the inclusion of English in the exam further disadvantages rural students because they often do not have qualified English teachers in their middle schools (Bradsher 2013).

In order to secure admission to one of the key universities, students need to take tutorial classes throughout all levels of schooling, and some start as early as kindergarten, with private English and mathematics tutoring. This so-called shadow education has become a large profit-oriented business in China and it shows that although the national exams are open to everybody, not everybody has the same chance to succeed since poorer families and families in remote regions have far fewer opportunities to provide tutoring for their offspring (Kipnis 2012: 190–193; Schulte 2014: 515–516). A clear proof of the discrimination in the Chinese education system is the fact that the majority of students in China's key universities are locals from big first tier cities (Schulte 2014: 519–520).

Additionally, migrant students are not allowed to take the *gaokao* in their place of current residence but must return to their home province, the location of their household registration (*hukou* 户口). Although these regulations are currently being reformed and are changing in some regions (OECD 2016b: 11), the overwhelming majority of migrant students have to enroll in vocational education on the higher secondary education level and thus will not have the opportunity to enter a university (OECD 2016b: 29–30). In compulsory education, there has been some progress in including migrant students in the education system in the place of residence. The *Notice of Improving Education of Children of Rural Migrant Workers* issued in 2003 bars state schools from charging fees for migrant students. Also, entrance exams and fees for choosing a school during compulsory education are illegal (OECD 2016b: 22). Yet, the implementation of the notice was proceeding at a different pace in different regions. Migrant students still had to pay extra fees to get into state schools, or they had to enroll in substandard private schools. According to a survey in the Pearl River Delta, quoted by Aris Chan (2009: 34–37), the attendance rate of migrant children in primary school was 91.7% compared to 99.8% among local children and in lower middle school it dropped to 75% compared to 99.9% among local children. Once enrolled, discrimination does not end, as Lan Pei-Chia (2014: 250–253) pointed out. Schools are not keen on educating migrant children because they are afraid that they will perform worse than locals and thereby lower average exam scores. Local parents do not want their children to have contact with migrant children because they are afraid of them having a bad influence on their own children's school performance, and therefore, some schools separate locals and migrants so that the latter are often assigned to a part of the school which is less well equipped. All of these obstacles result in migrant students being underrepresented in top education institutions in China (OECD 2016b: 29–30).

3.1.2 Diploma Inflation

As mentioned previously, a university degree is becoming more and more important in China. Gross enrollment in tertiary education has increased from 21% in 2006 to 39% in 2014 (OECD 2016b: 10–11), which is an increase of 1.75 million students (National Bureau of Statistics of China 2016).[5] Under Mao, simple workers were more respected than academics, but this has changed dramatically and urban middle class citizens with a high education and the means to consume become the new role models to which people aspire (Alpermann 2013: 294–295). Instead of recognizing that academic education might be suitable only for some people who are particularly interested in studying a certain subject, university education has become the goal for everybody (Kipnis 2012: 198). One of the consequences of the birth planning policy was that parents were able to concentrate their resources on one child, and they had to rely on this one child in old age. For parents, tertiary education became the key which would enable their child to find a well-paid job (Xu 2017b: 114–117). With Bachelor degrees becoming more and more common however, they can no longer guarantee good employment. With this so-called 'diploma inflation' tertiary education degrees become a requirement even for simple jobs. While children in today's China often achieve a higher level of education than their

---

5   Bachelor and vocational *dazhuan*.

parents, they cannot improve their social status; the higher degree merely prevents social descent. In order to compete successfully, candidates need to set themselves apart with an international or a Master's degree (Liu 2008a: 201; Hansen, Woronov 2013: 245–246). Thus, the Chinese education system is highly competitive and the competition does not only evolve around the university entrance exam, but also infiltrates every stage of education. Even after graduating from university the competition does not end – it continues in the labour market. Fresh graduates' unemployment rate six months after graduation is estimated to be anywhere between 15% and 30%, which means over one or two million young Chinese who followed the education ideal to higher education have difficulties finding a job. The unemployment rate for students without university degree is far lower since they are more willing to take blue-collar jobs (Sharma 2014). Clearly, university education is by no means a guarantee for professional success and social advancement in China.

3.2 Vocational Education in China

3.2.1 The Vocational Education System

There are four types of vocational schools on the upper secondary level: senior vocational schools (*zhiye gaozhong* 职业高中), secondary technical schools (*zhongdeng zhuanke xuexiao* 中等专科学校), skilled workers schools (*jixiao* 技校) and adult technical secondary schools (*chengren zhuanke xuexiao* 成人专科学校). Differences between the first three school types are being abolished and by now, enrollment criteria, the training courses offered and length of the education are the same (Li 2010: 168; Wang 2007: 168). Since most students attend a secondary technical school (close to 70% in Shanghai) this school type is the focus of the present study (Shanghai Bureau of Statistics 2015: 20.3).

There are also vocational schools on the lower secondary level. These junior vocational schools (*zhiye chuzhong* 职业初中) exist in central and Western China, and in rural and underdeveloped parts of the country (Jiang 2011: 6). Numbers are decreasing, with only 22 schools listed for 2015 (National Bureau of Statistics of China 2016: 21.1), yet, these schools shall be kept in underdeveloped regions where the government considers it necessary (Ministry of Education, Ministry of Development and Reform, Ministry of Finance, Ministry of Human Resources and Social Securities, Ministry of Agriculture, State Council Department for Aid-the-poor 2014). On the tertiary level, there are higher vocational colleges and senior skilled workers schools, which offer two to three year courses which end with a vocational tertiary education degree (*dazhuan* 大专) (Wang 2010b: 3).

The most common system in upper secondary vocational schools is the so-called '2+1 system'. Students spend two years in school and then do an internship in a company during the last year. Structures exist in which students alternate between school and company, or are educated on demand for one specific company, but these structures are not widespread (Cai 2008: 48–56).

The curriculum of vocational schools has three parts: general academic skills defined by the MOE, vocational skills also nationally defined and a third, locally determined part which teaches vocational skills relevant for the local industry (Kuczera, Field 2010: 14).

After finishing their education, students receive a graduation certificate (*xueli zhengshu* 学历证书) and, in addition, can obtain a vocational qualification certificate from the Ministry of Human Resources and Social Security (MOHRSS) by passing the verification for professional suitability, which then decides in which wage bracket students will be classified (*zhiye zige zhengshu* 职业资格证书) (Ministry of Human Resources and Social Securities 2005; Xu 2003: 58). The tests for the verification of professional suitability are the same nationwide (Schnarr et al. 2008: 30) and involve knowledge examination and operational skills assessment. Government approved agencies conduct these tests (UNESCO-UNEVOC 2013: 16).

Vocational education is financed by the state and society (Standing Committee of the National People's Congress 1996 §§ 26–35). School revenues come from school fees, the state and sometimes business activities (Franke 2003: 72). In 2006, 40.4% of schools' budgets came from the central government. Students' tuition constituted 32.0% and only 1.0% were company investments (Wang 2010b: 12) According to the law, enterprises need to finance the training of their employees, yet the central government has the leading role in financing vocational education (UNESCO-UNEVOC 2013: 12–13).

Schools recruit teachers themselves. Teachers need to have at least a Bachelor degree or a degree from a vocational college. They are required to train in a company for one month per year or two months every other year (UNESCO-UNEVOC 2013: 15). The aim is to have a certain percentage of dual-certified teachers – that is, teachers who have a vocational skill and are also qualified as teachers (State Council 2014), or to employ company employees as part-time teachers. In Shanghai, about one third of vocational education teachers also work for a company (Kuczera, Field 2010: 14).

Similar to the academic education system, there are a number of key national schools. They are required to meet certain standards concerning the number of teachers and students, teachers' qualifications, and so on. Key schools receive government grants and charge higher school fees. In Shanghai, more than half of the vocational schools on the upper secondary level are key national schools. They charge roughly double the school fees charged by average vocational schools.[6]

3.2.2 Reforms and Development

The history of vocational education in China goes back to the early 20th century when in 1903 various industrial schools were founded in Shanghai under a new school charter published by the Qing dynasty. Most of these schools were on the secondary level, specializing in commerce, telecommunications, manufacturing, agriculture and other subjects. (The Encyclopedia of Shanghai Editorial Committee 2010: 395–396). The expression 'vocational education' (*zhiye jiaoyu* 职业教育) was introduced in China after the fall of the Qing dynasty with the founding of the *Chinese Association of Vocational Education* under Huang Yanpei in 1917 (Schulte 2003: 221). During this warlord era, education was considered important to build a modern nation and to spread the knowledge and technical skills necessary for national survival. Vocational education had an additionally crucial role since it could educate social classes which had not had access to education before. Huang Yanpei wanted to replace social mobility, which the exam system provided, with social tranquility (Schulte 2013: 233). Vocational education was supposed to civilize people and provide them with a way to earn a living (Schulte 2013: 236). 'Vocational education to save the country' (*zhijiao jiuguo* 职教救国) was a popular slogan at the time (Schulte 2012: 9–11). In 1922, Huang Yanpei and the *Chinese Association for Vocational Education*, which had over 7000 influential members by the end of the decade, succeeded in integrating vocational education in the new education system, which included six years primary, plus three years lower and higher secondary education respectively (Schulte 2012: 19; The Encyclopedia of Shanghai Editorial Committee 2010: 395–396).

---

6   While average vocational middle schools charged between 1100 RMB and 1300 RMB depending on the training course (excluding art training courses) in 2016 in Shanghai, the schools of the present study (both key vocational schools) charged 2600 RMB and 1980 RMB respectively per semester for electrical engineering courses. However, one school stated that the government paid the fees for electrical engineering courses for all students, and both schools confirmed that students with rural hukou were not required to pay fees (Shanghai Fabu 2016).

After the founding of the People's Republic of China in 1949, vocational education again played an important role in the economic development of the new country. The implementation of the first five-year plan in the 1950s created a need for technical workers (Xu 2009: 46; The Encyclopedia of Shanghai Editorial Committee 2010: 395–396). With only a few university graduates, the economy depended on vocational education to satisfy labour demands, and the system underwent a positive development which included the formulation of education goals, standardization of education structures, improvement of school management, and development of curricula (Xu 2009: 49–52).

Despite its importance for the development of the country, vocational education was always considered inferior. Before 1949, primarily Confucian studies and a career as an official were highly respected, and after the founding of the People's Republic of China, only Marxism studies and a career as a party official earned people's respect. Manual labour was always looked down on by society (Schulte 2003: 222–223). In addition, during the Cultural Revolution, which started in 1966, many schools stopped working and were turned into factories. Due to the ongoing political power struggle, development of education did not pick up until the opening reforms at the end of the following decade when vocational education was back in focus to mitigate the lack of skilled workers and the bottleneck which the reinstated *gaokao* created in 1977 (Xu 2009: 73–76, 102–103).

Since then, vocational education has undergone different stages of reform and development. These stages can be grouped into three phases. In the first, between 1978 and 1998, the economy developed rapidly and China was in need of skilled labour. In order to develop the vocational education system, China started to cooperate with other countries, such as Germany, to try to first transfer and then learn from successful systems abroad (Xu 2009: 166–167). Roughly half the students at higher secondary level went to vocational schools (58% in 1996). The founding of the first higher vocational education colleges also falls in this stage. In 1995, the vocational education law was passed in order to regulate school systems, responsibilities and funding. Then between 1999 and 2002, development stagnated. Many schools were offering similar courses but lacked education quality. The system in which different entities, such as government departments, industry branches and local institutions ran their own schools, was not efficient enough. Student recruitment became a problem. The government started to merge schools and shift responsibilities to local governments but the shift of supervision was not well organized and some schools' quality descended further so that they lost student resources and industry support (Xu 2009: 149–152). In 2001, the government reacted to the diminishing attractiveness of vocational education and the desire for a higher education level by reforming the curriculum and including academic subjects, as well as introducing two graduation certificates: the graduation certificate from the school and the vocational qualification certificate from MOHRSS (Xu 2009: 154–155). Nonetheless, by 2002 only 38% of students at higher secondary level studied in a vocational school (Jiang 2011: 6).

The third phase started in 2003 and has lasted until today. During this last decade and a half, the central government has focused once again on the development and quality improvement of vocational education. The fourth National Conference on Vocational Education was held in 2002, and in the same year the *Decision of the State Council to Rapidly Expand Vocational Schooling, Reform and Development* was released. In 2005, the State Council released the *Decision to Vigorously Develop Vocational Education,* and during the fifth National Conference on Vocational Education held in the same year, the central government decided to invest ten billion RMB in vocational education (Liu 2008c: 2). Important goals included the improvement of school operations and management, the establishment of new training systems such as education on demand and intensified school-company cooperation in order to meet industry needs, the improvement of equipment, and school to school cooperation to improve the quality of rural and western schools by partnering them with urban and eastern schools (Xu 2009: 181–182). Another important element was the improvement of teachers' qualifications. Since 2006, every vocational teacher is required to do at least two months practice training in a company every other year (Xu 2009: 193–194), and during a national conference on teaching reform in vocational education in 2008 further improvements in education quality, teaching, school-company cooperation, teacher training, etc. were discussed (Liu 2008c: 7). Also in 2008, the MOE published its *Suggestions on Deepening the Reform of Teaching in Vocational Education.* Different from the top down approach met during previous curriculum reforms, the reform this time started from the bottom. The new curricula were developed in accordance with the work processes and focused on vocational skills (Xu 2009: 186–187). After 2010, three major documents regarding the strengthening of vocational education were released, namely the *National Outline for Medium and Long Term Education Reform and Development Plan (2010-2020),* the *Decision of the State Council to Accelerate the Development of Modern Vocational Education,* and the *Plan of Modern Vocational Education System Construction (2014-2020).* In order to further spread vocational education over the country, the government started an initiative to abolish school fees, and poor students started to receive subsidies of 1,500 RMB per year during the first two years of vocational education (Kuczera, Field 2010: 5). There are also other subsidy options but these are locally determined and, therefore, dependent on regional finances (Kuczera, Field 2010: 13).

In 2015, there were about 16.6 million students studying in vocational middle schools and about 24 million students attending higher academic middle schools on the upper secondary level. In the same year, 6 million students (43% of students entering upper secondary education) were newly enrolled in vocational schools while 8 million (57% of students entering upper secondary education) were newly enrolled in academic higher middle schools, which is just short of the government's goal of channeling equal numbers of students into vocational and academic education on the upper secondary level (National Bureau of Statistics of China 2016: 21.2).

3.2.3 Challenges for Vocational Education

Despite the improvement of vocational education during the last decade, crucial deficits persist which re-enforce each other and hinder the overall development of vocational education.

With the ongoing modernization of the economy and industrial production, it is impossible to predict which skills will be needed in the future. In addition, people do not work for one company in the same position for their whole working life anymore. Frequent job changes have become the norm. This trend exists in the West, as well as in China. Therefore, it is more and more important to impart so-called 'key competencies' instead of narrow, job-specific skills. Students have to learn how to learn. Graduates have to be able to teach themselves new skills and solve unseen problems in their later working lives (Jiang 2011: 9). This requires qualified teachers and the training of skills in production processes – still two big challenges for vocational education in China.

The lack of qualified teachers is considered one of the main obstacles for the development of vocational education. The central government is investing substantial amounts in the education and training of vocational teachers (Xinhua News Agency 2007), as the goal is to train dual-certified teachers (Sun, Zhang 2015) who have professional skills and are qualified teachers. So far, these teachers are too few in numbers (Zhang 2013b: 1). Too few adequately trained teachers compromise education quality, and compromised education quality leads to a poor reputation for vocational education in general (Sun, Zhang 2015). For technically skilled teachers, working in the industry is more attractive, not only because of the better reputation but also because of the higher income (Kuczera, Field 2010: 33).

Another factor leading to poor education quality is the insufficient engagement of companies in vocational education in China. A survey cited by the

Education Commission of Shanghai showed that companies were generally satisfied with vocational education, and observed that vocationally trained students are able to adapt to tasks in the company (Shanghai Education Commission 2015), but neither these generally positive opinions nor the demands for improvement voiced by some companies in the survey has led to further engagement and support of vocational education (UNESCO-UNEVOC 2013: 18; Zhang 2013b: 1; Sun, Zhang 2015). The state appeals to companies to invest in vocational education by financing workshops in schools, by training teachers and by sending technicians as part-time teachers to schools, and companies offering internships for students receive tax benefits (Jiang 2011: 8; State Council 2014). Still, companies do not contribute enough, often refusing to cooperate with schools at all or teaching their interns very specific skills which are not transferable across the industry (Kuczera, Field 2010: 5–7). Ultimately, the state has no control over companies and industry sectors, and schools depend on government finances, which differ regionally (Jiang 2011: 7). Therefore, schools in less developed regions are underfinanced and do not live up to national standards (UNESCO-UNEVOC 2013: 18). Companies' lack of engagement makes planning difficult and contributes to the fact that vocational education does not cater to the demands of the labour market as it should (UNESCO-UNEVOC 2013: 18). Another survey, though, showed that companies do criticize several aspects of vocational education: 79% of employers wish for better vocational accomplishment (zhiye suyang 职业素养) among the graduates, 75% want better curricula and 61% hope for better cooperation with the schools (Shanghai Education 2014: 1). When vocationally trained students still need on-the-job training after their graduation because their skills are out of date, companies continue to lose their motivation for engagement in vocational education. Ideally, schools and companies should share the responsibility of educating students to ensure that vocational education is closely connected and up to date with modern production. In China though, companies see themselves as being on the receiving end. They employ students after graduation, rather than training them during their education. As a result the lack of company engagement is one of the biggest obstacles for the modernization and quality improvement of vocational education in China.

Challenges for vocational education lie not only within the school system but also within society. The flipside of the aforementioned ideal of higher education is the low status of vocational education graduates and the low respect society has for manual workers (Renmin Ribao 2013: 1). Vocational education is considered a second class education, inferior to general education (Shieh et al. 2008: 1; Zhang 2013b: 1). Although reforms during the last few years have gradually opened the way from vocational education to the tertiary education sector, the options are still limited and vocational education is often a 'dead end education' (Zhou, Mao 2013: 1). Poor education quality, due to inadequately qualified teachers and the lack of company engagement, further contributes to the poor reputation of vocational education.

Only students who have no other options take vocational education into consideration, as will be confirmed in the study at hand. As a result, vocational students are considered poor students (Shieh et al. 2008: 1) and problematic (Renmin Ribao 2013: 1). Many teachers consider their own students lazy and/or stupid (Hansen, Woronov 2013: 249). In China, exam results are not only significant for judging performance in school, but also because they describe the value of a person (Woronov 2011: 83). Failing students are not only weak in mathematics or not good in written examinations; they are considered worthless as a person. Students apply this negative view to themselves and often suffer from a lack of self-esteem (Shieh et al. 2008: 1; Hansen, Woronov 2013: 249). Additionally, students are looked down on because of their family background. In 2012, 82% of vocational students had a rural *hukou*[7], 70% came from central or western China. According to a survey from 2008, the majority of parents were manual workers, farmers or independent traders and 45.7% of the families had an annual per capita income of 3,000 RMB (Da 2013: 1). After entering a vocational school, students face the challenge of bringing the societal opinions of vocational students in line with their own self-perception. They have to deal with the stigmas of having failed in school, being a vocational student and coming from a poor background.

Combined, all of these factors form a vicious cycle for vocational education in China. Vocational education has long been overlooked and has had the reputation of being a second class education. While universities and general education received government support early on, vocational schools were left with poor equipment and inadequately qualified teachers. This led to a bad reputation for vocational education and, consequently, only poor students who did not have a choice entered vocational schools. Their lack of success then leaves people with the impression that vocational education is the dead end of education. Companies thus prefer to hire university graduates for blue collar jobs (Shieh et al. 2008: 1) and have too few incentives to contribute to vocational education, which then suffers from inadequate school equipment and teachers lacking company experience. Additionally, the bad reputation of vocational education and vocational students makes teaching in this field an unattractive profession. In particular, dual-certified teachers prefer to work for companies where they also have higher salaries (Kuczera, Field 2010: 33). This, again,

---

[7]   Houshold registration (see below).

compromises education quality and leaves vocational education as an unattractive last resort for students who have no other options left (Shieh et al. 2008: 1; Hansen, Woronov 2013: 243). This vicious cycle hinders the development of vocational education and has a deep impact on students' identities.

3.3 Shanghai as a Special Case

Taking into consideration the vast differences between different regions in China, no education-related study can claim to capture the whole of the country. Economic development and education resources are unevenly spread across the country and some studies choose a variety of locations to include developed and backward regions and thereby try to create a picture which resembles the country's situation. The present study followed a different approach by choosing good schools in Shanghai, China's most developed city, where the government regularly tries out education reforms. The Shanghainese education system is China's flagship, particularly since the successful participation of the city in the PISA test[8] in 2009 (OECD 2010: 5). By choosing good vocational schools in Shanghai, we can see how persistent the problems of vocational education are or if they perhaps only exist in other provinces. We can also get an idea about future development in other provinces since the government tries to copy successful education models in other regions.

With a population of just over 24 million, Shanghai, one of the four directly administered municipalities, is China's most populous city and the 5th most populated city in the world. Its population density reaches 3,854 people per square kilometer in urban areas while the average density is 2,059 people per square kilometer overall, and it is still expected to grow further with some estimates expecting 50 million people in Shanghai by 2050 (Shanghai Population 2017 - World Population Review 2017).

Shanghai, which came into existence as a fishing village in the 10th century, is the financial and economic center of China, with double-digit economic growth almost every year for the last 20 years (Wu 1999: 207–208; Shanghai Population 2017 - World Population Review 2017). Its per capita GDP is considerably higher than the nationwide average and the service sector produces 65% of the city's economic output. Disposable income and consumption expenditure are higher than anywhere else in the country (National Bureau of Statistics of China 2015; OECD 2016b: 42). A special economic zone, a free trade zone, the world's busiest container port and the connection to China's

---

[8]   OECD Programme for International Student Assessment.

high-speed railway system make Shanghai the most important economic hub in China, and the city is leading in all kinds of reforms, including education (International Maritime Information Website 2017; OECD 2016b: 42). Career options, income, the health system and the quality of education are better than anywhere else in the country. The life expectancy is also over 80 years, not only the highest in mainland China but one of the highest life expectancies worldwide (Shanghai Population 2017 - World Population Review 2017). Therefore, it is not surprising that Shanghai is an attractive destination for China's domestic migrants as well as foreign expats.

According to official figures there are about 150,000 foreigners living in Shanghai with a majority coming from Japan, the US and Korea (Shanghai Population 2017 - World Population Review 2017). Apart from these expats, the population is separated into Shanghainese locals and non-Shanghainese migrants from other provinces. Everyone's origin is noted in the so-called *hukou* (户口), the household registration. The government employs the *hukou* system to control internal migration and to secure resources for local populations. This is particularly relevant in Shanghai where the best schools, universities and hospitals of the country are located and where land and water resources are limited (Wang 2010a: 335–337). Long-term migrants without Shanghai *hukou* constitute 39% of the population in Shanghai and while the Shanghainese population has a negative growth-rate, the number of migrants is growing, leading to an overall positive growth-rate in Shanghai's population (Shanghai Population 2017 - World Population Review 2017). Since 2007, employers need to purchase insurance for their migrant employees, but these migrants are still disadvantaged compared to local Shanghainese (Lan 2014: 248). While the city government tries to attract highly qualified personnel by offering special perks such as a 'naturalization' via a point based system, the migrant population is a very diverse group which not only includes highly qualified personnel with tertiary education degrees but also a huge number of uneducated labourers (Lan 2014: 248). Most migrants live in the suburbs and work in manufacturing, construction, real estate and commerce. Fengxian and Qingpu, the two districts where the schools of the present study are located, are among the districts with the highest number of migrant children (Minjin Shanghai Shiwei 2011).

A recent trend is the tendency of migrants to move to the city with their whole family and, as a result, numerous migrant children need to be enrolled in the local school system (Lin 2011: 315). In 2012, 46.2% of all children in Shanghai came from migrant families, which was a far higher proportion compared to 26.2% nationwide. The sex ratio among migrant children showed that parents were more likely to bring sons to the cities for compulsory education, and daughters only after they finished school (All-China Women's Federation 2013).

Each first-tier city in China enforces different rules concerning the education of migrant children in their jurisdiction. Shanghai is commonly seen as a model example for a successful integration of migrants into local schools. Not only was the city among the first to achieve universal compulsory education with an enrollment rate of 99.9%, and almost universal secondary education with an enrollment rate of 97% of the age cohorts according to official statistics from 2014, Shanghai was also a "national leader in dealing with the educational problem of migrant children" according to the OECD (OECD 2016b: 43). Shanghai was the first city to admit migrant children in public schools for compulsory education (Lan 2014: 247). Today, migrant children are eligible to receive their nine year compulsory education in Shanghai for free and the government controls the schools so that teachers' qualifications and equipment standards are met (Chen, Feng 2013: 77). Nonetheless, migrant children are still disadvantaged. In order to enroll in a school, their parents need to provide several documents to prove that they live in Shanghai legally. Some children are not registered in the city and, therefore, cannot be enrolled (Chan 2009: 48–56; Lan 2014: 250). Probably the most obvious discrimination is the fact that migrant children in Shanghai are not allowed to enroll in an academic higher middle school and they are not allowed to sit the *gaokao* exam in Shanghai. Instead, they are forced into vocational education if they want to continue their education in Shanghai (Ling 2015: 112). In the vocational education sector, not all courses are open to migrant students because the government tries to fill up less attractive courses by admitting non-locals (Lan 2014: 260–261). In the end, most vocational schools in Shanghai have a mix of migrant students and Shanghainese students who did not pass the *zhongkao* exam (Ling 2015: 128–130).

3.3.1 Vocational Education in Shanghai

In 2015, there were 98 vocational middle schools in Shanghai with 13,100 teachers and staff. In the same year, 32,400 students (37.8% of students enrolling in upper secondary education) were newly enrolled in vocational middle schools compared to 53,400 (62.2% of students enrolling in upper secondary education) in academic higher middle schools. In the same year, there were 104,400 students attending a vocational middle school, compared with 158,200 students enrolled in academic higher middle schools (Shanghai Bureau of Statistics 2016: 20.1). The ratio of students studying in vocational and academic higher middle schools in Shanghai and the country as a whole is roughly 4:6

which is, as mentioned before, still below the government goal of enrolling an equal number of students in both areas.[9]

In order to make vocational education more attractive, and to train the technical workers and midlevel management Shanghai's economy needs, the government started to introduce vocational training courses in 2010, in which students enroll in upper secondary level and after three years enter the tertiary level, from which they graduate with a vocational *dazhuan* degree. In 2014, additional programs finishing with an applied Bachelor degree (*yingyong benke* 应用本科) were established. This reform gives students the chance to get a higher education degree with vocational education.

By 2015, 72 training courses which last five to six years and end with a *dazhuan* degree, and 14 training courses which last seven years and end with an applied Bachelor degree, were offered in Shanghai. All courses have a consistent, newly designed curriculum in order to avoid repetition of content between the secondary and tertiary education level, and local media proudly reported that in 2015 over 4000 students whose *zhongkao* results would have allowed them to enroll in an academic higher middle school instead chose one of these so-called 'run-through' vocational education courses (*guantong zhiye jiaoyu* 贯通职业教育) (21 Shiji Jiaoyu Yanjiuyuan 2016).

Activity rates (including employment and further education) for students who graduated from upper secondary vocational schools in Shanghai are consistently high. In 2014, the activity rate reached 97.9%. Of these students, 44.0% pursued further studies. Among migrant students the activity rate was even higher, at 98.8%, but only 23.4% pursued further studies. These numbers have been consistent for some years. The activity rate for all students who graduated between 2010 and 2014 is 97.8%; 59.9% started to work after finishing vocational education, 37.9% pursued further studies. The activity rate among non-Shanghainese students who graduated between 2010 and 2014 is 98.5% (Shanghai Education Commission 2015).

In 2014, 13.4% of students in Shanghai who started to work received a starting salary under 2000 RMB per month; 23.1% received a starting salary between 2000–2500 RMB per month; the majority, 56.1%, received between 2500–3000 RMB and 7.5% received more than 3000 RMB per month. The highest salaries at the beginning of their career are for flight attendants (3263 RMB/month), mechatronics (2989 RMB/month) and chemical engineers (2929 RMB/month).

---

[9] In 2015, there were 16,6 million students enrolled in secondary vocational schools (incl. adult vocational schools) and 24 million students were enrolled in academic middle schools on the upper secondary level (National Bureau of Statistics of China 2016: 21.2).

After three years most students (56.5%) earn between 3000–5000 RMB per month (Shanghai Education Commission 2015).

A majority of working students, 87.3%, has jobs that completely or basically match their education (Shanghai Education Commission 2015), but, as pointed out by teacher Zheng Lina during the interview, there is no definition for what a matching job is. Among the students who graduated between 2010 and 2012, 42.9% had changed jobs at least once by 2014 (Shanghai Education 2014: 1).

If students choose to pursue further studies and then look for a job, their employment rate is apparently higher than the employment rate of university graduates who had attended an academic higher middle school (Shanghai Education Commission 2015). The number of tertiary education graduates with vocational education at secondary level is far smaller than the number of graduates with academic middle school education, however, and it is unclear what the income differences are. One therefore has to be careful with drawing quick conclusions. Still, China is suffering from a lack of skilled workers and this deficit will continue in the future (Da 2013: 1). Many workers are close to retirement; their skill set is no longer up to date (Shieh et al. 2008: 1). Therefore, vocational education will continue to be a fairly secure route to employment, but the government also has to work on making vocational education more attractive, and it needs to further strengthen development opportunities for vocational education graduates.

4 Methodology

4.1 Mixed Methods Design

The present study is based on a mixed methods design which uses a panel to combine qualitative and quantitative data. Over three years students have been interviewed up to three times, and student cohorts filled in questionnaires up to two times. With the triangulation of questionnaires and interviews, it was possible to check how common certain opinions voiced during interviews were in the whole cohort, while agreement or disagreement with certain questionnaire statements could be explained with the background information in the interviews. The panel design allowed a repeated, targeted adjustment of interview manuals and questionnaires to get further insights. Applying mixed methods is becoming more and more popular with researchers in the field of social sciences because it can compensate for weak points in quantitative and qualitative methods, and matching interview and questionnaire results are an additional validation of the conclusions.

Table 4.1: Data Collection - Overview.

Data Collection - Overview	
Autumn 2013	Interviews
Spring 2014	Questionnaire: first and third year
Autumn 2014	Interviews
Spring 2015	Questionnaire: second year
Autumn 2015	Interviews

Source: Author's own illustration

4.2 Two Vocational Schools

Two key vocational schools on the outskirts of Shanghai were chosen for the present study, one was located in Fengxian district, hereafter called Fengxian School, and the other one was located in Qingpu district – Qingpu School.[10]

Qingpu district became a part of Shanghai in 1999. It is known for its big parks and greenery, as well as for having Shanghai's only fresh water reservoir. With the recent development of an airport, train station and the exposition center in nearby Hongqiao district, and the few international schools located in Qingpu, the district is becoming more and more urbanized. A subway connection to the city center was in the planning at the time of research.

Fengxian district is located 58 km from the city center and People's Square. The district only became a part of Shanghai in 2001. It is still a rural area where cotton, grains, rice and fruits are grown. In summer 2014 Fengxian School moved to a new, smaller campus in the more centrally located Minhang district. A subway line connects this district to central Shanghai and many factories are located in the area. Yet, all students in the sample spent at least two years in the more remote Fengxian campus and, therefore, this surrounding was formative for their experiences in school.

Qingpu and Fengxian Schools are both key vocational schools and, as a result, their equipment is modern, and school personnel were adequately trained, including overseas training for principals and about 50% of the teachers. In comparison to other studies on vocational education in China, these two schools were privileged because of their status as well as their location in Shanghai, which is an attractive destination for migrant workers and promises a higher income than anywhere else in the country. Admission to both schools was based on points derived from lower middle school exams – with a cut-off line close to the upper limit of secondary vocational schools' admission range – and, in some cases, interviews. With the present study's focus on better vocational schools, it became possible to find out if the frustration of students and the bad reputation of vocational education also persist under relatively good circumstances.

To ensure comparability, the focuses of the present study were the electrical engineering and mechatronics courses. The first major differences between the two schools was the size: in Qingpu School the electrical engineering cohort consisted of four classes with 40 students in each, on average, while the Fengxian School cohort had only one class with about 30 students. The organization of the courses also differed: Qingpu School's course used to take four

---

[10]   All names of people, schools and companies are anonymized throughout the thesis.

years. In the first year students focused on general subjects, the second and third years introduced technical skills, and in the fourth year, they did an internship with a company. Due to the standardization of vocational education, Qingpu School had switched to the most common education structure, called the 2+1 system, where students spend two years learning technical skills in school and then do their internship in the last year. Most of the Qingpu School students in the sample were enrolled in a 2+1 course. Fengxian School, though, had a long history of cooperation with Germany, which resulted in a different education system. With the German dual system as an inspiration, students were enrolled in an alternating system. Starting from the second year, they alternated on a bi-monthly basis between school and factory. Fengxian students also sit an additional exam, organized by the German Chamber of Commerce, which is recognized by German companies, and they have the chance to participate in a student exchange in Germany. Additionally, Fengxian School occasionally trains classes of students specifically for one company. After successful graduation, all students have the opportunity to start working for that company. One of these classes was trained for Mechatronic Company at the time of the research and these students have been included in the interviews and surveys.

Access to the schools was gained through my former employer, a German foundation which had cooperated with both Fengxian School and a tertiary vocational school located on the same campus for close to 30 years. The principal of the school, whom I knew personally for a few years, agreed to support me and through her connections, I came in contact with Qingpu School where the Dean of the electrical engineering department had some genuine interest in my research and made sure I had all the access I needed for the following years. In both schools I had my gate keepers whom I contacted whenever I needed to gather some data, and after the first year, the teachers knew me as well which further facilitated my access. None of the school personnel seemed to be worried that my results might shed a negative light on the schools; on the contrary, they always expressed the hope that my findings might help them understand their students better and improve their education. This awareness of existing strength and willingness to face potential deficits suggests that the schools were indeed among the top schools in Shanghai.

4.3 The Research Process

4.3.1 The Interview Data

Several students in different stages of their education were interviewed up to three times between spring 2013 and winter 2015/16. The manuals for the semi-structured interviews started with an easy open question such as 'Please describe an average day in school' to get the students talking. The different questions were discussed beforehand with a native Chinese speaker to make sure they were phrased correctly and were as easy to understand as possible. The first manual was geared towards getting a broad picture of students' backgrounds and their everyday lives. The following manuals became more refined and differed for each student, since they included an individual follow-up and additional questions concerning new topics that came up during other interviews or which appeared to be relevant in the questionnaires. After each interview the students filled in a short form concerning their demographical data, and the interview situation including students' non-verbal behavior was documented in a detailed field diary. All interviews were conducted in Mandarin and audio recorded with a mobile phone. A native Chinese speaker and professional transcript writer transcribed each interview. The transcripts were additionally proof-read by me and were then analyzed without further translation.

Following is an overview of the main topics in each round of interviews. Aside from the general, easy, opening question, the order of the topics was not set in advance but depended on students' accounts.

First round of interviews – Focus: students' backgrounds

- School and training course
- Family background
- Friendships and interests
- Generational differences
- Future and ideal life

Second round of interviews – Focus: School and internship

- Individual follow up
- Opinions on vocational education
- Relationships with teachers

- Internship and future work
- Personality self-assessment

Third round of interviews – Focus: Future and retrospect

- Individual follow up
- Vocational education in comparison to general education
- Internship and work
- Goals and future plans

Interviews with graduated students[11] - Focus: Development

- Review vocational education
- Current situation: work, private life
- Regrets and success
- Personality self-assessment

Students were either randomly chosen by the teacher or myself, or they volunteered, or they were selected according to a theoretical sampling to include both migrant and Shanghainese students, both girls and boys. Some students were proud to be part of my research and others were very nervous and insecure. Only one female student refused to speak to me. After the interview, they received some German chocolate as a thank-you and during the follow up interviews most students were able to relax more than they had done during the first interview. In spring 2013, I noted down mobile numbers of the graduating cohorts in both schools and with this information I was able to contact graduated students in autumn 2015 and include them in the survey.

Most students were interviewed in the schools, either in an empty classroom or in a conference room. Except for one occasion, where there were other teachers in an office, all interviews were conducted with only the interviewed student present. I met graduated students wherever it was convenient for them, either at their workplace, in a park, or in a café where we sometimes encountered very noisy backgrounds. Students' willingness and ability to reflect and elaborate differed vastly, and consequently interviews lasted between eight and 45 minutes despite being based on similar interview manuals.

---

[11]   Topics were included in second- and third-round interview if students had already graduated by then.

My interview analysis was based on Philipp Mayring's (2003) approach to qualitative interview analysis. In a first step, I grouped central statements and important passages together according to their general topics, such as life in school, family background, or work experiences, which resulted in a clearly arranged interview summary. The main part of my analysis focused on the development of categories. I had several deductive categories prior to my data interpretation, based on my research questions as well as on my previous studies. These categories included among others 'family', 'work' and 'vocational education'. After the first rounds of data interpretation several of these categories became more refined, for example 'work' was split into 'internship' and 'work' and 'vocational education' was split into 'life in school' and 'vocational education'. During this process, I also added several inductive categories which were developed from the interview material itself, e.g. 'motivation', 'communication' and 'independence'. I defined each category and added one or more anchor examples, for example: category: 'motivation', definition: reasons for doing something, anchor example: 'In future, I cannot rely on my parents anymore. This always motivates me'; or category: 'belief', definition: opinion, dogma, anchor example: 'My generation has big financial pressure'. The categories were then structured into broader main categories and sub-categories with, for example 'internship' being a main category and 'entering society' being an inductive sub-category. Additionally, I wrote short memos about ideas, insights and questions that came to my mind during the analysis, e.g. 'Frequent use of proverbs' and 'Contradicts himself concerning future plans: staying with internship company and finding employment himself'. Using a Microsoft Excel spread sheet, I grouped all statements together according to their category. In subsequent interviews, I could then see what each student had said about each category over the years, and I could compare the development of a single student, as well as the differences between the students. In a final step, I wrote a summary for each category.

All the names of interviewed students were anonymized and further information is displayed as follows: (No. of interview_sex/school initial year of study or G for graduated). (1_F/F2) would be information derived during a first interview with a female student in Fengxian School in her second year of study. (3_M/QG) would be information derived during a third interview with a male Qingpu student who already graduated. After a direct quotation the initial of the student's anonymized name and the interview location are provided. Thus, (LQ1_75) would be a quote from a student whose pseudonym starts with L and Q, e.g. Lei Qiang, who provided the cited information in the 75th statement in his first interview.

In 2013, 17 students in total were interviewed, about half of them being first year students. The average age of students was 17 years with the youngest one being 15 and the oldest being 21. In 2014, 15 of these 17 students were interviewed for a second time. The average age of the students was 18 years with the youngest one being 16 and the oldest one 22. In 2015, 11 students were interviewed for a third time. Their average age was 19 years with the youngest one being 17 and the oldest one 22. Additionally two graduated students from each school were interviewed. Three of them were 20 or 21 years and one of them was 38 years.

Table 4.2: Interviews 2013 – Overview.

2013 Interviews		Fengxian School		Qingpu School	
		Male	Female	Male	Female
First year	Shanghai		1	2	
	Migrant	2	1	2	
Second Year	Shanghai	1			
	Migrant	1	1		1
Third Year	Shanghai	1			
	Migrant		1		
Fourth Year	Shanghai		1		
	Migrant			1	1
Graduated	Shanghai				
	Migrant				

Source: Author's own illustration

Table 4.3: Interviews 2014 – Overview.

2014 Interviews		Fengxian School		Qingpu School	
		Male	Female	Male	Female
First Year	Shanghai				
	Migrant				
Second Year	Shanghai		1	2	
	Migrant	2	1	2	
Third Year	Shanghai	1			
	Migrant	1	1		
Graduated	Shanghai	1			
	Migrant		1	2	

Source: Author's own illustration

Table 4.4: Interviews 2015 – Overview.

2015 Interviews		Fengxian School		Qingpu School	
		Male	Female	Male	Female
First Year	Shanghai				
	Migrant				
Second Year	Shanghai				
	Migrant				
Third Year	Shanghai	1	1	1	
	Migrant	2		2	
Graduated	Shanghai	2	1	1	1
	Migrant	1	1	1	

Source: Author's own illustration

4.3.2 The Questionnaire Data

The first 17 interviews in 2013 were followed by a survey in 2014. Concepts appearing during the interviews were included in the questionnaire in order to find out how relevant they are in general (e.g. 'If you don't go forwards, you go backwards'). In addition to this inductive method, several concepts prevalent in other related studies were included as well (e.g. 'Higher middle school students hardly ever have the chance to get in touch with society'). Altogether, there were six main topics closely linked to the categories which were developed from the interviews: vocational education (choosing school, opinions on vocational education, expectations on education), family background, self-assessment, expectations and wishes concerning the future, opinions on society, plus demographical information. During the interviews, most students were comfortable answering questions about school and daily life. Therefore, the questionnaire started with this topic. Questions about self-perception and society which required more reflection and were generally more difficult to answer were placed at the end of the questionnaire. The questionnaire contained three different question types:

-   Multiple choice questions with one possible answer
-   Multiple choice questions where more than one answer could be chosen
-   Questions requiring a rating of agreement from 'not at all' to 'very much' on a 1 to 5 Likert scale

Some questions included the option to give an open answer ('Other, please explain: …'). The last section of the questionnaire concerned demographical data (age, hometown, former school, brothers or sisters, etc.) and gave the option to write a comment or volunteer additional information.

The questionnaire was proofread by a native speaker. A professional interpreter and native Chinese speaker made a translation back to German. Then, the questionnaire was tested with two students, one second year student from Fengxian School and one third year student from Qingpu School. Both students were able to understand the instructions given and filled the questionnaire in just under 20 minutes.

The survey was conducted in classrooms and teachers explained the importance of filling in the questionnaire according to one's own opinion without thinking about right or wrong. It turned out to be difficult to get the third year students since in both schools they only came back for the graduation ceremony. In Qingpu School the students had no interest in sitting down and focusing on a questionnaire after they had just been handed their graduation certificates. Teachers did their best to get them to concentrate one last time and after few minutes the atmosphere became quieter. Yet, some students did not fill in the questionnaire. Fengxian School had their graduation ceremony at a time when I was not in China and, therefore, the students filled the questionnaires in my absence.

In 2015, a second survey was conducted. The new questionnaire partly included the same items as the 2014 questionnaire as well as some new additions. Topics were students' motivation, sense of belonging, opinions on school and classes, self-assessment, family relationships, and plans and wishes concerning students' future. The first part, on sense of belonging, motivation and opinions on school and education, consisted of new items. The family-related items were items from the first questionnaire complemented by new items. Self-assessment items were repeated from the first questionnaire, values were mainly repeated with a few new items added. Future plans were repeated while items concerning leisure activities were new. The demographical data stayed the same. With the mix of old and new items, changes in the opinions of students could be identified and, at the same, time a broader, more complex picture of the research sample evolved. The questionnaire was proofread by, and discussed with, a native Chinese speaker. Except for the question on leisure activities, all items required the same Likert scale rating from 1 to 5 as it had already been used in the first questionnaire. The survey was again administered in the classroom with the support of the classroom teachers.

4.3.2.1 Sample Composition and Analysis

With the two questionnaires two different sets of data were created. The first one is a large sample including all students who filled in the first questionnaire, hereafter called questionnaire A.

These are Qingpu School first, third and fourth year electrical engineering students[12], as well as Fengxian first and third year students and Mechatronic Company class students in their second year. Since the cohorts in Fengxian School were considerably smaller than in Qingpu School, the questionnaire had been administered for a second time in 2015 with the new first year electrical engineering cohort in Fengxian School. The questionaire is able to give a broad overview of the student population enrolled in electrical engineering in both schools.

---

[12]   Both, third and fourth year electrical engineering students were graduating in 2014.

Table 4.5: Questionnaire A – Overview I.

Questionnaire A	No. of students in the cohort	Valid question-naires
Qingpu School – Electrical engineering first year 2014	145	128
Qingpu School – Electrical engineering third and fourth year 2014	167	101
Fengxian School – Electrical engineering first year 2014	32	32
Fengxian School – Electrical engineering first year 2015	31	30
Fengxian School – Mechantronic Company class second year 2014	32	32
Fengxian School – Electrical engineering third year 2014	31	30

Source: Author's own survey 2014, 2015

Table 4.6: Questionnaire A – Overview II.

Questionnaire A	Percentage (N)		
Students' school	Fengxian School	Qingpu School	n/a
	35.8% (128)	64% (229)	0.3% (1)
Students' sex	Male students	Female students	n/a
	78.5% (281)	17.3% (62)	4.2% (15)
Students' hukou	Shanghainese students	Migrant students	n/a
	45% (161)	42.2% (151)	12.8% (46)

Source: Author's own survey 2014, 2015

The second questionnaire, hereafter referred to as questionnaire B or 'Panel Data – Second Year', was administered in 2015 in the second year electrical engineering cohort in both schools. To analyze changes between the first and the second year, a panel data set was created by using all first year electrical engineering data sets from 2014, and all second year electrical engineering data sets from 2015. For a few specific analyzes a real panel data set was created by only selecting students who could be clearly identified as having participated in both surveys. These students were identified by their birthdates and other demographic data such as school, year of study and *hukou*. In the end, there were 91 students who participated in both surveys and provided sufficient demographical data to unambiguously identify them.

Table 4.7: Questionnaire B – Overview I.

Questionnaire B	No. of students in the cohort	Valid question-naires
Qingpu School – Electrical engineering second year 2015	145	105
Fengxian School – Electrical engineering second year 2015	31	31

Source: Author's own survey 2015

Table 4.8: Questionnaire B – Overview II.

Questionnaire B	Percentage (N)		
Students' school	Fengxian School	Qingpu School	n/a
	22.8% (31)	77.2% (105)	0.0% (0)
Students' sex	Male students	Female students	n/a
	79.4% (108)	17.6% (24)	2.9% (4)
Students' *hukou*	Shanghainese students	Migrant students	n/a
	44.1% (60)	39.0% (53)	16.9% (23)

Source: Author's own survey 2015

SPSS was used to analyze the data sets. For the five point Likert scale items, means and standard deviations were computed, and in a second step, differences between school, sex, *hukou* and year of study were checked for each item. Correlations between two items were identified with Pearson's Chi Square.

After this descriptive assessment, a principal axis factor analysis with oblique rotation (direct oblimin) was conducted on some items to create factors. A factor analysis can measure so-called latent variables which cannot be measured directly such as attitudes or positive and negative experiences in school. It is also a useful way to reduce a data set with many items. Sampling adequacy was verified with the Kaiser-Meyer Olkin measure. Scree plot and eigenvalues helped to define the appropriate number of factors. The reliability of each factor was assessed with Cronbach's Alpha. Factor scores for each individual case were attained by computing the mean of sum scores of all item loading >0.4 on a factor.

Finally, in order to identify opinion groups within the sample, clusters were computed. In a first step, Ward method and squared Euclidian distance created hierarchical clusters which indicated the ideal number of clusters. These were then produced using K-Means analysis (Voß et al. 2012; Field 2013).

4.3.3 Additional Data

4.3.3.1 Teacher Interviews

In 2015, two teachers from each school were interviewed. In Fengxian School the classroom teachers of the electrical engineering and the mechatronics company classes were chosen as interview partners. In Qingpu School the classroom teachers were not willing to participate in the interview and instead two senior teachers who had worked for the school for many years volunteered. The interviews were used to validate the results from student interviews and questionnaires. Interestingly, all four teachers from both schools had very similar opinions which also matched my own findings. Therefore, no additional teachers were interviewed.

4.3.3.2 Tutor Interviews

In 2013, two of the students' tutors in companies were interviewed. These tutors are experienced workers who introduce the students to their tasks during the internship. In my case both workers were low-skilled, female workers who took care of female students. Unfortunately, companies were reluctant to allow tutors to participate in interviews, and therefore, only two interviews were conducted.

4.3.3.3 Classroom Observations

Between 2013 and 2015, I observed several theory and practice lessons in both schools. This gave me a feeling for classroom dynamics and for the different teaching styles employed by the teachers during different kinds of lessons. I documented my impressions in a detailed field diary.

4.3.3.4 Factory Visits

Unfortunately, only a couple of factory visits were possible during my research and only during one visit was I allowed to see the actual workshop and a students' work station. Visits to the dormitory or observations of the work were not possible and most companies refused a visit altogether.

5   Students' Lives

This first empirical data-based chapter will approach students from their environment. In order to understand how they feel and see the world, we first must understand which surroundings they live in and how their daily lives are structured. Focusing on students' living circumstances, this chapter shows what vocational education students have in common, what sets them apart from other youth in Shanghai, and it highlights differences within the group. Since family relations, gender, native place and relationships with peers and teachers all turned out to have important influences on students' opinions on vocational education and their assessments of their own situations, this chapter provides important background information.

The first part focuses on students' families. Differences in parents' education levels and origins, as well as the resulting implications for students, are analyzed. While the majority of students lived in nuclear families and enjoyed positive relationships with their parents, some students grew up in divorced families or were 'left-behind children' during lower middle school in their hometown because their parents had moved to Shanghai for work. Here it becomes clear that vocational education is not necessarily a bad choice because it actually raises children's education level above their parents' and in some cases makes a family reunion possible.

The second part of this chapter turns to students' lives in school. Students talk about their daily routines, their relationships with each other and with teachers and they describe how they spend their leisure time. The positive overtones with which most students speak about their regular school days are surprising at first, and they emphasize the fact that most students did not have an easy time in their lower middle schools. It turns out that at least to some degree vocational education does provide more happiness and freedom.

5.1   Family Life

Almost all the students grew up in nuclear families who usually lived close to school – no matter if they were Shanghainese or migrants. Some students lived on campus during the week and returned home during weekends but even if students were boarding, they still referred to themselves as living with their parents.

According to the questionnaire, 46.6% of the students had siblings but during the interviews, it became clear that some students referred to cousins as brothers or sisters. Therefore, the questionnaire results on this question must be interpreted with caution. Significantly more migrant students than Shanghainese had siblings, which is plausible because the one-child policy had been strictly enforced in Shanghai whereas in other parts of China a second child was permitted under specific circumstances. Among the interview sample, 50% of migrant students had siblings but all Shanghainese students were only-children. A few students also mentioned grandparents whom they visit or to whom they were close.

Table 5.1: Questionnaire A – Siblings.

Questionnaire A (First, third, fourth year electrical engineering, second year Mechatronic Company Class)		Valid percent (cases)
Having siblings - Yes		46.6% (158)
Having siblings - Yes	Shanghainese students	28.6%* (46)
	Migrant students	64.7%* (97)

Notes: * = sign .05

Source: Author's own survey 2014, 2015

Students' parents were simple workers or self-employed in Shanghai's suburbs. In the questionnaires, the majority of students either did not answer the open question on parents' profession or simply wrote 'worker' (*gongren* 工人). During the interviews it was confirmed that almost all of the parents either worked in factories or were small traders. Among the fathers' jobs were breeding fish, working in a post office, being a driver, selling ping-pong tables, being a wood worker and working in a car repair shop. Among the mothers' jobs were doing laundry for the elderly, working in a restaurant, in a weaving factory, in a glass factory and in a printing company. All of these jobs are relatively lowly paid and parents were probably trained on the job.

5.1.1 Parents' Educational Background

The majority of parents, Shanghainese as well as migrants, had low education levels. 70% attended school for nine years or fewer, and as we have seen, they were unqualified workers and, therefore, had a relatively low income.[13] The studies by Chen and Ling confirm that there usually is no big income difference between Shanghainese and migrant families living in Shanghai's suburbs (Chen, Feng 2013: 79; Ling 2015: 128–130).

Table 5.2: Questionnaire A – Parents' Education Level I.

Highest education level		
Questionnaire A (First, third and fourth year electrical engineering, second year Mechatronic Company Class)	Father Valid percent (cases)	Mother Valid percent (cases)
Primary school	12.3% (41)	21.2% (68)
Lower middle school	56.9% (189)	50.2% (161)
Higher middle school	20.5% (68)	17.4% (56)
Vocational school	4.2% (14)	4.4% (14)
Tertiary education	6.0% (20)	6.9% (22)

Source: Author's own survey 2014, 2015

While parents' overall education levels were low, they nonetheless correlated with *hukou* and Shanghainese parents had more years of schooling. Additionally, there was a strong link between fathers' and mothers' education; most fathers and mothers shared the same education level.

---

[13] Questions on income were not included in the questionnaire. During interviews, some students found it difficult to describe their parents' profession and it seemed unlikely that they would be able to make a reliable statement on their parents' income.

Table 5.3: Questionnaire A – Parents' Education Level II.

Highest education level				
Questionnaire A (First, third and fourth year electrical engineering, second year Mechatronic Company Class)	Father Valid percent (cases)		Mother Valid percent (cases)	
	Shanghai	Other	Shanghai	Other
Primary school	8.8%* (14)	16.4%* (24)	8.9%* (14)	37.3%* (53)
Lower middle school	51.9%* (83)	63.0%* (92)	45.9% (72)	52.8% (75)
Higher middle school	21.9% (35)	18.5% (27)	23.6%* (37)	9.9%* (14)
Vocational school	8.1%* (13)	0.7%* (1)	8.9%* (14)	0%* (0)
Tertiary education	9.4%* (15)	1.4%* (2)	12.7%* (20)	0%* (0)

Notes: * = sign .05

Source: Author's own survey 2014, 2015

Differentiating by school, it became apparent that parents whose children went to the German-influenced Fengxian School had a higher education level than parents who sent their children to the more traditional Qingpu School. A significantly higher percentage of Fengxian School students' fathers had vocational education or a higher education degree, compared to Qingpu School students' fathers. They were also less likely to have only primary school education, although this difference was not significant. Fengxian School students' mothers were also significantly more likely to have a vocational education or higher education degree, and they were less likely to have only primary school education compared to Qingpu School students' mothers, but schools and *hukou* correlate. There were more Shanghainese students in Fengxian School, and therefore the differences between schools and parents' education level might be down to *hukou*. A partial correlation proved that *hukou* and having a father who attended school nine years or fewer significantly correlated while controlling for students' school (sign .01). The same was true for mothers with an education level of nine years or fewer. The correlation was not significant, however, when correlating students' school and one parent's education level of nine years or fewer while controlling for *hukou*.

Table 5.4: Questionnaire A – Parents' Education Level III.

Questionnaire A	Highest education level			
	Father		Mother	
(First, third and fourth year electrical engineering, second year Mechatronic Company Class)	Valid percent (cases)		Valid percent (cases)	
	Fengxian School	Qingpu School	Fengxian School	Qingpu School
Primary school	7.9% (10)	15.0% (31)	15.4%* (19)	24.7%* (49)
Lower middle school	55.6% (70)	57.8% (119)	44.7% (55)	53.5% (106)
Higher middle school	19.0% (24)	21.4% (44)	20.3% (25)	15.7% (31)
Vocational school	7.9%* (10)	1.9%* (4)	8.1%* (10)	2.0%* (4)
Higher education	9.5%* (12)	3.9%* (8)	11.4%* (14)	4.0%* (8)

Notes: * = sign .05

Source: Author's own survey 2014, 2015

Previous studies have pointed out that socio-economic factors, such as parents' education level and occupation, impact on students' chances to attend university (Chen 2016: 158–159). The low level of parents' education in the present sample is likely to have influenced students' performance in lower middle school and contributed to their failure in the final lower middle school exam.[14] According to Bourdieu, education claims to be objective while in reality fortifying existing differences in society (Hepp 2009: 24–25). Students only perform well in schools when they have acquired the right *habitus*, the habit of thinking and acting that fits the school, beforehand. Students learn their *habitus* through parental education and conditioning (Kupfer 2014: 145).

---

[14] Chapter 6.1 will show that having failed the lower middle school exam was one of the main reasons students entered vocational education.

Studies in China revealed that students struggle when they enter social environments in educational institutions which differ from their family environment. During his research at a key university in Beijing, Li He (2013) found that rural students had considerable difficulties adjusting to their new environment and becoming accustomed to the urban lifestyle. Chen Yu (2016) confirmed that the examination-based school system with key schools on the upper secondary and tertiary education level favors students with good financial, political (party membership) and academic family backgrounds and it leads to an unequal distribution of social, economic and academic resources for certain groups of people. Lin Yi (2005) showed how Muslim children's reputation as poor students turns into a self-fulfilling prophecy, thereby leading to a vicious cycle in which Muslim minorities have lower education levels and are considered more backwards than the *Han* Chinese majority (*hanzu* 汉族) or other ethnic minorities.

Parents' education level in the present study suggests that the majority of students would not have had the right *habitus* for an academic higher middle school. Even in a vocational school, it is questionable whether students whose parents only have primary or lower middle school education would be able to adapt. Following Bourdieu, one would have to assume that students without the right *habitus* will struggle with vocational education. However, as will be shown later in this chapter, students' *habitus* did fit their education, but at the same time more years of schooling did not raise their relative status in society.

In fact, students' educational aspirations were linked to parents' education level. In the sample 69.2% of students' fathers had an education of nine years or fewer (230 cases). On a five point Likert scale ranging from 1 (= 'no agreement at all') to 5 (= 'completely agree'), these students had a significantly lower agreement rate with the statement that 'After vocational education, I want to get a higher education degree' than students whose fathers had more than nine years of schooling. The same is true on the mother's side: 71.4% of students' mothers had an education of nine years or fewer (292 cases) and their children agreed significantly less with this statement. The agreement rate with the statement that 'Not being able to go to a higher middle school gave me a feeling of frustration' rose with a rising education level on the fathers' side. The same was true for mothers' education level except for mothers with tertiary education, where the agreement rate dropped. Equally relevant was *hukou*. For both statements – 'After vocational education, I want to get a higher education degree' and 'Not being able to go to a higher middle school gave me a feeling of frustration' – the agreement rate among Shanghainese students was significantly higher than among migrant students – but as mentioned above, *hukou* and parents' education level correlated as well.

A partial correlation analysis revealed that the correlation between 'hukou' and 'After vocational education, I want to get a higher education degree' was significant while controlling fathers' education level as well as while controlling mothers' education level (sign .01).[15] It was not significant when 'hukou' was used as the controlling variable. Therefore, the conclusion must be that while parents' education level certainly does have an influence, the broader environment is an even more important factor determining students' educational aspirations and tertiary education is still more common and more important in Shanghai than in other less developed parts of the country. In summary, migrant students are more likely to come from families with relatively low education levels and they are also more likely to be content with their secondary vocational education degree.

This result confirms what has been put forward by other studies on social mobility in China as well: Parents' education levels, occupation and income, as well as, socio-economic status and home background, are among the factors which influence the likelihood of students attaining tertiary education levels (Chen 2016: 158–159).

My sample supports the theory that school reproduces society (Kramer 2014: 432; Furlong, Cartmel 1997: 19). The students came from families with a low educational background and, due to diploma inflation, they will be considered people with low educational background themselves once they finish school. The 'elevator effect' which Beck formulated in order to describe the social development in Germany after the Second World War also applies in China (Beck 1986: 122). The parents' generation worked hard and their children will have a better education and a higher income but, at the same time, education level and income will be relatively low in their children's generation. This may not be the case when compared to the average of all of China since there is a massive developmental difference between eastern, central and western parts, but it will certainly be low when compared to the rest of society in eastern China, where the students lived.

---

[15] The dichotomous variables 'father attended school for nine years or fewer' and 'mother attended school for nine years or fewer' were controlled.

Table 5.5: Questionnaire A – Fathers' Education / 'After vocational education, I want to get a higher education degree'.

'After vocational education, I want to get a higher education degree'	
Questionnaire A (First, third and fourth year electrical engineering, second year Mechatronic Company Class)	Mean
Father <= 9 years education	3.5**
Father > 9 years education	4.0**
Mother <= 9 years education	3.6**
Mother > 9 years education	4.1**
Shanghainese Students	4.0**
Migrant Students	3.3**

Notes: ** = sign .01; Likert Scale 1 = 'Do not agree at all' – 5 = 'Totally agree'

Source: Author's own survey 2014, 2015

Table 5.6: Questionnaire A – Parents' Education / 'Not being able to go to higher middle school gave me a feeling of frustration'.

'Not being able to go to higher middle school gave me a feeling of frustration'				
Questionnaire A (First, third and fourth year electrical engineering, second year Mechatronic Company Class)	Primary school	Lower middle school	Higher middle school	Higher education
Fathers' highest education	2.2	2.7	3.1	3.2
Mothers' highest education	2.6	2.7	3.2	2.3

Notes: Likert Scale 1 = 'Do not agree at all' – 5 = 'Totally agree'

Source: Author's own survey 2014, 2015

It is important to recognize that, as Ling pointed out, for migrant families this reproduction of society in Shanghai happens with no exception due to government regulations which do not allow migrant students to enter an academic higher middle school (Ling 2015: 131). The fact that less well-off Shanghainese families also do not manage to climb up the social ladder suggests that these regulations only cement a social reproduction that would have been likely anyway.

5.1.2 Family Relationships

Most students had a good relationship with their parents and felt that their parents supported and cared for them. Many students considered their parents the biggest influence in their lives. The Chinese word 'family'/'home' (*jia* 家) had solely positive associations such as harmony, happiness, warmth, and good food. Students recognized that their parents work for the family. Xue Mei (1_F/Q4): "I know how hard my parents work...how they brought us up." (XM1_10). They recognized that their parents' lives were bitter (*ku* 苦) and they showed a lot of empathy for them. Students strongly agreed with the statement that 'My parents' generation had a hard life' and 'My parents' generation lived for the children and the family'. The agreement rate with the latter statement was significantly higher among older students. This suggests a growing understanding which students also mentioned during the interviews. They also strongly agreed with the statement that 'I respect my parents', 'My parents love me', 'I have a good relationship with my parents' and 'Family is my harbor'. Family was valued importantly by the students and as such will be further discussed in Chapter 8.1.1.

Students did mention fights with their parents but usually described them as either negligible or as a thing of the past which does not happen anymore because they gained a better understanding of their parents. Nineteen year old Xue Mei (1_F/Q4), for example, used to fight with her parents but she claimed to have stopped because she started to understand their hard life. Fifteen year old De Hua (1_M/Q1) had not reached this point in 2013. Although he knew his parents meant well, he did not listen to them. Analyzing the causes for his own behavior, he said that it was age-related. Overall, the agreement rate with 'I often fight with my parents' was low but Shanghainese students agreed more with this statement than migrant students. Interestingly though, Fengxian School students (who were mainly Shanghainese) agreed more with 'I respect my parents' and 'I have a good relationship with my parents' in the second year of their education.

The relationship between students and their parents was generally harmonious but parents' education, family *hukou*, and the students' schools were influential factors. The relationship between migrant students and their lesser-educated parents appeared to be better than between Shanghainese students and their better-educated parents. In the second year, Shanghainese students also agreed more with the statement that 'I disappoint my parents', whereas migrant students agreed more with 'My parents are proud of me'. If the mother has had more than twelve years of schooling – which was true only in a few cases – students were less likely to agree with 'My parents are proud of me'. This is in line with what has been discussed previously: parents' education shapes children's aspirations and influences how students experience their parents' feelings towards them. Including the *hukou*-related correlations, it became clear that being Shanghainese and having better-educated parents led to students feeling different expectations, and the greater likelihood that they would feel that they were not living up to these, which in turn stressed the relationship between parents and children.

Besides parents with better education having higher expectations, the parental pressure to succeed in school and find a good job has also been linked to the fact that the majority of the younger generation in China grows up without siblings (Fong 2004: 28–29), and media has been blaming this pressure as a cause for suicides and mental illness (Fong 2004: 87). Only-children carry the sole responsibility when it comes to taking care of parents in old-age and living up to their expectations. In fact, agreement rates with the statement that 'My parents put big pressure on me' was higher for students without siblings irrespective of *hukou*.

Being an only child not only increases pressure but also the likelihood of being spoiled (Fong 2004: 29). This phenomenon of the spoiled only-child generation has been frequently discussed in the media as 'Little Emperor Syndrome'. Student Li An (1_F/F1) described the phenomenon:

> I think my generation is quite precocious and quite spoiled [...]. Precocious because their fathers and mothers did not look after them because they [parents] were working a lot [...]. Some turned from being pure to being spoiled. I think some people think they are amazing, they just are too spoiled. Then parents are not with them, they [children] are with their grandparents. The grandparents love them dearly and do not have them do anything. They are like flowers in a greenhouse. My generation, if they are not spoiled they are precocious. (LA1_84)

Table 5.7a: Questionnaire A + B – Family Relationships.

Questionnaire A (First, third and fourth year electrical engineering, second year Mechatronic Company Class)		Mean
My parents' generation had a hard life.		4.4
My parents' generation lived for the children and the family.		4.2
My parents' generation lived for the children and the family.	First year	4.0**
	Third year	4.3**
I have a good relationship with my parents.		4.2
Family is my harbor.		4.3
I often fight with my parents.		2.3
I often fight with my parents.	Shanghainese students	2.4*
	Migrant students	2.1*
The 1990s Generation is spoiled.		3.0
The 1990s Generation is spoiled.	Male students	3.2**
	Female students	2.5**

Notes: * = sign .05, ** = sign .01; Likert Scale 1 = 'Do not agree at all' – 5 = 'Totally agree'

Source: Author's own survey 2014, 2015

Zhang Hua (1_F/F3) linked the spoiled 1990s Generation not to parental education but to the economic development:

The older generation says they [1990s Generation] are spoiled and pampered. Actually, being pampered and spoiled is also what this decade gave us because before it was enough to have enough to eat. Now after being full, there are more material needs. There is continuous development in this decade and people have more and more needs. (ZH1_62)

Table 5.7b: Questionnaire A + B – Family Relationships.

Questionnaire B (Panel Data – Second Year)		Mean
My parents love me.		4.3
I respect my parents.		4.3
I respect my parents.	Fengxian School students	4.7*
	Qingpu School students	4.2*
I have a good relationship with my parents.	Fengxian School students	4.5*
	Qingpu School students	4.0*
I disappoint my parents.	Shanghainese students	2.8*
	Migrant students	2.2*
My parents are proud of me.	Shanghainese students	3.3*
	Migrant students	3.8*
My parents are proud of me.	Mother's education > 12 years	2.8*
	Mother's education <= 12 years	3.6*
My parents spoil me.		2.3

Notes: * = sign .05, ** = sign .01; Likert Scale 1 = 'Do not agree at all' – 5 = 'Totally agree'

Source: Author's own survey 2014, 2015

Interestingly, Zhang Hua assessed her generation similar to Yunxiang Yan's description of the 1980s' generation. Yan pointed out that the 'frail pragmatists' born in the 1980s were commonly considered spoiled because of their circumstances: their parents were able to provide for them materially and they never missed out on anything. In return, the younger generation had to give up their carefree childhood and study hard in order to satisfy parents' expectations. Yan concluded that young people do not feel that they are spoiled because they had to make this tradeoff (Yan 2006: 261–262). His argument has limited explanatory power in the case of vocational education students because they dropped out of the arduous study regime in academic middle schools and therefore do not trade their childhood for material benefits anymore. Also, Li An's frank description of her own generation would indicate that other students might admit as well to being part of a spoiled generation. Nevertheless, this was not the case.

Participants overall had a very low agreement rate with the statement that 'My parents spoil me', and they were neutral towards the general statement that 'The 1990s Generation is spoiled'. Male students agreed slightly with this statement while female students disagreed, which suggests that male students were more often pampered. However, as Yan pointed out, there is no definition or agreement on what 'being spoiled' involves and every assessment depends on what is considered normal standard. Parents' limited financial assets compared to the Shanghainese middle class could therefore explain why students in the sample did not feel spoiled.

Table 5.8: Questionnaire B – Pressure from Parents.

'My parents put big pressure on me'					
Questionnaire B (Panel Data – Second Year)	All students	Shanghainese students	Migrant students	Male students	Female students
Having siblings - yes	2.5	2.7	2.4	2.4	2.9
Having siblings - no	3.0	3.0	3.2	2.9	3.0

Notes: Likert Scale 1 = 'Do not agree at all' – 5 = 'Totally agree'

Source: Author's own survey 2014, 2015

5.1.3 Divorce and Separation

The divorce rate in China has been rising for the last 30 years (Xu 2017c: 153) and several students in the sample had divorced parents. According to one Qingpu School teacher, about 20% of the students live with only one parent. In the interview sample four of the initial 17 students' parents were divorced. In the questionnaire, 12.5% of the students said that their parents were divorced and 14.6% of the students said that they come from a one-parent family. These numbers are significantly higher than China's nationwide refined crude divorce rate of 7% in 2010 as quoted by Xu (2017: 154) referring to the national census.[16] This strongly suggests that students coming from broken families are more likely to leave the academic education system and to enter vocational education.

A divorce ultimately changes family structures and the relationship between students and parents. There were a few students who shared their experiences during the interviews. Zhao Jing (1_M/F1), a tall, slightly cross-eyed Fengxian School student, was struggling with his parents both having new partners. In 2013, he said that his mother, who lived in Shenzhen, never cared about him and never got in touch.

> My former mom, in one sentence, is a slave to money (*cainu* 财奴); my current mother [fathers' new wife], how to say...is... a bit mischievous (*tiaopi* 调皮), really mischievous, just like her daughter, the same personality. (ZJ1_56).

He applied two metaphors to describe his family. He compared his first family, his biological parents, with a broken vase that cannot be fixed anymore. His new family, his father and his new stepmother, he compared with a plant that yields limitless harvest. Considering that Zhao Jing did not speak at all fondly of his stepmother, the reality did not seem to be as nice as this metaphor suggests. In 2015, Zhao Jing had visited his mother and her new partner in Shenzhen and, subsequently, decided not to visit her again. His parents' influence in his life was showing him the frustrations of life, said Zhao Jing in that year. He prided himself as one of the best students in class but he had gotten in trouble with his superior during his internship and was sent back to school early where he kept himself busy with founding a Lego group. Clearly, a troubled home can add to the difficulties of coping with the challenges of vocational education.

Two female students lived with their divorced fathers. Both said that they have to take care of the household for their fathers. Li Miao (1_F/Q2): "If I did not take care of my father, then he would have nobody who would take care of him" (LM1_96) and Wen Qing (3_F/F3):

> Because he is a man, some chores he does not like to do. When I'm at home during the weekend, then I do it. Every week, I clean up, I do the kitchen, my room, his room, cleaning, doing chores, cooking. This is only a little time. (WQ3_90)

---

[16]   The refined crude divorce rate is the number of divorces per 1000 women married to men in a given year. A refined crude divorce rate of 7% means that there is one divorce per 143 married couples (Xu 2017c: 154).

Wen Qing, the latter student cited, spoke very openly about her broken family during her three interviews. Wen Qing's father was from Anhui province and her mother from Sichuan. Her mother wanted to go to university but lacked funding. She came to Shanghai to work where she met Wen Qing's father. They married. When Wen Qing was four, her mother went to her home in Anhui and never returned. Wen Qing did not know where her mother was and her father got angry when she asked about her. He told her that her mother does not miss her. Wen Qing missed her mother, however, and wanted to look for her once she had the financial resources to do so on her own. Her father worked for a relative in Shanghai but Wen Qing did not know his position or what exactly he did. She said that she and her dad were middle class (*zhong deng* 中等) but rather poor compared to Shanghainese families. The relationship between Wen Qing and her father was difficult and defined by conflict. In 2013, during the first interview, she said that she had a good relationship with her father; that her father treasured her and that she loved him, but the rest of the interview revealed that the father-daughter relationship was more complicated. Her father preferred boys and, at the same time, scolded her for her boyish behavior. He was annoyed by Wen Qing. As a result, she chose not to talk to him. In 2014, Wen Qing said that her relationship with her dad was getting better and that they were sometimes able to talk with each other. She dared to voice her opinion and they had a discussion. In 2015, it almost sounded like a breakthrough: Wen Qing recounted a big fight with her father and afterwards they talked things out. Since then, the relationship was very good according to her. She explained that her father had a bad temper and he took it out on her. She told him that she cannot take it anymore and since then they listened to each other and communicated on an equal level. Wen Qing still had no contact with her mother. It looked as if Wen Qing's growing up and being able to reason with her father led to the relationship improving and the biggest fights being avoided. It also seemed as if Wen Qing's mother was occupying a less prominent space in her mind. When asked about her during the last interview, Wen Qing did not go into details anymore and did not mention earlier plans of earning enough money to go after her and find her. Wen Qing had learned to accept her family situation the way it was and was also learning how to deal with her father.

Even if parents were not divorced, any separation was hard to handle for the students. With more than 200 million migrants living in Chinese cities, the problems their left-behind children encounter in the home provinces have attracted the attention of the government (Chan 2009: 5). Drawing on a population survey from 2010, the All-China Women's Federation claims that 21.9% of all children in China are left-behind. When both parents are gone, most children live with their grandparents (32.7% of left-behind children) or with other people (10.7%) (All-China Women's Federation 2013). Most of these children see their parents only once or twice a year. They often lack supervision and are more likely to be involved in accidents or become victims of crime compared to children living with their parents. Also, their caretakers often care about physical safety only and neglect children's psychological needs, which leads to depression, anxiety, and low-self-esteem (Chan 2009: 7–18).

For parents who were working in Shanghai while their children were in their home provinces, the vocational education policies in Shanghai made family reunions possible. Especially when students did not pass the lower middle school exam, enrolling in a vocational school in Shanghai and living with their parents became the preferred choice for many families, and thus the number of migrant children in cities is growing quickly. In Shanghai, four out of ten children are migrants. The statistics published by the All-China Women's Federation showed that the sex ratio among younger children aged between three and 14 is higher than among the left-behind children, meaning that parents are more likely to take their sons to the cities for schooling. Daughters on the other hand are more likely to be brought to the cities after compulsory education so that they can find work. As we know, however, once they settle in the cities, migrants and their children still face different social, cultural and economic discrimination due to the *hukou* system, such as not being allowed to enter an academic higher middle school in Shanghai. Yet, research has shown that children want to be united with their parents (All-China Women's Federation 2013) and the biographies of some of the students in the present study demonstrate the difficulties left-behind children face and how coming to Shanghai to reunite with their parents can be a positive turning point in their lives.

Migrant student De Hua (1_M/Q1) moved to Shanghai with his parents in the first grade of primary school. During lower middle school, he was sent back to his hometown in Jiangsu where he lived with his uncle. During these years he saw his parents only during summer and winter holidays when he visited them. They hardly ever came to see him which was very difficult for De Hua. In 2015, he still mentioned his aunt and uncle as being the biggest influence in his life because they taught him how to behave. During lower middle school, his uncle, who himself only had nine years of schooling, tutored him. De Hua failed the lower middle school exam and, subsequently, came to Shanghai to live with his parents again and go to a vocational school. His parents worked long hours and came home late. His father was a wood worker and his mother worked for a relative in a restaurant. By 2015, however, De Hua did not have a lot of contact with his parents anymore. He still returned home during the weekends but sometimes his parents were out working.

Wang Ming (1_M/F2) had a similar biography. He was originally from Sichuan. During lower middle school, he lived there with his grandparents; his parents, his little sister and two cousins lived in Shanghai. His mother was born in Anhui, where he also spent two years of his life with his uncle, while his mother was sick. Although he had lived only a couple of years in Sichuan, Wang Ming refered to himself as being Sichuanese. He said that his grandparents in Sichuan, as well as his uncle in Anhui, were all good to him, but the majority of his friends are in Shanghai. His homeroom teacher spoke very fondly of Wang Ming. She explained that Wang Ming used to get into fights when he was living with his grandparents, and one time his father had to return to Sichuan to sort things out. Once enrolled in the vocational school, Wang Ming underwent a very positive development and turned out to be one of the best students in the class, according to his teacher. In 2015, he only rarely visited his parents who were still living in Shanghai but were likely to return home soon to take care of Wang Ming's grandparents. Wang Ming himself was planning to stay in Shanghai. He was enrolled in a work and study program, where he was doing a tertiary vocational education degree while working part-time.

Although commonly seen as a second class education, vocational education in Shanghai is not necessarily a worst case scenario when the alternative is growing up with relatives and going to an academic middle school or a vocational school in the provinces. Migrant children in cities still face many difficulties such as unaffordable health care, discrimination in education, social segregation and a higher risk of becoming involved in crime (Chan 2009: 27–44) but the stories of De Hua and Wang Ming show the difficulties left-behind children face in the countryside and how coming to Shanghai and living with their parents was a positive development. Studies on vocational education often approach the subject from the perspective of urban families aspiring upward social mobility. In their case, vocational education is undesirable and a setback. For left-behind children in the provinces, on the other hand, coming to Shanghai and attending a vocational school might be a great opportunity for family reunion and further education.

5.2 Life in School

The influence of family on students' lives cannot be overestimated, but in their day to day lives students on the secondary level spend more time in school than with their families. Therefore, school must be considered an equally important environment.

Students' school days start with exercises in the school yard followed by classes until around 3pm. In Fengxian School, which cooperates with German companies, there were 30 to 32 students in one class. In Qingpu School there were 40 students in one class, but classes were split for practical lessons. In both schools the majority of students were male and there were boarding as well as day-students. Some students knew each other from lower middle school and some were completely new.

Entering a new school is usually a challenge. Students have to get to know new teachers, new peers, adjust to new teaching methods and a new surrounding (Schaupp 2014: 747). They need to recognize what is expected from them in the new school and develop their new role in accordance with their own history (Kramer 2014: 424). A successful school change, however, enables students to manage other changes in their future lives successfully as well (Schaupp 2014: 753–754).

In reality, though, students mastered the school change well. When they entered the vocational school, they did not know what their electrical engineering training would be like. The agreement rate with the statement that 'I did not understand anything about electrical engineering when I came to this school' was high. Yet, they found themselves with classmates who performed equally poorly in their former school and they had different subjects that focused on manual skills instead of theoretical knowledge. Additionally, in these subjects no previous knowledge was required. Students effectively got a second chance. The adjective used most often to describe vocational education was 'relaxed' (*qingsong* 轻松). Students had a good time, at least, compared to their experiences in lower middle school. This is in line with the findings of youth studies conducted in Germany. Students who failed to enter their desired school underwent a positive development. Their grades improved and so did their self-worth (Schaupp 2014: 748–750). This positive experience strengthens students and they regain motivation.

In both schools, students depicted their environments in positive ways. Fengxian School was described as a familiar environment with a good and harmonious atmosphere; Qingpu School's environment was described as good, nice and green. Initially, students liked the big campuses of both schools but after moving, Fengxian School students were less satisfied because the new campus was closed off and students were not allowed to leave anymore. Additionally, the dormitories lacked hot water and had no heating facilities which made the winter very hard. Nonetheless, students generally liked their schools, their peers and their teachers, and only a few criticized the food in the canteen or the dormitories. Life in school was characterized as fun, happy, quiet, harmonious and relaxed. Students enjoyed the community with their peers. The daily routine was shaped by learning, with breaks during which they played sports in the courtyard or chatted with their friends. Students in the second year of their education agreed more with the statement that 'My life in vocational education is happier than in lower middle school' than with the statement that 'My life in lower middle school was happier than in vocational school'. Fengxian School students were happier in their school than Qingpu School students. They agreed significantly more with the statement that 'My life in vocational education is happier than in lower middle school' and with the statement that 'I'm always happy when I get to the classroom in the morning'. Whereas in the first year of their education male students agreed more than female students of the same cohort with the statement that 'During vocational education, life is happy', one year later the differences had disappeared, with both female and male students agreeing that 'My life in vocational education is happier than in lower middle school'.

In the second year of their education most students described a positive development. They got to know their classmates, improved their social contacts and in class they understood more and studied better. De Hua (2_M/Q2):

> When I just entered the school, I was not used to the atmosphere and I studied a bit sluggishly. In class, I was a bit absent minded. Now in the second year, I know the technique of my training course. I have a new understanding. Now, I listen diligently every day in class and I do my tasks with all my capability. This is the biggest change concerning my studies. (DH2_2)

Many students mentioned that they did not need tutoring during the weekends and they also did not have a lot of homework. Vocational education students have a lot of spare time during the first two years of their education.

In the last year with their graduation approaching, students felt pressure in school. Fengxian School students criticized the alternating system, which left them not enough time to study for the exams in the third year. Many students also took *gaofu* (高复) classes, which prepare them for an exam that allows vocational students to enter tertiary vocational education colleges. These classes were held either in the evening or during the weekends and students needed to pay for them. In Qingpu School, some students took *gaofu* classes instead of doing an internship.

When it comes to performance in school, migrant students are often considered weak and less well equipped to adapt to schools in Shanghai. The lower education background of migrant parents would suggest that there is indeed a connection. Chen and Feng (2013) compared the test results of migrant students in public and private schools with Shanghainese students and found that

Shanghainese students had the best results, followed by migrant students in public schools. Migrant students in private schools performed worst of all.

Table 5.9: Questionnaire A + B – Life in Vocational School.

Questionnaire B (Panel Data – Second Year)		Mean
My life in vocational education is happier than in lower middle school.		3.4
My life in vocational education is happier than in lower middle school.	Male students	3.5
	Female students	3.4
My life in lower middle school was happier than in vocational education.		3.0
My life in vocational education is happier than in lower middle school.	Fengxian School students	4.0*
	Qingpu School students	3.3*
I'm always happy when I get to the classroom in the morning.	Fengxian School students	3.4*
	Qingpu School students	2.8*
Questionnaire A (Panel Data – First Year)		Mean
During vocational education, life is happy.	Male students	4.2*
	Female students	3.6*

Notes: * = sign .05; Likert Scale 1 = 'Do not agree at all' – 5 = 'Totally agree'

Source: Author's own survey 2014, 2015

Additionally, the longer migrant students had been living in Shanghai, the better their results, and students whose families had a higher income also had better results (Chen, Feng 2013: 79). Yet, what Chen and Feng did not compare were migrants and people who had been granted an urban *hukou* following the expansion of the city area. Lin Yi (2011) studied a primary school in a suburban village of Xiamen and concluded that teachers generally considered migrants to be striving and hardworking while children from newly urban *hukou* holders were seen as having similar disadvantages while additionally lacking motivation (Lin 2011: 320–321). This would explain teachers' different opinions on their Shanghainese and migrant students in the present sample.

The Fengxian School teachers I interviewed agreed with migrant students being weaker, whereas Qingpu School teachers had a more positive opinion on migrant students' skills. Fengxian School teacher Lin Keping said that Shanghainese students have better basics and adapt better; there is a bigger difference between weak students and strong students. Fengxian School teacher Zheng Lina agreed that migrant students tend to be poor in mathematics and English. They tend to give up and need extra motivation. On the other hand, Qingpu School teacher Zhao Shaofan said that migrant students adapt well and are more simple and plain (*zhipu* 质朴), as well as closer to the teacher than Shanghainese students. Qingpu School teacher Zhang Yuzhou agreed with his colleague: migrant students adjust well since most of them have been living in Shanghai for many years already. Since I did not collect any school results or rural-urban *hukou* information, it is not possible to find out if Shanghainese students or students with urban *hukous* performed better than migrants or students with rural hukous. Teachers' different opinions suggest that there is no evident trend though. With only very few exceptions, all interviewed students said that they were satisfied with their personal grades and that they were improving. Migrant students agreed only slightly more with the statement that 'Chances and difficulties in life depend on *hukou*'.

Perhaps differences in performance were not necessarily linked to *hukou* but without a question students had different levels and were either more or less interested. Some students complained that unmotivated students disturbed the class. Zhang Hua (2_F/FA) complained that students with a poor attitude towards studying had a negative influence on the overall atmosphere of the class. According to her, the school should be stricter and put more pressure on those students. Also Zhao Jing (2_M/F2) mentioned that both good and poor students were in one class, which was not ideal. Wen Qing (3_F/F3) added that teachers were young and often couldn't control the students who disturbed the class. The atmosphere was loud and teachers had to use a microphone.

Table 5.10: Questionnaire A – 'Chances and difficulties depend on *hukou*'.

Questionnaire A (First, third and fourth year electrical engineering, second year Mechatronic Company Class)		Mean
Chances and difficulties in life depend on *hukou*.	Shanghainese students	3.3
	Migrant students	3.5

Notes: Likert Scale 1 = 'Do not agree at all' – 5 = 'Totally agree'

Source: Author's own survey 2014, 2015

5.2.1 Relationships with Teachers

The atmosphere in school depends to a high degree on the teachers. Most students had a close and positive relationship with their teachers, especially the homeroom teacher with whom they spent many hours a day together. These teachers played an important role. They were like a family member and some students considered them the biggest influence in their lives. Students described their teachers as good, humorous, happy, responsible and friendly. The statement 'Teachers are role models for students' had an agreement rate of 4.0.[17] During the interviews, some migrant students also compared their teachers in Shanghai with teachers in their home town who were rude and punished students physically, so a positive relationship with teachers is not a given but a characteristic of the student-teacher relationship in the two vocational schools studied here.

Students preferred strict but humorous teachers. They recognized that they would use any freedom they had in class to do other things, but they also recognized that the consequences would be bad. Therefore, students wanted to have teachers with authority; a few students criticized teachers as not strict enough. Another important characteristic was the sense of humor. Students wanted to be able to laugh with their teachers, and they enjoyed having their attention drawn back to the subject with some jokes. After class, students enjoyed communicating with teachers the same way they communicated with friends. In essence, popular teachers needed to be able to maintain their authority, not allowing the students to disturb the class or miss their homework while at the same time, being able to entertain the students with jokes and make it easier for them to follow the class by presenting study content in a humorous way.

Overall, teachers were hardly ever criticized by the students. Two exceptions were Wen Qing and Li An, both female students in German-influenced Fengxian School but not from the same class. Wen Qing (3_F/F3) complained that teachers did not prepare the classes properly and did not care about the weaker students. They lacked responsibility, according to her. Li An (3_F/FA) made a similar point, saying that teachers did not explain clearly enough and did not check whether students understood.

Despite these two examples, Fengxian School students had a more positive relationship in general with their teachers. The agreement rate with the statement that 'Teachers often scold us students' was significantly lower than for Qingpu School students. Fengxian School students also agreed more with the

---

[17]   Questionnaire A (First, third and fourth year electrical engineering, second year Mechatronic Company Class), Likert Scale 1 = 'Do not agree at all' – 5 = 'Totally agree'.

statement that 'Teachers let us actively participate in class', and 'Teachers often praise us students'. Although the majority of Fengxian School students had a Shanghai *hukou,* the differences are not linked to *hukou.* Migrant students agreed more with 'Teachers consider students interests' and there were no differences in agreement towards the other mentioned statements. Smaller class size in Fengxian School is likely to be one of the factors contributing to a more positive evaluation of their teachers. Teachers can keep a smaller class better under control and students have more opportunities to be active.

Students liked classes in which they did well. For most students these were vocational and practical classes, as well as, sports. When asked about the differences between teaching and learning in lower middle school and vocational school, Li An (1_F/F1) replied:

> There is a big difference. In lower middle school [...] the teachers for example gave us more to learn; we had a lot of homework at home. Now, there is basically no homework and if there is, it is done very quickly. Most of the content is taught by the teacher in class and during our spare time he has us understanding it by ourselves. In lower middle school, this was different. (LA1_34)

Lei Qiang (1_M/F1) described the teaching methods in Fengxian School, where teachers first introduced the theory and later linked it with work-related processes. Theory was applied in practice and the whole training course started from scratch with the very basics.

Teacher-centered teaching, which has students memorizing large amounts of theory and neglects creativity, is often criticized and, generally, considered to be too prominent in Chinese classrooms (Halpin 2014: 2), but when Fengxian and Qingpu School teachers described their teaching methods, a different picture appeared. It became clear that they cared about students' interests. They were aware that students struggled with the memorizing-oriented teaching style in Chinese academic schools. To prevent students from falling behind, teachers had the following approaches: Fengxian School teacher Lin Keping said that he started with the interests of the students and then led over to the actual subject. Fengxian School teacher Zheng Lina focused on lively and flexible teaching and let the students be active. Qingpu School teacher Zhou Shaofan said that she put herself into the position of the students and thought about what they would like. She focused on encouragement instead of scolding and fostered their independence by giving them time to read or discuss on their own. Qingpu School teacher Zhang Yuzhou designed his lessons to be task-oriented. Teachers' own accounts do not necessarily mean that they did not use lecture-style teaching but it certainly shows that they knew which other, more learner-oriented teaching methods exist. Practical lessons held in workshops also contributed to the fact that the oft-criticized teacher-centered teaching was less prominent or at least seemed to be complemented with other teaching methods in the two schools of the present study.

Table 5.11: Questionnaire B – Relationship with Teachers.

Questionnaire B (Panel Data – Second Year)		Mean
Teachers often scold us students.	Fengxian School students	1.8**
	Qingpu School students	2.9**
Teachers often praise us students.	Fengxian School students	3.2
	Qingpu School students	3.0
Teachers let us actively participate in class.	Fengxian School students	4.2**
	Qingpu School students	3.4**
Teachers consider students' interests.	Fengxian School students	3.0
	Qingpu School students	2.9
Teachers consider students' interests.	Shanghainese students	2.8
	Migrant students	3.2

Notes: ** = sign .01; Likert Scale 1 = 'Do not agree at all' – 5 = 'Totally agree'

Source: Author's own survey 2015

In summary, there were three reasons why students had a good relationship with their teachers: First, teachers in both schools were well-trained and had the skills to plan their lessons according to students' needs. Second, vocational education includes practical and manual activities, and the vocational lessons did not require any prior knowledge. Therefore, students had the opportunity to discover new strengths and a feeling of success in class. Third, some students had had negative experiences with former teachers and were glad that their current teachers were more agreeable and understanding. Contrary to this, Hansen and Woronov (2013: 249) found that teacher-student relationships were neither friendly nor respectful in the vocational schools they observed in Nanjing. The good relationships in the present sample are a clear indication for these schools' quality.

5.2.2 Circles of Friends

In their schools, students not only interacted with their teachers but also with friends, and peers are indeed one of the most important influences on youth during adolescence (Ecarius et al. 2011: 113). Students described the atmosphere in their classes as harmonious. They were neutral towards the statement 'My class is a close unit', and they tended to agree with the statement that 'I have many friends in school' but standard deviations for both questions were rather high. During the interviews most students said that they liked peers with open and optimistic personalities as their friends (*kailang* 开朗); other valued traits were loyalty, team spirit, humor, generosity and honesty.

Table 5.12: Questionnaire B – Friends.

Questionnaire B (Panel data – Second year)	Mean	Standard deviation
My class is a close unit.	3.2	1.3
I have many friends in school.	3.8	1.1

Notes: Likert Scale 1 = 'Do not agree at all' – 5 = 'Totally agree'

Source: Author's own survey 2015

Friendships were considered important – not least as a resource for one's future career. Li An (2_F/F3) quoted a Chinese saying to illustrate this importance: "There is a sentence that says it well: what your friends are like determines what your future life will be like." (LA2_84). A few students considered their friends the biggest influence in their lives and some studies have shown that peers can be as important as family since adolescence as a phase of life is becoming longer and youth are spending more free time with their peers (Ecarius et al. 2011: 113, 121). Contact with peers allows students to train their social and professional competencies (Hurrelmann et al. 2014: 67). Friends were also important for the students when they encountered difficulties and they usually stayed in touch at least for some time after changing from lower middle school to vocational school, after moving and also after their graduation.

In Qingpu School, Shanghainese and migrant students were not put in the same class. In Fengxian School, where there is only one electrical engineering class per year, students learn together. Shanghainese student Lei Qiang (3_M/FA) said that despite different family backgrounds and different financial situations, all classmates got along well but, nonetheless, migrant students stuck together and Shanghainese students stuck together. Sometimes they worked together, and sometimes they had different opinions. Lei Qiang also mentioned the different Chinese dialects migrants had, which made it hard to understand each other, and the general prejudice that Chinese people have towards migrant students. "I always feel these are two levels", summarized Lei Qiang (LQ3_22). Shanghainese and migrant students were neither close friends, nor did they fight with each other. The spatial and social segregation as described by Lan Pei-Chia (2014: 255–256), in which migrant students are separated from Shanghainese students and discriminated against by locals, was hardly a topic during the interviews for the present study. This suggests that students do not experience any discrimination, even though locals and migrants are separated in different classes in Qingpu School, or it means that *hukou*-based segregation and discrimination is taken for granted to such an extent that it becomes negligible in students' perceptions.

Fights or bullying in general were never mentioned and teachers confirmed that there were no serious fights because students were educated appropriately. Qingpu School teacher Zhou Shaofan recounted:

> Since we had our first class together, when we went into the workshop, I asked them to be quiet and not to disturb. If something is the matter you have to talk to the teacher. Therefore they developed good manners. After class when I'm not in the classroom for example, they will not make noise. Everybody is very peaceful. (ZSF1_24)

Students were not all friends with each other but there were no open conflicts either. Woronov (2016) who studied students in vocational schools in Nanjing came to a similar conclusion. According to her, friendships were formed without taking *hukou*, gender or family background into consideration (Woronov 2016: 47). The long hours spent in the same classroom, studying the same vocational training course, reduces the differences students perceive between themselves and their classmates.

Students could be divided into two categories depending on how they defined friendship and made friends. Either they had many friends and were friends with all their classmates, or they divided their peers into acquaintances and close friends. Most students belonged to the first group. Students belonging to the latter group had certain criteria that defined a close friendship, and usually had one close, long-lasting friendship with a classmate or neighbour.

Han Feng (1_M/F3), for example, had one very close friend: "All my life we were close… this kind of thing, maybe you never have this in your life, therefore, it is very treasured." (HF1_90). De Hua (1_M/Q1) made a distinction between regular friends and close friends. In his first year in the vocational school, he analyzed the relationships with his peers more thoroughly and, therefore, needed more time to figure out who in Shanghai would become his friend. His close friends were in his hometown. One year later, De Hua was very happy to have made two or three friends in school. Li Qing (1_M/Q3) also had specific assumptions that defined friendship: the relations had to be empathetic (*jiangxin bixin* 将心比心 = to put oneself in somebody else's shoes), there had to be mutuality and support among friends (*xueli song tan, er bu shi xueshang jia shuang* 雪里送炭，而不是雪上加霜 = to send charcoal when there is snow and not to put frost on top of snow) and he was not interested in superficial friendships (*jiurou pengyou* 酒肉朋友 = wine and meat friends). When it came to friends he aimed for quality not quantity. He mentioned one very close friend whom he had known for four years by 2013. One year later, Li Qing's friend was married and had a child. Li Qing considered his number of friends average but felt alone because he did not have a relationship. In 2015, Li Qing was in a relationship and said that he finds friends fairly easily despite being stubborn. His new relationship might have substituted his need for a very close friend.

Most students had their first relationship at a younger age than Li Qing who was already 22 when he talked about his girlfriend in 2015. Close to the graduation from their vocational school, most students had had a relationship and a few students had been together with their girl-/boyfriend for several years, but none of them was planning to get married before finding a stable job.

5.2.3 Interests and Hobbies

Compared to students attending academic higher middle school, vocational education students have a lot of free time. School finishes around 3pm and students, at least for the first two years of their education, usually do not have homework and no tutorial classes. Therefore, the question arises of how they fill their free time.

Different kinds of sports were the most popular pasttime for students when they were together with friends, basketball being the most common one. Other sports mentioned included badminton, ping-pong, running, soccer, pool, tennis and swimming. When students were alone, they spent their time playing computer or online games, browsing the internet, or playing with their mobile phones. The overall agreement rate with the statement that 'The 1990s Generation spends too much time online and playing games' was 3.6. which is relatively high for a statement with a negative connotation. The standard deviation was quite high because there were different opinions among different groups of the sample. Students from Fengxian School, plus Shanghainese and male students, all had a significantly higher agreement rate, which suggests that male Shanghainese students spent more time playing games than female migrant students (see Table 5.13). Students were usually slightly embarrassed when they admitted that they like playing games. In her study on internet usage among the younger generation, Liu Fengshu (2011: 11) confirmed that vocational students tend to spend more time in internet cafes compared to students from general higher middle schools who have to study for longer hours. Li Qing (1_M/Q3) explained his motivation: "I like to play these two games [computer games] when I'm feeling very tired. This makes me feel better and it is a way to give vent (*faxie* 发泄)." (LQ1_74). Similar explanations for recreational internet usage were given by Liu's interviewees.

Table 5.13: Questionnaire A – 'The 1990s Generation spends too much time online and playing games'.

'The 1990s Generation spends too much time online and playing games'	
Questionnaire A (First, third and fourth year electrical engineering, second year Mechatronic Company Class)	Mean
All Students	3.5
Students' school — Fengxian School students	3.8*
Students' school — Qingpu School students	3.5*
Students' *hukou* — Shanghainese students	3.8*
Students' *hukou* — Migrant students	3.4*
Students' sex — Male students	3.7**
Students' sex — Female students	3.2**

Notes: * = sign .05, ** = sign .01; Likert Scale 1 = 'Do not agree at all' – 5 = 'Totally agree'
Source: Author's own survey 2014, 2015

Other leisure activities mentioned were music/singing, movies/TV, reading, shopping, talking or going out with friends, Chinese chess, etc. Students enjoyed spending time with their friends and some preferred weekdays over weekends because they felt useless or got bored in their parents' homes. A few students had part-time jobs, for example at fast food joints, but most of these jobs were limited to the holidays.

Students liked a broad variety of celebrities from movies and the music scene such as the singers Zhou Jielun, Huang Jiaju, Chen Yixun, and Ma Tianyu; or the actors Liu Yifei, Jackie Chan and Zhou Xingchi. The only non-Asian celebrity mentioned was Michael Jackson. The majority of these celebrities are from Hong Kong. Japanese Mangas were also popular among the students, and when it came to reading, fantasy was one of the preferred genres.

Despite not having a lot of money to spend, consumer-oriented activities were still part of students' leisure activities. The top three leisure activities which students enjoyed at least twice a month were: going to friends' homes (52.2%), going shopping (50.0%) and going to restaurants (44.1%). One has to keep in mind, though, that neither Fengxian nor Qingpu had high-end shopping malls or fancy restaurants at the time of research. Students frequented simple Chinese establishments and, according to the interviews, hardly ever went to the city center. Surprisingly however, a relatively high percentage of students went outdoors in natural areas on a regular basis. This gives an idea of how rural the locations of Fengxian and Qingpu School in Shanghai were. A higher percentage of Qingpu School students and migrant students went routinely to a natural environment, which is related to the fact that Qingpu is well-known as a very green district of Shanghai, and there were more migrant students among Qingpu School students. A higher percentage of Fengxian School students went regularly to a cinema which is likely to be related to having a cinema close by. Internet cafés were frequented on a regular basis by more migrant students than Shanghainese students. The logical conclusion would be that fewer migrant families have internet access at home. Additionally, there was a distinct difference between male and female students with more female students going to restaurants, going shopping or going to sing karaoke as part of their usual leisure activities.

A consumer-oriented lifestyle creates peer pressure (Fong 2004: 82, 85) and students do experience pressure to consume. Migrant student De Hua (2_M/Q2): "Difficulties? Not enough money. That is my money is not enough for me. Every time I clearly have a lot of money on me, I spend it without even realizing…" (DH2_66). Another example was migrant student Wen Qing (2_F/F2):

> I think money is one of my difficulties… For example, when I broke my phone and I did not dare to tell my father… I have no pocket money, only the money for lunch, so I had to take the money from my lunch money. That is very difficult… or for example when I want to have new shoes or some cloths; I do not have any money and my father does not give me any… and if I take it from my lunch money, I have nothing to eat. (WQ2_125)

Wen Qing's account illustrates not only the pressure experienced by the students but also on which level consumption happens. Importance of clothing brands or (among the older students) entertainment at expensive restaurants or bars and dance clubs were never mentioned during the interviews and, in conclusion, not part of students' lives. Students came from families not affluent enough to finance such a lifestyle and consumption happened on a much lower level by going out to eat at local restaurant or going shopping at the local mall.

Another indicator that students did not belong to Shanghai's relatively well-off middle-class was the fact that parents did not require them to pursue specific hobbies, such as learning an instrument, and none of the interviewed students participated in any structured leisure activities like playing sports in an official team. Generally, middle-class youth are more culturally active than working-class families (Furlong, Cartmel 1997: 58) and Andrew Kipnis (2012: 187) observed the popularity of extra-curricular courses among families in a rapidly urbanizing county in Shandong province. Students there were enrolled either in prep courses for the *gaokao*, or in art-, music- or sport-related courses which are supposed to enhance students' quality (*suzhi* 素质). Different from Kipnis' findings, parents in the present sample did not have the means or the interest in investing in organized extra-curricular activities. As such, the vocational education students were left to decide on their own how to fill their time.

Table 5.14a: Questionnaire B – 'Which of these activities do you do at least twice a month? To which of these places do you go at least twice a month?'.

'Which of these activities do you do at least twice a month? To which of these places do you go at least twice a month?'		
Questionnaire B (Panel data – Second year)		Valid percent (cases)
Friends' homes		52.2% (71)
Shopping		50.0% (68)
Shopping	Male students	44.4%* (48)
	Female students	79.2%* (19)
Restaurant		4.1% (60)
Restaurant	Male students	38.9%* (42)
	Female students	75%* (18)
Nature		35.3% (48)
Nature	Shanghainese students	21.7%* (13)
	Migrant students	43.4%* (23)
Nature	Fengxian School students	16.1%*(5)
	Qingpu School students	41.0%* (43)
Cinema		30.1% (41)
Cinema	Fengxian School students	48.4%* (15)
	Qingpu School students	24.8%* (26)

Notes: * = sign .05

Source: Author's own survey 2015

Table 5.14b: Questionnaire B – 'Which of these activities do you do at least twice a month? To which of these places do you go at least twice a month?'.

'Which of these activities do you do at least twice a month? To which of these places do you go at least twice a month?'		
Questionnaire B (Panel data – Second year)		Valid percent (cases)
Sports event (participating)		30.1% (41)
Sports event (watching)		27.2% (37)
Shanghai sights		27.2% (37)
KTV		26.5% (36)
KTV	Male students	23.1%* (25)
	Female students	45.8%* (11)
Library		25.7% (35)
Internet café		25.0% (34)
Internet café	Shanghainese students	15.0%* (9)
	Migrant students	35.8%* (19)
Concert/ Dancing		7.4% (10)

Notes: * = sign .05

Source: Author's own survey 2015

5.3 Conclusion

After entering secondary education, most students had already spent more years in school than their parents and will have an education degree higher than their parents once they graduate from the vocational school. Yet, due to diploma inflation in China and the spread of university education, this achievement loses its relevance in society.

Shanghainese parents had a higher education level than migrant parents, and their children had a higher motivation to pursue further studies. Parents' expectations regarding students' education influenced their attitude towards education, but even more relevant was the broader environment. Shanghainese students had higher educational aspirations compared to migrants and, additionally, felt more pressure. They were more likely to agree that they were not living up to their parents' expectations.

Apart from this, social differences between local and migrant students were of minor relevance. Data on income level was not collected in the present study, but other studies have found that Shanghainese and migrant vocational education students come from similar economic backgrounds and have the same chances and experiences in a vocational school since the majority of parents are unskilled workers and live in the suburbs of Shanghai (Ling 2015: 128–130). This is also the case in the present study. The interviews with students and teachers suggested that social differences between Shanghainese and migrant students exist but are not prominent in students' daily lives in school. Differences were only mentioned in response to an explicit question. This came as a surprise since Shanghainese and migrants do have different opportunities linked to their *hukou*, namely the exclusion of migrants from academic higher middle schools in the city, which would have suggested a more obvious separation between the two groups. In the more conventional Qingpu School, where migrant and Shanghainese students were split into different classes, there was naturally very little interaction. In German-influenced Fengxian School, students as well did not seem to mix despite being in one class, but neither did they fight with one another. Overall, in regard to family backgrounds, Shanghainese vocational education students shared more similarities with their migrant peers than with Shanghainese students in academic education. This might be explained by the fact that the Shanghainese parents' *hukou* were in Shanghai's new suburban districts which could be linked to an even lower quality (*suzhi* 素质) than a migrant's *hukou*, as Lin (2011) has observed in Xiamen's suburbs. Segregation and discrimination, as it has been described by Lan (2014) in academic schools in Shanghai were not an influential element in the vocational schools and the following chapters will check to which extent *hukou* still correlates with different attitudes and opinions.

With divorce becoming more common in China, several students in the sample lived with only one parent or in a patch-work family which rendered family relationships more difficult. Nonetheless, the majority of students had a good relationship with their parents which then would contribute to a positive attitude towards themselves and their school, as according to Rohlfs (2011), and students indeed managed the change to vocational education well and developed positive attitudes. They enjoyed the new classes and the new teaching style, and they made new friends. Additionally, they were satisfied with their performances in school. Many students had a feeling of success – maybe for the first time. This was facilitated by the teachers. Both schools in this study were key schools and teachers were educated well. They not only showed a high level of understanding of students' family backgrounds and living circumstances during the interviews, but students themselves also spoke very fondly of their teachers. This is in stark contrast to Hansen and Woronov (2013) who discovered that teachers in two Nanjing schools had very negative opinions of their students and did not display any affection at all. The fact that many vocational teachers have very low opinions of their students has even been discussed in the news (Renmin Ribao 2013: 1). Teachers in the two schools of the present study, on the other hand, speak in a very different tone, which is a clear indication of the qualitative differences between the sample schools and other vocational schools in China.

During the first year of their vocational education, students experienced a big and positive contrast to what lower middle school had been like for them. The focus lay on practical lessons instead of cramming theory which benefitted the students, and having more spare time also contributed to them liking the new school. In their second year, they got used to their new surroundings, their subjects, and their teachers, and they made new friends. Besides playing computer games – their favorite pastime – students spent most of their free time with their peers playing sports. Restaurants and shopping malls were visited on a regular basis by most students, and particularly by female students. Some students had part-time jobs. They did experience consumption-related pressure but, coming from low-income families, their aspirations as consumers were basic and did not involve high-end luxuries. Somewhat unexpectedly, several students said during the interviews that they did not have a preference for weekdays or weekends since they can do whatever they want during weekends but weekdays are used more productively. Ling (2015), who found that with all of their spare time vocational education students actually like to be controlled, linked this desire to socialization in an exam-oriented school system.

In essence, this chapter has shown that the life of a vocational education student differs from the stereotype of a Chinese student as it is frequently portrayed by Chinese and foreign media (China Daily 2007; Kaiman 2014). These 'typical' students spend around nine hours a day in classrooms and attend cramming schools and music or sports lessons during the weekends. Every day is structured and planned from early morning until late evening and parents expect educational success. The students in the present sample, however, come from families with low education levels where parents work long hours, usually as unskilled workers, in order to feed the family. After school and during weekends students might help their parents in the household but otherwise are left to their own devices. What defines the stereotypical students' lives – studying to make parents proud and become a top student – is not relevant for vocational students anymore. The pressure seems to have disappeared.

Considering all of this, it is less surprising that students' descriptions of their daily lives in school was overwhelmingly positive, and the next chapter will examine if their opinions on vocational education were in fact as positive as initially suggested.

6 Vocational Education through Students' Eyes

The previous chapter described students' environment, i.e. their social background and their schools. It became clear that they, as a group, differed from the stereotypical student in an academic middle school because their parents were less well-off, had fewer years of schooling and students themselves had more free time. Everyday life in the vocational schools was described in a very positive way. Students pointed out their relaxed schedule and their good relationships with teachers and peers. The present chapter will proceed with a more in-depth analysis of students' experiences with and opinions on vocational education. It will be discussed how these opinions changed throughout the training and what students thought they gained from their education.

Both questionnaires designed for the present study included several questions requiring students to assess vocational education. Some of these items have been clustered which resulted in a more complex picture of different types of experiences and the interviews allowed an even more differentiated insight into students' attitudes.

This chapter starts with raising the question of why the students entered a vocational school and how they chose their training course. In the second part, students' attitudes towards vocational education and their experiences with their education are explored through their answers in interviews and questionnaires. It was confirmed that students overall had a positive attitude and made positive experiences but they were also aware of the bad reputation society ascribes to vocational education students. This led to conflicting feelings in which academic education was ultimately preferred despite understanding the value of skilled work. The final part of this chapter looks at the skills students acquired and it finds that vocational education trained social skills which students used in their working life, whereas technical skills appeared to be of less importance to them. A last subchapter takes the Chinese human quality (*suzhi* 素质) discourse into account and examins if students did improve their quality through their education.

6.1 Entering Vocational Education

The majority of the students in this study did not choose vocational education freely but were forced out of the academic education system. Migrant students living in Shanghai were not allowed to enter an academic higher middle school at the time of research; for them the only options were to start working after lower middle school, return to their home province or enter a vocational school. Students agreed that they were too young and inexperienced after lower middle school to enter the labour market. Returning to their home province was not attractive either and in some cases not even possible, since most of the parents of migrant students in the sample were working in Shanghai. Also, schools in the home provinces were not considered good and some students recounted bad experiences with provincial teachers. Shanghainese students, meanwhile, are not admitted in academic higher middle schools if they failed the lower middle school exam, as did the majority of Shanghainese students in the sample: 59.6% agreed that they failed the lower middle school exam. Out of 312 students in the sample who provided information on their *hukou*, 65 (20.8%) were Shanghainese students who did *not* agree that they entered vocational education because they failed the lower middle school exam. The actual number was probably even smaller since students were likely to be embarrassed about their failure and therefore might have concealed this fact in the questionnaires. To put it another way, almost 80% of students enrolled in one of the two schools did not have the opportunity to choose general education in Shanghai. Consequently, the question "Why did you choose vocational education?" was inappropriate since most of the students did not have a choice and it could not be expected that they would show any bias for vocational education. It was more likely that their attitudes would be defined by aversion.

Overall, including migrant students, close to 50% 'chose' vocational education because they failed the lower middle school exam. When asked during the interviews, students admitted that they did not study well or that they were weak in general subjects. The second major reason given was being interested in technical subjects. Also relevant were both a high employment rate for vocational education graduates, and recommendations by others. Looking at students' origins again, migrant students were more interested in technical subjects and it was more likely for them that vocational education had been recommended by others. Strikingly, during the interviews, no migrant student challenged the policy that they were not allowed to take the university entrance exam in Shanghai and therefore, had to enter a vocational school. Instead, many migrant students admitted that their grades were not good enough for university anyway.

Looking at the differences between schools and students' sex, more male students chose vocational education out of interest, and a high employment rate mattered significantly more to students in German-influenced Fengxian School.

Table 6.1: Questionnaire A – 'Why did you choose vocational education?'.

Why did you choose vocational education? (You can choose multiple answers)		
Questionnaire A (First, third and fourth year electrical engineering, second year Mechatronic Company Class)		Valid percent (cases)
Did not pass lower middle school exam		46.6% (164)
Did not pass lower middle school exam	Shanghainese students	59.6%* (96)
	Migrant students	31.3%* (47)
Interested in technical subjects		38.0% (135)
Interested in technical subjects	Shanghainese students	33.5%* (54)
	Migrant students	44.7%* (67)
Interested in technical subjects	Male students	41.9%* (112)
	Female students	22.6%* (14)
High employment rate		39.6% (105)
High employment rate	Fengxian School	40.6%* (52)
	Qingpu School	23.5%*(53)
Recommended by others		35.6% (91)
Recommended by others	Shanghainese students	34.7%* (52)
	Migrant students	18.0%* (29)

Notes: * = sign .05

Source: Authors' own survey 2014, 2015

6.1.1 Choosing the School and Training Course

The vocational school was usually chosen together with parents while focusing on schools close to home and relying on what others had to say. In 33.3% of the families, parents or relatives chose the school, while 24.9% of the students said they followed personal intuition. Having friends in the same school also influenced the decision.

During the interviews, some students said that their lower middle school teacher took them to visit the vocational school, and this had a decisive influence. When choosing a school, location close to where parents lived was more important for migrant students, probably because they were faced with the option of returning to their home province for schooling. Shanghainese students, though, were more likely to look at the school profile, and for 50% of the female students, parents decided in which school to enroll, a significantly higher number compared to male students.

Although 34.2% of the students said they chose electrical engineering out of interest, their overall influence on in which course to enroll was limited. For 26.8% of students it was their parents' decision. Li Miao (1_F/F2) described how little she had to do with the decision: "I also never thought I would enroll in electrical engineering. This was my dad's decision. My dad said that electrical engineering is pretty good [sigh]." (LM1_75). Usefulness and high employment rates were important arguments for enrolling in a certain training course, and in some cases the course of choice was already full. During the interviews, several students said that teachers recommended a course – and again the employment rate of graduates was being stressed; a particular interest in electrical engineering was only expressed by a few students during the interviews. It might come as a surprise that salary expectations were not mentioned in this context and were also not relevant according to the questionnaire results, which suggests that students did not have a concept of how their income level would influence their lives – or they simply might not have had any information on the average income of vocational graduates – although this kind of data is available. Overall, despite some students' research of institutions, they did not seem to be well informed about their school's profile or the different training courses on offer. This phenomenon has also been described by Ling Minhua in 2015, who wrote that as a result students entered schools nearby or followed their classmates (Ling 2015: 118).

When it came to choosing a training course, migrant students were more likely to listen to others' recommendations and to be interested in courses which were already full. Shanghainese students, on the other hand, were more likely to follow their interests. Also, male students were more likely to choose their training course out of interest, because of the good employment rate or because they considered it a useful course. Female students were interested in booked-out courses more often than their male peers.

Table 6.2: Questionnaire A – 'Why did you choose your current school?'.

Why did you choose your current school? (Can choose multiple answers)		
Questionnaire A (First, third and fourth year electrical engineering, second year Mechatronic Company Class)		Valid percent (cases)
Parents / Relatives decision		33,3% (118)
Parents / Relatives decision	Male students	30.1%* (84)
	Female students	50.0%* (31)
Personal intuition		24,9% (88)
Friends are in the same school		21,2% (75)
Other people's recommendation		20,3% (72)
Location close to where parents live		19,8% (70)
Location close to where parents live	Shanghainese students	14.3%* (23)
	Migrant students	28.0%* (42)
School's profile		16.4% (58)
School's profile	Shanghainese students	23.0%* (37)
	Migrant students	11.3%* (17)

Notes: * = sign .05

Source: Author's own survey 2014, 2015

Looking at differences between the two schools, it became clear that parents were the dominant decision makers in both schools but Qingpu School students had to deal with fully booked courses more often. In 38% of Fengxian School families, parents decided on the training course. In Qingpu School, 21% of the parents made the decision, and 23% of Qingpu School students could not enroll in their first choice of training course because it was full. This basically did not happen in Fengxian School.

Students' narratives on how they ended up in their current school and training course reflected the results from the questionnaires. Migrant student De Hua (1_M/Q1), for example, had failed the lower middle school exam in his home province. When he discussed the issue with his parents, the family came to the conclusion that a vocational school in Shanghai would be better than one in his home town. Finally, Qingpu School was chosen because De Hua had a cousin who had graduated from that school already.[18] He first wanted to enroll in computer technique but he was too late and ended up choosing between two training courses; he picked the more useful one: electrical engineering. Migrant student Huang Gui (1_M/F1) came with a teacher to visit Fengxian School and liked what he saw. He enrolled in electrical engineering since his uncle had a factory where he could potentially start working after his graduation. After doing online research, migrant student Zhang Hua (1_F/F3) chose Fengxian School because of its good reputation. She enrolled in electrical engineering because it was a popular subject. Plus, the technical modernization created a need for skilled workers and Zhang Hua saw an opportunity for professional development. Shanghainese student Lei Qiang (1_M/F2) failed the lower middle school exam; he and his mother decided that he should enter a vocational school and they chose one close to home. Lei Qiang had always been interested in physics and chemistry, and therefore chose electrical engineering.

---

[18] De Hua talked about an 'older brother' but he mentioned only one older sister when asked about siblings, therefore, he probably referred to a cousin.

Table 6.3: Questionnaire A – 'Why did you choose your training course?'.

Why did you choose your training course? (Can choose multiple answers)		
Questionnaire A (First, third and fourth year electrical engineering, second year Mechatronic Company Class)		Valid percent (cases)
Interested in electrical engineering		34.2% (121)
Interested in electrical engineering	Male students	39.8%* (111)
	Female students	12.9%* (8)
Interested in electrical engineering	Shanghainese students	41.6%* (67)
	Migrant students	30.7%* (46)
Parents' decision		26.8% (95)
Useful course		25.1% (89)
Useful course	Male students	27.2%* (76)
	Female students	14.5%* (9)
High employment rate		21.8% (77)
High employment rate	Male students	23.7%* (66)
	Female students	9.7%* (6)
Other courses already fully booked		16.9% (60)
Other courses already fully booked	Male students	14.7%* (41)
	Female students	27.4%* (17)
Other courses already fully booked	Shanghainese students	11.8%* (19)
	Migrant students	23.3%* (35)
Recommended by others		13.6% (48)
Recommended by others	Shanghainese students	9.3%* (15)
	Migrant students	20.0%* (30)

Notes: * = sign .05

Source: Author's own survey 2014, 2015

6.1.2 Summary

Vocational education was not a matter of choice. More than three-quarters of the students in the sample did not have the opportunity to enter an academic higher middle school in Shanghai. Also when it came to choosing a school and a training course, students' influences were limited. As a result, students had neither a particular interest in their training course nor an aspiration to a career as a blue collar worker.

Shanghainese students were more likely to be forced into vocational education but then appeared to make a more conscious decision – selecting their school according to school profile, and choosing their course according to their interests. Migrant students, generally, were more likely to choose vocational education because they were interested in technical subjects, but subsequent decisions were determined by other circumstances, such as location of residence, availability of courses and the recommendations of others. Male students were more likely to choose vocational education and their training course out of interest. They also considered the usefulness of the course and the employment rate. For female students, the parents often chose in which school to enroll – and then the desired courses were already fully booked.

Woronov (2016) asked students in Nanjing why they entered a vocational school and how they chose their courses. Like the students in the present study, many of these Nanjing students were equally open to admitting that they were not good enough in lower middle school to go to an academic higher middle school. Others provided explanations such as wanting to save their parents expensive tuition fees, or being too busy helping with their parents' business and therefore lacking the time to study well (Woronov 2016: 50–52). None of the students in the present sample cited similar family-related considerations as the reason for entering vocational education, even though their families played an important role in their lives. Also, when it came to choosing a training course, processes were similar and often the decision was made by parents and with very little information. In some cases friends had an influential role as well. Generally, neither in my nor in Woronov's sample was it common to make decisions based on interests (Woronov 2016: 52–53). Instead, students' agency was restricted and their way into an electrical engineering course in a vocational school was largely determined by others. Decisions were based on limited or no information about what the specific training course would involve and which future prospects it might have.

This would suggest that students' attitudes towards vocational education would be in line with the negative attitude towards vocational education held by the population in general and it would predict that migrant students and male students have a more positive attitude towards vocational education – and consequently they might have better experiences and development during their vocational education. Yet, in the previous chapter we have already seen that students are generally quite content with everyday life in vocational education. In the following, students attitudes and experiences will be evaluated to greater depth and also placed in relation to how they entered vocational education in the first place.

6.2 Opinions and Experiences

Although the majority of students did not select vocational education voluntarily, their attitudes were nevertheless not all negative. They described vocational education as a second chance after failing lower middle school. In questionnaire A, the statement 'Vocational education is a new starting point for me' had the highest agreement rate (4.1) with the lowest standard deviation (1.2) among all the statements related to vocational education.[19] During the interviews, students gave two reasons why vocational education, for them, might not be a bad alternative to an academic education after all: good employment rate due to the lack of skilled workers, and the opportunity to get a higher vocational education degree.

Several students pointed out that China is lacking skilled workers and therefore, they will themselves be sought after once they enter the labour market. High activity rates among vocational education graduates supported this idea. In 2014, 98% of graduates from vocational schools in Shanghai either found a job or proceeded with further studies (Shanghai Education Commission 2015). Once they entered their vocational school, students realized that higher middle school followed by an university degree is not the only path leading to professional development and employment. With a rather pragmatic attitude, Han Feng (2_M/FG) recognized that not all students study well enough for university. For them, vocational education and learning in practice would be suitable. Former poor students would start to focus again, and with the lack of technicians in today's China, they might even have better future prospects than white collar workers, he explained.

The debate about the difficulties university graduates encounter when looking for jobs supports the argument of good employment opportunities for voca-

---

[19]   Questionnaire A (First, third, fourth year electrical engineering, second year Mechatronic Company class), Likert Scale 1 = 'Do not agree at all' – 5 = 'Totally agree'.

tional education. While arguing that China needs to strengthen its vocational education system, Chinese scholar Wang Qiang (2003) cites some interesting numbers: seven out of ten graduating university students were without an employment contract in April during their last semester, and in Harbin just under 3,000 graduates – including 29 with a higher degree – applied for 457 jobs as street cleaners, whereas in Guangdong there was a shortage of one million skilled workers (Wang 2013: 381). He does not cite the source of his numbers but the general difficulties of university graduates finding a job are indisputable. According to official sources such as the Shanghai Education Commission, graduates with a higher education degree who went to a vocational middle school have better chances finding a job than university graduates (Shanghai Education Commission 2015). Also, when directly comparing graduates from a vocational middle school with Bachelor and Master graduates, vocational education graduates still have the higher activity rate (Zhang 2013a: 1). This certainly says nothing about the working conditions or the income but it gives the students a sense of security and some future prospects. In the beginning of their education, students were confident that they could hold their ground in the labour market competition. Additionally, vocational schools refer jobs to their graduating students – something which was considered another perk of vocational education. Students stressed the value of vocational education in comparison to university education. Lei Qiang (2_M/F3) explained just after he entered his third year of education:

> In China, everybody wants to go to university. They think working in an office is most relaxed but too many people take this road. Therefore, there are few skilled workers like us. [...] Teachers told us, [...] society really needs these kinds of people [skilled workers]. (LQ2_68)

While students pointed out the good employment prospects for vocational education graduates compared to university graduates, the new opportunity to get a higher education degree after finishing vocational middle school was probably the most important argument for students as to why vocational education is not so bad after all. With the ongoing reform of the education system, it is becoming more common for graduates of vocational middle schools to sit an alternative *gaokao* exam which allows them to enter a vocational college on tertiary level if their result is good enough (Ministry of Education 2014; Shanghai Education Commission 2016). According to the Shanghai Education Commission, among the 98% of vocational middle school graduates in 2014 who either found a job or proceeded with further studies, 44% did the latter. This number has increased during the last few years (Shanghai Education Commission 2015). During the interviews, students emphasized that they had not yet lost the opportunity to get a higher education degree, and therefore they had not lost anything at all for the time being. Li Tao (3_F/F3) was a typical example of how students adjust their outlook. Her parents wanted her to go to university but after entering vocational education, she was convinced that she still could achieve development and get a higher education degree if she wanted to. In the last year of her education, Li Tao described China's lack of blue collar workers and surplus of university graduates. Consequently, vocational education students would have an advantage when looking for employment. Vocational education was never her first choice but having no alternatives she concentrated on the positive aspects.

With his longitudinal study in Germany in the 1980s, Klaus Hurrelmann evaluated the influence of failure in school on students. He showed that a poor performance in school has a long-term effect on students' lives and they lose their self-esteem as one of the consequences (Kramer 2014: 425–426). Yet, once the failure in school has forced students to enter an undesired school form, such as *Hauptschule*[20] in Germany, then these students often experience a positive development. Grades improve, they are no longer at the bottom of the class and they regain (some of) their self-esteem. Several youth studies conducted in Germany focused on this phenomenon[21] (Schaupp 2014: 748–750).

Here we can explain once again students' positive descriptions of their everyday lives as recounted in Chapter five. Like their peers in *Hauptschule* in Germany, the Chinese vocational education students experienced a similar positive development after having been forced out of the academic education system. They were no longer the weakest students in the cohort and with new technical subjects students who struggled with mathematics and Chinese could have a new start. Written exams were no longer the one and only assessment method. Now, manual precision mattered more than academic subjects and students regained their motivation. The positive experiences with vocational education during the first and second year also influenced students' general opinions on vocational education. Despite their different family backgrounds, different places of origin and different experiences in their past lives, students' outlooks on vocational education were surprisingly similar and consistently positive during the first two years of their education. Negative attitudes in society towards vocational education lost relevance in students' everyday lives. To

---

[20] A secondary school form to which all primary school graduates can be admitted and where students study five to six years before they graduate. *Realschule* and *Gymnasium*, the other school forms on the secondary education level, require better grades and students spend six and eight to nine years in these schools. Only graduates from the *Gymnasium* can enter university.

[21] For example: Buff (1991), Valtin and Wagner (2004).

quote Lei Qiang (1_M/F2) again: "We are skilled workers and therefore later, we will be a big help for the development of the country" (LQ1_14).

Although several students stress the lack of skilled workers and how they, as vocational education graduates, will be sought after in the labour market, Lei Qiang was the only one to speak with a clearly patriotic overtone, stressing their contribution to the nation as skilled workers. He fits in with the concept of 'patriotic professionals', a term coined by Hoffman (2006) after interviewing graduates from Dalian University of Technology where she found that her interviewees' personalities combined neoliberal goals such as career, development and obtaining opportunities, with socialist goals such as serving the country and society. Hoffmann argued that the co-existence of neoliberal and socialist regimes in China creates 'patriotic professionals'. Similar to Hoffman's university graduates, Lei Qiang, in his second year of vocational education at the time of the interview, expressed a high motivation and the ability to lay out his future including measures for self-improvement: "I want to study well and then change my destiny with my future work" (LQ1_8) and then, as shown above, he put his own improved self in the bigger picture and explained how he and his peers will aid the nation. Yet, his narrative is quite unique among my interviewees, the majority of whom recited what they had been told by others, namely that there is a lack of skilled workers, but they neither concluded how this will shape themselves and their future, nor did they outline in which ways they, by easing the lack of skilled workers, might contribute to society, the economy or the nation as a whole. Nelson et al. (2007: 88) explain this focus on themselves among young Chinese with social changes and the development of a market economy, and they also suggest that schools support this self-centeredness. Hansen (2015) interviewed several middle school teachers and, just like the vocational education students, they wanted success for themselves and their families, and not for the nation. Putting these results into perspective it seems that for the most part young Chinese do not take over the patriotic ideals of the party state and they are not politically interested. Yet, there are also some exceptions who are motivated by the idea of contributing to the development of the nation.

Getting back to students' opinions on vocational education, the vast majority shared a positive outlook during the beginning of their education. However, these lofty ideals clashed with the realities soon enough. For most students, their attitudes started changing when they got in touch with a regular work life during their internships. They encountered long work hours filled with monotonous, dull tasks in factories and realized that the jobs they would be qualified for are physically tiring, lowly paid and unattractive. Negative experiences during the internship provoked some students' changes in attitude towards vocational education in general. When Qian Qin (2_M/Q2) was in his second year of study, he was convinced that vocational education would be helpful for finding a job. One year later though, he had changed his opinion and considered vocational education a waste of time. Li Qing (2_M/QG) also changed his opinion. After his graduation, he said that vocational education furthers students' development and leads to stable employment. One year later, he was more critical and argued that graduates of both vocational education and university were competing for the same jobs, and therefore a vocational middle school degree would not be sufficient anymore. While students at the beginning of their education were likely to stress the value of vocational education and the chances they will have after graduation, they tended to be disillusioned towards the end and wanted to avoid working in their field of training. These results show the limitations of non-longitudinal studies, such as the one done by Woronov (2016). The trajectory, where students express a very positive and sometimes almost euphoric attitude at the beginning of their vocational education after having experienced a negative school selection, followed by a downward trend which for most students hits a low during the internships and/or close to their graduation, can only be brought to the fore with a panel design. Further experiences during the internship will be discussed in detail in Chapter 7.1.

6.2.1 Opinions on the Alternating System

It has been pointed out that the schooling system in Qingpu and Fengxian School was different. In Qingpu School students studied two years and finished their education with a yearlong internship. This so-called 2+1 system is the most common one in China. Fengxian School, on the other hand, employed a German-style alternating system which is rare. After the first year of school, students alternated every other month between school and the company for two years.

Among Chinese education experts, the German vocational education system is often considered the key to that country's strong economy (Jiang 2011: 6; Wang 2013: 381). China has cooperated with Germany since the early 1990s, first with the goal to copy the dual system and later just with the intention to learn from Germany's experiences. Fengxian School is one of the projects that developed through this cooperation. The school had connections to several German companies who accepted students as interns, teachers were trained by German experts, and some students had the chance to go to Germany on a student exchange. There were also groups of German students visiting Fengxian

School for a couple of weeks each year. The goal of this project was to train skilled workers with strong practical skills especially for, but not limited to, German companies in and around Shanghai.

The hallways of Fengxian School were lined with pictures of German students and teachers working with the Chinese students and staff of Fengxian School. Therefore, it came as a surprise that, although they were speaking to a German interviewer, the vast majority of Fengxian students did not mention this connection to Germany. When asked about the alternating system, many third year students criticized it. Two female students suggested that it would be better to finish the exams and then do an internship. With the alternating system, they felt pressured because they did not have enough time to prepare for exams. An exception was Lei Qiang (2_M/F3) who described the alternating system as a combination of learning and working, knowledge and experience, which helps to understand the theory. He did not see any disadvantage in the system itself but suggested that the school should have more company connections to place students as interns and that these companies should be more closely related to the students' study courses. Lei Qiang was the only student who spoke about his admiration for German products and German engineering. Overall, students were not identifying with the German aspects of their school; they were not even very aware of them in their everyday lives, and in their opinion the alternating system was more a burden than a benefit. This of course does not consider learning benefits which the students might have had but were not aware of.

6.2.2 Opinions during the First Year of Vocational Education

The analysis above, which was based on repeated interviews over three years, discovered a general trend for students to see vocational education in a positive light at the beginning and then develop more negative attitudes at a later stage. This had been explained by the effects of negative school selection and the disillusionment which follows, in many cases, during the internships. The two questionnaires which students completed in their first and second year of vocational education can now shed a light on additional factors, such as *hukou*, sex, reasons for choosing electrical engineering, and so forth, which influenced opinions and experiences and therefore were important elements which added to more stability in students' outlooks.

In 2014, first year electrical engineering students of both schools answered several questionnaire items concerning vocational education. The analysis of their answers showed which attitudes were dominant in the cohort just after entering the new school (see Table 6.4).

In order to identify latent variables, a principal axis factor analysis was conducted on these nine items with oblique rotation (direct oblimin). The Kaiser-Meyer-Olkin measure verified the sampling adequacy for the analysis, KMO = .69, which is considered an acceptable value (Field 2013: 706). The KMO values for individual items were all over .57, which again is an acceptable value. During an initial analysis three factors came out with an eigenvalue of >1, but retaining only two factors was found to be more meaningful especially since the eigenvalue of the third factor was barely over 1.0. These two factors together explained 33.2% of the variation. Factor 1 had a good reliability, Cronbach's α = .740. Factor 2 had a relatively low but still acceptable reliability, Cronbach's α = .529. Factor scores were obtained by computing the mean of all items loading with ≥ 0.4 on one factor.

Items loading on factor 1, 'Likes Vocational Education', suggest that students with a high factor score had a positive attitude towards vocational education. They liked technical subjects and were interested in vocational study. For them, vocational education was a new starting point and they were happy. Factor 2, 'Prefers General Education', has two items loading with ≥ 0.4. These items suggest that students with high factor scores would have preferred to continue academic education. They agreed that they planned to go to a higher middle school and were frustrated when they had to enter a vocational school (see Table 6.5).

Overall, students were neutral towards factor 2 and slightly agreed with factor 1. Looking at the schools, Fengxian School students who were going to study in the alternating system had a higher agreement rate with factor 1 and a lower agreement rate with factor 2 compared to Qingpu School students. This suggests that Qingpu School is faced with a less motivated group of students. Male students had a significantly higher agreement rate with factor 1 than female students who agreed more with factor 2 compared to their male peers, which is in line with the gender stereotype that men have more technical interests and pursuits while women prefer humanities. Chapter 9.4 will take a closer look at how gender expectations influence students' outlooks. There were no differences between Shanghainese and migrant students (see Table 6.6).

Table 6.4: Questionnaire A – Opinions during the First Year of Vocational Education.

Questionnaire A (Panel Data - First Year)	Mean	Standard deviation
During lower middle school, I planned to go to higher middle school.	3.3	1.5
During vocational education, life is happy.	4.1	1.2
I always liked technique.	3.6	1.3
I am interested in vocational subjects.	3.3	1.5
I am interested in general subjects.	3.5	1.3
Vocational education is a new starting point for me.	4.3	1.2
Not being able to go to higher middle school gave me a feeling of frustration.	2.6	1.6
During lower middle school, I was satisfied with my grades.	2.7	1.4
I am satisfied with my current grades.	3.1	1.3

Notes: Likert Scale 1 = 'Do not agree at all' – 5 = 'Totally agree'

Source: Author's own survey 2014

Table 6.5: Questionnaire A – Opinions on Vocational Education Factor Analysis I.

Questionnaire A (Panel Data – First Year)	Pattern Matrix	
	Factor 1 'Likes vocational education'	Factor 2 'Prefers general education'
I always liked technique.	.876	
I am interested in vocational subjects.	.662	
During vocational education, life is happy.	.605	
Vocational education is a new starting point for me.	.511	
I am interested in general subjects.	.302	
I am satisfied with my current grades.		
During lower middle school, I planned to go to higher middle school.		.774
Not being able to go to higher middle school gave me a feeling of frustration.		.460
During lower middle school, I was satisfied with my grades.		

Notes: Extraction Method: Principal Axis Factoring; Rotation Method: Oblimin with Kaiser Normalization

Source: Author's own survey 2014

An additional test revealed that the factors do not correlate negatively. Students scoring high on factor 1 did not have a low score for factor 2 but scored similarly to the overall average. The same was true for students scoring low on factor 1. Also students scoring high or low on factor 2 had average scores for factor 1. Providing socially desirable answers might explain why students who admitted that they would have preferred a general middle school had high scores for positive vocational education related items similar to their peers, but there is also another reason: the interviews provided a more detailed insight into students' attitudes and it turned out that the majority of the interviewed students would have, at least to some extent, preferred to go to an academic higher middle school – while still seeing the value of vocational education and generally being happy in their schools (see Chapter 6.2.4). Similarly to the interviews, the questionnaires did not convey an either-or attitude. Since both quantitative and qualitative research approaches demonstrated considerable ambivalence on the part of the students, the computation of clusters would only have obscured this phenomenon.

Table 6.6: Questionnaire A – Opinions on Vocational Education Factor Analysis II.

Factor 1 'Likes Vocational Education'		Mean	Standard deviation
All students		3.8	1.0
Students' school	Fengxian School	4.0	0.9
	Qingpu School	3.8	1.0
Students' sex	Male students	3.9**	0.9
	Female students	3.3**	1.2
Factor 2 'Prefers General Education'		Mean	Standard deviation
All students		3.0	1.3
Students' school	Fengxian School	2.6	1.2
	Qingpu School	3.1	1.3
Students' sex	Male students	2.9	1.2
	Female students	3.1	0.8

Notes: ** = sign .01; Factor scores 1 = very low – 5 = very high

Source: Author's own survey 2014

6.2.3 Experiences during the Second Year of Vocational Education

In 2015, while former first year students were in their second year of vocational education, they were asked again to answer several questions, this time concerning their experiences with vocational education.

Table 6.7a: Questionnaire B – Experiences during the Second Year of Vocational Education.

Questionnaire B (Panel Data – Second Year)	Mean	Standard deviation
My school is better than others.	3.0	1.3
My life in vocational school is happier than in lower middle school.	3.4	1.5
My life in lower middle school was happier than in vocational school.	3.0	1.4
I am always happy when I get to the classroom in the morning.	2.9	1.3
Class is easy.	3.2	1.3
Class is boring.	3.3	1.4
I am afraid of exams.	2.9	1.5
In school, pressure is big.	2.5	1.3
Vocational education is an education degree too low.	3.6	1.3
Teachers consider students' interests.	2.9	1.3
Teachers often praise us students.	3.1	1.2
Teachers often scold us students.	2.6	1.4

Notes: Likert Scale 1 = 'Do not agree at all' – 5 = 'Totally agree'

Source: Author's own survey 2015

Table 6.7b: Questionnaire B – Experiences during the Second Year of Vocational Education.

Questionnaire B (Panel Data – Second Year)	Mean	Standard deviation
Teachers let us actively participate in class.	3.6	1.2
I have many friends in school.	3.8	1.1
Teachers all like me.	3.2	1.2
My class is closely unified.	3.2	1.3
The classroom teacher is like family.	3.2	1.4
Technical skills are more useful than higher middle school knowledge.	3.4	1.4

Notes: Likert Scale 1 = 'Do not agree at all' – 5 = 'Totally agree'

Source: Author's own survey 2015

As before, a principal axis factor analysis was conducted on these 18 items, with oblique rotation (direct oblimin). The Kaiser-Meyer-Olkin measure verified the sampling adequacy for the analysis, KMO = .74, which is considered an acceptable value (Field 2013: 706). The KMO values for individual items were all over .56 which again is an acceptable value. During an initial analysis, six factors with an eigenvalue of >1 were retained but the scree plot suggested retaining only four factors. These four factors together explained 40.1% of the variation. Here, the structure matrix was used for interpretation. Although usually the pattern matrix is interpreted, in this case the structure matrix was found to represent the empirical data best since it retains the information that factor 1 and 4 are closely related. Factor 1 had a good reliability, Cronbach's α = .793. Factor 2, 3 and 4 had relatively low but still acceptable reliabilities, Cronbach's α = .591, α = .602 and α = 598 respectively. Factor scores were obtained by computing the mean of all items loading on one factor ≥ 0.4.

Table 6.8a: Questionnaire B – Experiences with Vocational Education Factor Analysis I.

Questionnaire B (Panel Data -Second year)	Structure Matrix			
	Factor 1 'Good Experience'	Factor 2 'Pressure'	Factor 3 'Preferred Lower Middle S.'	Factor 4 'Good Social Relations'
I'm always happy when I get to the classroom in the morning.	.693		-.328	
Teachers often praise us students.	.683			
The classroom teacher is like family.	.661			.402
My school is better than others.	.587			
Teachers let us actively participate in class.	.574		-.324	.456
Teachers consider students' interests.	.573			
Class is easy.	.399	-.397		
Technical skills are more useful than higher middle school knowledge.	.311			
Teachers often scold us students.				
I'm afraid of exams.		.792		
In school, pressure is high.		.619	.323	

Notes: Extraction Method: Principal Axis Factoring; Rotation Method: Oblimin with Kaiser Normalization

Source: Author's own survey 2015

Table 6.8b: Questionnaire B – Experiences with Vocational Education Factor Analysis I.

Questionnaire B (Panel Data -Second year)	Structure Matrix			
	Factor 1 'Good Experience'	Factor 2 'Pressure'	Factor 3 'Preferred Lower Middle S.'	Factor 4 'Good Social Relations'
My life in lower middle school was happier than in vocational school.			.718	
My life in vocational school is happier than in lower middle school.	.379		-.707	.302
Class is boring.	-.348	.399	.412	
Vocational education is an education degree too low.				
I have many friends in school.				.703
My class is a closely unified.	.310			.334

Notes: Extraction Method: Principal Axis Factoring; Rotation Method: Oblimin with Kaiser Normalization

Source: Author's own survey 2015

Items loading on factor 1, 'Good Experience', suggest that students with a high factor score were content overall with their education. They had positive opinions of their teachers and their school and were happy to be there. The average of students' factor loading was 3.1 which means that they were neutral. Splitting the sample according to schools showed that Fengxian School students had more positive experiences with their teachers and their school.

Factor 2, 'Pressure', has only two items loading on it. Students with high factor scores were afraid of exams and felt a lot of pressure in school. The average factor loading was 2.7 – relatively low, meaning that students did not generally feel pressure, but this was higher for Shanghainese students than for migrant students. The high educational aspirations prevalent in Shanghai influenced local students more than migrant students who might come from regions where people are still impressed by someone with a vocational education degree from Shanghai. This is in accordance with the fact that Shanghainese parents have higher education degrees on average, and it shows the different realities which exist in today's China. What is a failure for one group of people might be a success for a different group of people.

Factor 3, 'Preferred Lower Middle School', consists of three items, two stating that lower middle school was better than vocational school and the third one stating that class is boring. Students, again, were neutral overall but there was a slightly higher average factor score among Qingpu School students, which was in line with them also having lower factor scores than Fengxian School students for factor 1, 'Good Experience', and higher factor scores in 2014 for factor 2, 'Prefers General Education'. Qingpu School students' attitudes towards vocational education were less positive than Fengxian School students' attitudes.

Items loading on factor 4, 'Good Social Relationships', suggest that students with high factor scores had many friends, were active in class and had good relationships with their teachers. The overall average factor score was comparably high (3.5) which confirmed what teachers said during their interviews: students generally get along well and fights are the exception. Factor loadings for Fengxian School students were significantly higher than for Qingpu School students. This is connected to the higher loading for factor 1, 'Good Experience' (see Table 6.9).

These four factors were clustered hierarchically using Ward method and squared Euclidian distance. The results indicated that three clusters would be an adequate option. In a second step, the clusters were produced with K-Means analysis. By creating these attitude-based groups, comparisons which go beyond the usual sociodemographic variables such as sex and *hukou* became possible, and in a second step, by creating a real panel, changes in attitudes between the first and the second year could be traced.

Cluster 1 'Preferred Lower Middle School' was, with only 26 students (19.7%), the smallest cluster. These students had a higher-than-average factor score for factor 3, 'Preferred Lower Middle School'. Cluster 2, 'Happy in School', was, with 54 students (40.9%), the biggest cluster, where students had higher-than-average factor scores for factor 1, 'Good Experiences', and factor 4, 'Good Social Relationships'. Cluster 3, 'Pressure', was almost equally big. The 52 students (39.4%) belonging here had higher-than-average factor scores for factor 2, 'Pressure', and slightly higher scores for factor 3, 'Preferred Lower Middle School' (see Table 6.10).

Table 6.9: Questionnaire B – Experiences with Vocational Education Factor Analysis II.

Factor 1 'Good Experience'		Mean	Standard deviation
All students		3.1	0.9
Students' school	Fengxian School	3.4	0.8
	Qingpu School	3.0	0.9
Factor 2 'Pressure'		Mean	Standard deviation
All students		2.7	1.2
Students' hukou	Shanghainese students	2.9	1.1
	Migrant students	2.5	1.2
Factor 3 'Preferred Lower Middle School'		Mean	Standard deviation
All students		2.9	1.1
Students' school	Fengxian School	2.7	0.8
	Qingpu School	3.0	1.1
Factor 4 'Good Social Relationships'		Mean	Standard deviation
All students		3.5	0.9
Students' school	Fengxian School	3.9**	0.8
	Qingpu School	3.4**	09

Notes: ** = sign .01; Factor scores 1 = very low – 5 = very high

Source: Author's own survey 2015

A further analysis of the differences between the clusters concerning professional plans, family and personality brought more insights forward and proved the content validity of the clustering.

Students who were happy in school also strongly agreed that technical skills were the foundation for their future development, whereas students who preferred life in lower middle school were neutral towards this statement – but strongly disagreed with the statement that 'Later, I want to work in a factory'.

For this statement, students happy in vocational school had the highest agreement rate. Students feeling pressure in school, and also happy students, agreed with the statement that 'The purpose of work is to realize one's value'; however students preferring lower middle school stayed neutral (see Table 6.11a).

Table 6.10: Questionnaire B – Experiences with Vocational Education Cluster Analysis I.

	Cluster 1 'Preferred Lower Middle school'	Cluster 2 'Happy in School'	Cluster 3 'Pressure'
Factor 1 'Good Experiences'	2.20	3.67	3.04
Factor 2 'Pressure'	1.87	1.96	3.83
Factor 3 'Preferred Lower Middle School'	3.87	2.13	3.30
Factor 4 ,Good Social Relationships'	2.74	4.08	3.33

Notes: Factor scores 1 = very low – 5 = very high

Source: Author's own survey 2015

Students' attitudes towards their education and their relationships with their parents were closely related. Students who were happy in their school agreed strongly that their parents loved them, and the standard deviation was especially small here. These students also agreed strongly with the statements that 'Family is the foundation of happiness' and 'Family is my harbor'. For students who were happy in school the family is a supporting institution. Cluster 3, 'Pressure', students considered their parents their role models and they agreed more than the other two student groups that they study to fulfill their parents' expectations. Happy students, on the other hand, agreed more than their peers that they study because they like to learn. They also had the highest agreement rate with the statement 'My parents are proud of me'. Students who preferred their life in lower middle school had the lowest agreement rate with this statement. Therefore, students' preference when it comes to school was likely to be influenced by their parents. Pressured students and students preferring lower middle school life both agreed more than happy students that they disappoint their parents. Overall, students did not agree that they are being spoiled by their parents. Students who had the highest agreement rate here also felt pressured in school as if they felt obliged to repay their parents with good results. Appealing to students' filial piety to motivate and pressure them to study harder for their parents is not uncommon in Chinese classrooms (Hansen 2015: 140–141).

Looking at prevalent personality traits in the different groups, there were similarities between happy and pressured students. Both liked interaction with other people and considered a harmonious living environment to be important. Additionally, pressured students agreed more than students in the other two clusters that they were shy, quiet, lazy and underestimated. These students generally had low self-esteem, which can be both a result and a cause of their exam nerves and pressure.

The only noteworthy differences between school, sex, *hukou* and cluster belonging, were the higher percentage of Fengxian School students who belonged to cluster 2, 'Happy in School', and the higher percentage of Qingpu School students who belonged to cluster 3, 'Pressure'. There were only minor, insignificant differences between male and female students, and Shanghainese and migrant students. It is clear that conventional analyzes along sociodemographic lines cannot bring the attitude-based divisions among the students to the fore.

Table 6.11a: Questionnaire B – Experiences with Vocational Education Cluster Analysis II.

	Cluster 1 'Preferred Lower Middle School'		Cluster 2 'Happy in School'		Cluster 3 'Pressure'	
	Mean	Standard deviation	Mean	Standard deviation	Mean	Standard deviation
Technical skills are the foundation of my future development.	3.1*	1.5	4.2*	0.9	3.9*	1.2
Later, I want to work in a factory.	1.8**	1.0	3.2**	1.3	2.9**	1.4
The purpose of work is to realize one's value.	3.1*	1.6	3.9*	1.1	3.9*	1.2
My parents love me.	3.7	1.5	4.6	0.8	4.4	1.0
My parents spoil me.	1.7**	1.0	2.1**	1.3	2.6**	1.4
My parents are my role models.	3.0**	1.5	3.8**	1.1	4.0**	1.2
Family is the foundation of happiness.	3.3	1.5	4.2	1.2	4.2	1.2
Family is my harbor.	3.4*	1.9	4.3*	1.0	4.2*	1.1
My parents are proud of me.	2.7	1.4	3.9	1.2	3.4	1.2
I disappoint my parents.	2.8	1.5	2.2	1.3	2.9	1.3
I study to fulfill my parents' expectations.	2.8	1.5	2.3	1.0	3.0	1.3

Notes: * = sign .05, ** = sign .01; Likert Scale 1 = 'Do not agree at all' – 5 = 'Totally agree'

Source: Author's own survey 2015

Table 6.11b: Questionnaire B – Experiences with Vocational Education Cluster Analysis II.

	Cluster 1 'Preferred Lower Middle School'		Cluster 2 'Happy in School'		Cluster 3 'Pressure'	
	Mean	Standard deviation	Mean	Standard deviation	Mean	Standard deviation
I study because I like to learn.	2.3	1.4	3.2	1.1	2.8	1.3
I like interaction with other people.	3.3*	1.5	4.0*	1.2	4.0*	1.2
I often feel that I'm inferior to other people.	2.3**	1.5	3.3**	1.3	3.5**	1.3
I am quiet.	3.0*	1.4	3.6*	1.3	3.8*	1.2
I am shy.	2.9*	1.3	3.4*	1.4	3.7*	1.4
I am lazy.	2.2**	1.4	2.6**	1.3	3.0**	1.4
I am underestimated.	2.2*	1.4	2.6*	1.4	3.0*	1.2
Important for me – Harmonious living environment	3.8*	1.5	4.6*	0.8	4.5*	0.9

Notes: * = sign .05, ** = sign .01; Likert Scale 1 = 'Do not agree at all' – 5 = 'Totally agree'

Source: Author's own survey 2015

Table 6.12: Questionnaire B – Experiences with Vocational Education Cluster Analysis III.

		Cluster 1 'Preferred Lower Middle School' Valid percent (cases)	Cluster 2 'Happy in School' Valid percent (cases)	Cluster 3 'Pressure' Valid percent (cases)
Students' School % in school (cases)	Fengxian School	16.1% (5)	54.8% (17)	29.0% (9)
	Qingpu School	20.8% (21)	36.6% (37)	42.6% (43)
Sex % in sex (cases)	Male students	20.2% (21)	40.4% (42)	39.4% (41)
	Female students	16.7% (4)	37.5% (9)	45.8% (11)
Hukou % in hukou (cases)	Shanghainese students	18.6% (11)	40.7% (24)	40.7% (24)
	Migrant students	17.3% (9)	46.2% (24)	36.5% (19)

Source: Author's own survey 2015

In order to check changes between opinions on vocational education at the beginning and experiences with vocational education after one year in school, a real panel was used. The birthdates made it possible to identify all students who participated in the first and second questionnaire survey. Other demographical data such as school, year of study and *hukou* was used to filter students who shared the same birthdates but were not identical. In the end the data set included 91 students (see Table 6.13).

Comparing factor scores for students' opinions on vocational education in 2014, differentiated by their experiences they had in 2015, proved that, although not statistically significant, students who were happy in school in 2015 scored highest for the factor 'Likes Vocational Education', whereas students who preferred lower middle school in 2015 scored highest for 'Prefers General Education' in 2014 (see Table 6.14). Despite the finding that students' attitudes resemble a trajectory, with an initial surge of positive development followed by disillusion later on, there is also some consistency in students' attitudes. This means that the trajectory can have different shapes, steeper and flatter, and also that it can start at different levels, more positive or negative. It also hints at a bigger ambivalence within students' attitudes towards vocational education, which will be analyzed in detail in chapter 9.7.2.

Table 6.13: Real Panel Data – Overview.

Real Panel Data (First and second year electrical engineering)		First year electrical engineering Valid percent (cases)	Second year electrical engineering Valid percent (cases)
All students		100% (91)	100% (91)
Students' school	Fengxian School	27.5% (25)	27.5% (25)
	Qingpu School	72.5% (66)	72.4% (66)
Students' *hukou*	Shanghainese students	52.7% (48)	51.6% (47)
	Migrant students	44.0% (40)	39.6% (36)
	Missing value	3.3% (3)	8.8% (8)
Students' sex	Male students	83.5% (76)	79.1% (72)*
	Female students	16.5% (15)	19.8% (18)*
	Missing values	0	1.1% (1)

Notes: * Misrepresentation of sex

Source: Author's own survey 2014, 2015

It turned out that the reasons for choosing vocational education, school and training course correlated with the experiences students had had in their second year and, consequently, these reasons are important factors explaining the more consistent attitudes students display until their second year.

When looking at the most common reasons for choosing vocational education, the first striking fact was that the majority of the students who experience pressure and exam nerves in their second year in vocational school left the academic education system because they failed the lower middle school exam. Also, half of the students who preferred lower middle school in comparison to vocational school did not pass this exam either. A high employment rate was the most common reason for choosing vocational education among the students who turned out happy in school. It was also important for pressured students, but it was significantly less important for students who preferred lower middle school. Being interested in technical subjects was one of the most common reasons for all students, except the pressured ones.

Many students who preferred lower middle school claimed one year earlier that they followed their personal intuition when choosing their vocational school, and as many of them said they chose a school close to home. Half of the pressured students relied on their parents to make a decision, which was also the most common way happy students decided, and both student groups had friends in the same school. Additionally, a significantly higher proportion of happy students chose their school because of its reputation. Thus in all three groups, often the parents made the decision for their children and chose schools close to their homes (see Table 6.15).

Table 6.14: Real Panel Data – Opinion Changes.

Real Panel Data (First and second year electrical engineering)	Factor 'Likes Vocational Education' – first year Mean (Standard deviation)	Factor ' Prefers General Education' – first year Mean (Standard deviation)
All students (N=91)	3.8 (0.9)	2.9 (1.2)
Cluster 'Preferred Lower Middle School' – second year (N=18)	3.7 (1.1)	3.2 (1.2)
Cluster 'Happy in School' – second year (N=37)	4.1 (0.6)	2.8 (1.1)
Cluster 'Pressure' – second year (N=34)	3.7 (0.9)	3.0 (1.4)

Notes: ** = sign .01, * = sign .05; Factor scores 1 = very low – 5 = very high

Source: Author's own survey 2014, 2015

How students felt about their education was again closely connected to the reasons why they had ended up in a specific training course, and whether they were able to carry out their agency. Many students who preferred lower middle school were interested in electrical engineering, but many also had faced the fact that their course of choice was already fully booked. A relatively high number of students who experienced pressure and exam nerves later on had no choice because courses were already full and their parents made the decision. The most common reasons for choosing their training course among students who turned out happy in school were very different from the other two groups. Many of them were interested in their course and considered it a useful subject. Also, a significantly higher proportion of students chose it because of the salary expectations, and a significantly lower proportion had to choose their course because other courses were already fully booked. Here it becomes very clear that being able to act as an active agent in making strategic decisions leads to more positive experiences later on, whereas students who are condemned to passively follow whatever others or the circumstances dictate are far more likely to face difficulties or be unhappy. This, of course, is a strong argument for giving students more freedom and more information in order to let them make their own, informed choice when it comes to choosing a training course.

Table 6.15: Real Panel Data – Opinions on and Reasons for Choosing Vocational Education.

Most common reasons for:	Choosing vocational education Valid percent	Choosing the vocational school Valid percent	Choosing the training course Valid percent
Cluster 'Preferred Lower Middle School' N=18	50% 'Did not pass the lower middle school exam' 33.3% 'Recommended by others' 33.3% 'Interested in technical subjects 11.1% 'High employment rate'*	38.9% 'Personal intuition' 38.9% 'Close to where parents live' 27.8% 'Parents decided'	38.9% 'Interested in electrical engineering' 38.9% 'Other courses already full'
Cluster 'Happy in School' N=37	45.9% 'High employment rate' 43.3% 'Interested in technical subjects 43.3% 'Did not pass the lower middle school exam'	37.8% 'Parents decided' 27% 'Close to where parents live' 27% 'Friends are in the same school' 24.3% 'Good reputation'	43.2% 'Interested in electrical engineering' 43.2% 'Useful course'* 16.2% 'Good salary expectations'* 13.5% 'Other courses already full'*
Cluster 'Pressure' N=34	64.7% 'Did not pass the lower middle school exam' 38.2% 'High employment rate'	50% 'Parents decided' 26.5% 'Friends are in the same school'	38.2% 'Parents decided' 38.2% 'Other courses already full'

Notes: *= sign .05

Source: Author's own survey 2014, 2015

6.2.4 Vocational Education vs. General Education

Once they had entered their vocational schools, students emphasized how much more relaxed their lives had all of a sudden become. They recounted the bitter daily routine in lower middle school, which involved the pressure of studying for long hours, strict rules enforced by rude teachers and the setback of failing exams. As a result, they entered vocational school with a feeling of greater ease and were open to listen to their new teachers telling them about the advantages of vocational education, which they repeated during the interviews. Da Ming (2_M/Q2):

> Two years they make you learn, one year they make you do an internship. You have experiences with society and can directly adjust to it. Besides, in this vocational school you can learn how to behave... You do not need to be disadvantaged. If you are going to a general higher middle school, [...] you need to get to university and when you graduate you do not have any experience, [...] and only having knowledge simply does not work, right. (DM2_53)

In vocational schools, students still learn general subjects in addition to technical knowledge and practical skills, and there is enough time for sport lessons or extra-curricular activities. Therefore, students found the curriculum in their new school more varied. Some students, such as Wen Qing (2_F/F2), advocated at the beginning of her second vocational education year that technicians were more useful for society than university graduates. Lei Qiang (3_M/FG), who had continued to a vocational school on the tertiary level, saw vocational and general education as equal:

> Knowledge and manual work complement each other. You cannot do anything only with knowledge. Therefore, I think that China needs more technically skilled people... Only then can China advance. (LQ3_43)

Apart from educational content, the most important difference between a vocational and an academic middle school is the fact that students in a vocational school do not participate in the *gaokao*, the university entrance exam which determines if and into which university students will be allowed to enroll. Academic higher middle school students in their final year spend twelve hours and more per day preparing for this important exam. Diligence and ambition bind them together and are widely admired in society. Newspapers report extensively about the exam and thereby contribute to creating a heroic aura which surrounds the preparation marathon and the *gaokao* itself. In her article published in 2015, Ling Minhua explained that since vocational education students are excluded from the *gaokao*, they have no means to earn this kind of respect in society or form a feeling of belonging and a shared identity similar to their peers in academic middle schools (Cockain 2011: 116; Ling 2015: 119). In reaction to this lack of exam experience, vocational education students pointed out that their peers in academic education lack experience with society. They tried to regain their self-worth by portraying themselves as savvy when dealing with social relations and knowledgeable when it comes to technical matters. In the manner Zhang Hua (2_F/FG) described how she and her classmates assembled their first products in the school workshop, she copied the typical *gaokao* story of hardship which is endured together and followed by success as a reward:

> Although I was very tired that time, I was also very happy because you can successfully make something so that it fits the standards. [...] I had blisters all over my hands but not only me, many students were the same. This was the first time we did something like that, so there was a lot of pressure too [...]. (ZH2_17)

Knowingly or unknowingly, students took the notions of academic education prevalent in society and positioned themselves towards them. Their views on vocational education were different from the common discourse, yet they were formed in direct relation to or depended on it. The students were not ready to take on the label 'education loser'; instead they tried to find their self-worth by using academic education as a contrast. Zhang Hua was successful with this endeavor: she created her own success story and was able to draw self-worth and a feeling of belonging from it (Harbrecht 2018).

Although the students did have positive experiences with vocational education, which led to a generally positive attitude towards this type of education, they nonetheless preferred general education. When answering the question of why they would have preferred general education, students did not consider or were not aware of better career chances with a university degree; their preferences were influenced by other people's opinions and reactions. Qian Qin (3_M/Q3) and Wen Qing (3_F/F3) for example both argued that university education sounded better or was more impressive.

In Chinese society, vocational education students are considered difficult, lazy and stupid, and, poor performance in school is ascribed to a poor personality. Therefore, vocational education students not only are considered poor learners but their whole personality is considered to be problematic. They have a lower value than students in academic education (Shieh et al. 2008: 1; Renmin Ribao 2013: 1; Ling 2015: 120). Consequently, students feel inferior. De Hua (3_M/Q3) spoke about his feelings: "If you want to go to university, you have to fulfill some harsh requirements. I do not fulfill them, so I can only feel power-less and incompetent (*wang yang xing tan* 望洋兴叹)." (DH3_120). Wen Qing (3_F/F3) said that students with a good brain would choose an academic higher middle school. Vocational education was a good choice for weak learners and manually talented students. As a migrant in Shanghai, she regretted not return-ing to her hometown to go to an academic higher middle school and university. Wen Qing felt embarrassed when she admitted to other people that she was a vocational education student.

> Vocational school is lower than general education. People think that vocational education students were bad students in lower middle school. Otherwise, why would they go to a vocational school? (WQ3_18)

When asked where she got this idea, Wen Qing answered that this was her own opinion, as well as what she heard from other people. Students were sus-ceptible to what was said by other people, which could lead to a contradictory narrative: many students were happy in their vocational schools, they recog-nized the value of what they learned, they made progress and they were aware that their skills were needed in the labour market, they knew their peers in general education might have more difficulties finding a job after they graduat-ed from university. Yet still, they thought they were worth less than these coun-terparts and wished they would have the chance to return to general education – which had all the pressure they were actually happy to have escaped. The bad reputation of vocational education in society stigmatized the students, and neither school quality, nor a happy everyday life in school, nor future prospects, nor a new found sense of success enabled the students to distance themselves from society enough to defeat the stigma.

Students were also asked in the survey to value vocational education in comparison to general education. This allowed analyzing students' attitudes divided by school, sex and *hukou*. During their first year in vocational school, students strongly agreed with the statement that 'During lower middle school, my life was happy', and that 'In vocational education, life is happy'. After one year, students agreed more with the statement that 'My life in vocational educa-tion is happier than in lower middle school' and less with the statement that 'My life in lower middle school was happier than in vocational education'.

In 2014, during their first year, Qingpu School students studying in the 2+1 system had higher factor scores than Fengxian School students for factor 2, 'Prefers General Education', whereas Fengxian School students scored higher for factor 1, 'Likes Vocational Education'. Qingpu School students also agreed less than Fengxian School students with the statement that 'Graduates from higher middle school and vocational school have the same development opportunities'. Although in their second year, Fengxian School students agreed more with secondary vocational education being a degree too low, they also agreed significantly more than Qingpu School students with the statement that 'Technical skills are the foundation of my future development' and with 'My life in vocational education is happier than in lower middle school'. Comparing the two schools, it turned out that Fengxian School students had a more positive attitude towards vocational education when juxtaposed with general education.

Male students scored significantly higher than their female peers for factor 1 'Likes Vocational Education' in 2014. Female students on the other hand scored higher for factor 2 'Prefers General Education'. In 2015, more male students planned to rely on their acquired skills. They agreed more with the statements that 'Technical skills are the foundation for my future development' and 'Technical skills are more useful than higher middle school knowledge'. Many female students did not choose their major in the beginning and the present statements continued to show their preference for general education compared to technical education.

In 2014, migrant students and Shanghainese students had similar factor scores. Also in their second year, differences were minimal and not statistically significant. Altogether, male Fengxian School students were most likely to accept vocational education, have positive attitudes towards it and rely on their skills to further their careers.

Table 6.16: Questionnaire A – Opinions on Vocational Education.

Questionnaire A (Panel Data – First Year)		Mean	Standard deviation
During lower middle school, life was happy.		4.1	1.2
During lower middle school, life was happy.	Male students	4.0	1.3
	Female students	4.3	1.1
During vocational education, life is happy.		4.1	1.2
During vocational education, life is happy.	Male students	4.2*	1.1
	Female students	3.6*	1.6
Graduates from higher middle school and vocational school have the same development opportunities.		4.1	1.2
Graduates from higher middle school and vocational school have the same development opportunities.	Fengxian School	4.3	0.9
	Qingpu School	4.0	1.3

Notes: * = sign .05; Likert Scale 1 = 'Do not agree at all' – 5 = 'Totally agree'

Source: Author's own survey 2014

Table 6.17: Questionnaire B – Opinions on Vocational Education.

Questionnaire B (Panel Data – Second Year)		Mean	Standard deviation
My life in lower middle school was happier than in vocational school.		3.0	1.4
My life in vocational school is happier than in lower middle school.		3.4	1.5
My life in vocational school is happier than in lower middle school.	Fengxian School	4.0*	1.0
	Qingpu School	3.3*	1.5
Technical skills are the foundation of my future development.		3.9	1.2
Technical skills are the foundation of my future development.	Fengxian School	4.4**	1.0
	Qingpu School	3.7**	1.3
Technical skills are the foundation of my future development.	Male students	4.0**	1.2
	Female students	3.1**	1.3
Vocational education is an education degree too low.		3.6	1.3
Vocational education is an education degree too low.	Fengxian School	4.1*	1.1
	Qingpu School	3.4*	1.3
Technical skills are more useful than higher middle school knowledge.		3.4	1.4
Technical skills are more useful than higher middle school knowledge.	Male students	3.4	1.3
	Female students	3.0	1.3

Notes: * = sign .05, ** = sign .01; Likert Scale 1 = 'Do not agree at all' – 5 = 'Totally agree'

Source: Author's own survey 2015

6.2.5 Summary

Although the majority of students did not choose vocational education out of interest, the hypothesis that they would therefore have a generally negative attitude towards it was proved wrong. On the contrary, their overall attitudes were positive to begin with. According to the questionnaires, they were interested in technical subjects and they were not frustrated to enter vocational education. They also believed that vocational and general education graduates would have the same development opportunities. What they agreed with in the questionnaires differed substantially from general opinions on vocational education in society. Giving 'positive' answers or repeating what teachers had said certainly had a distorting influence on questionnaire results but students also showed positive attitudes during the interviews.

The interviews confirmed what other research projects on entering undesired school forms, undertaken in different social and cultural contexts, already discovered: being together with peers who share a similar performance level led to positive experiences for the majority of students in their vocational schools, and this again triggered a positive view of vocational education. Students experienced a new sense of achievement and focused on chances they still had with vocational education.

Students' opinions on vocational education in comparison to general education brought another aspect forward which gave a more differentiated picture of how they felt about vocational education. Although their lives had improved since they entered a vocational school, students were nonetheless deeply affected by the bad reputation vocational education and vocational education students have in Chinese society. As a result, they wished they could re-enter the academic education system despite being happy in vocational education. This contradictory attitude was also found in the questionnaire where first year students might score highly for the factor 'Prefers General Education' while still scoring on the average for the factor 'Likes Vocational Education', and vice versa. Chapter 9.7 will take a closer look at how students dealt with this complex sentiment.

Attitudes towards their education correlated with students' feelings about their families. Students with a positive opinion on vocational education were more likely to feel loved and supported by their parents, whereas students who preferred their lives in lower middle school were more likely to feel that they had disappointed their parents. Therefore, family background is an important influence on how students feel about their education. It also turned out that male students and students in the German-influenced Fengxian School were more likely to share positive attitudes towards vocational education than female and Qingpu School students. *Hukou*, on the other hand, did not have a significant correlation with attitudes, which is a surprising result considering that it was their non-Shanghai *hukou* which had forced the migrant students into vocational education. Despite the fact that *hukou* still determines life chances in China and effectively divides Chinese society (migrants-locals, rural-urban) it does not shape students' outlook. Additionally, experiences students had had by their second year were related to their initial reasons for choosing vocational education and their training course in particular. Students who chose their training course out of interest and/or because they considered it useful were more likely to be happy in school. Students who failed their lower middle school exam and subsequently had their parents making decisions for them were more likely to feel pressured or to prefer life in lower middle school.

Once students entered the labour market, which happened for the first time during their internships, their experiences stopped being mainly positive and, as a result, their outlooks became more critical. Students were disappointed by the type of jobs which would be available to them. How things changed for the students once they were confronted with day-to-day work will be discussed in Chapter 7.1.

6.3 Skills and Knowledge Acquired

How students judge vocational education is also significantly influenced by how they perceive their progress and how they think about skills and knowledge they acquired during their training. In vocational education, curricula include general academic subjects, in which the content is defined by the MOE, and vocational subjects, in which the content is partly defined by the MOE for the whole country and partly defined on a local level according to a region's particular economic situation (Kuczera, Field 2010: 14). The focus however is on vocational theory and practice. When graduating, students receive the graduation certificate from their school and they can obtain a technical skills certificate issued by the MOHRSS. Fengxian School students additionally sit an exam organized by the German Chamber of Commerce and receive the corresponding certificate recognized by German companies. The basic knowledge in general subjects and technical skills imparted by the schools enable students to work in a related field without further training on the job.

In the context of vocational education, different kinds of competencies are distinguished. Professional competence includes vocational knowledge and the understanding of operational structures in a company. Social competence includes the acceptance of others and acting cooperatively. Self-competence is the third competence, including self-awareness and the ability to judge (Grabowski 2007: 175). These three competencies were first introduced by Heinrich Roth in 1971 with the realization that vocational skills alone are not sufficient in professional life (Boer 2014: 24). As a consequence of technological development and organizational changes in industrial production, skill requirements are rising. Workers not only need professional knowledge and technical skills but also social skills and the ability to learn how to handle newly developed technologies (Lappe 2006: 80). Therefore, in Germany the goal is to provide a 'holistic' vocational education which confers all of these competencies, summarized as *Handlungskompetenzen*: the ability to use knowledge and technical skills, as well as personal, social and methodical skills, in a work or learning environment in order to achieve professional or personal development (Grabowski 2007: 12; Deutscher Bundestag 7/5/2013 3). The situation in China is similar to Germany: the ongoing development of technology changes the organization of production and makes it impossible to predict which technical skills will be needed in the future. Social competence, self-competence and the ability to learn have become as important as professional competence (Jiang 2011: 9–10). Therefore, vocational education must impart a range of competencies.

Measuring the acquired technical and social competencies of the students would go beyond the scope of the present study. Instead, the *perceived* acquired skills and competencies will be analyzed. Students can only gain self-worth and a sense of success if they are *aware* of a certain newly acquired skill; or to put it another way: If students do not realize that their education in school taught them a certain skill, then they will not be aware of their improvement and consequently they will not credit their education for the improvement. Analyzing which acquired skills the students consider most important does not answer questions about the overall qualification of students or the quality of their education, but it allows another insight into what students think is the value of vocational education, and into whether they are able to find self-worth, development and success through their education, which will then once more influence their opinions on vocational education in general.

It turned out that the development of their social and self-competencies played a bigger role for the students than the technical skills they acquired. Knowledge from general subjects such as Chinese or English was never mentioned. Following are some examples: Shuang Shuang (1_F/QG) said that she gained vocational knowledge, as well as soft skills during her education. She learned how to behave well in school and described this good behavior as knowing how to deal with life and setbacks, how to make choices and follow one's own ideas without parents' help. Wang Yuan (1_M/QG) was a student cadre during his education. He organized events and united his peers. Consequently, communication with fellow students was the most important thing he learned. Ai Wu (1_M/FG) also learned and started to enjoy communication during his vocational education, which – according to him – was the most important thing he learned. Vocational education made him more extroverted. Wen Qing (2_F/F2) became more mature and less naïve during her education. She learned a lot, improved her technical skills and bettered her behavior. She learned how to deal with people. Zhang Hua (2_F/FG) mentioned the progress she made in refined manufacturing during her education. Additionally, she learned how to learn and how to avoid mistakes by being diligent. In summary, students identified two improvements as a result of their education: better communication skills and better behavior.

Communication and communication skills were, in fact, focal points when students spoke about their improvements during their education. Several students worked in sales after their graduation, and according to them, success depended solely on their communication skills. Ai Wu (1_M/FG) explained that companies not only looked at professional skills but actually concentrated on personal skills, such as in communication, when hiring someone. Students often said that they were good communicators. They contrasted this skill with their poor performance in academic subjects as if to make up for this shortcoming. Communication skills were a source of pride and self-worth for the students.

As mentioned above, the second positive change students noticed in themselves was an improvement in their behavior. Again, the internship triggered this development. Life in the company was much stricter than in school and students had no choice but to adhere to the rules. In the hierarchy of the company they, as interns, were at the bottom and needed to listen not only to their superiors but also to senior workers. Only with discipline were the students able to maintain the quality standards and assemble the products within the given time. Zhang Hua (1_F/F3) explained: "This is what I have to work on every day: Increasing my speed while keeping the quality [of the product]." (ZH1_2). While they experienced the hardship of work life, students also started to have a better understanding and more empathy for their parents. Li Tao (3_F/F3): "I think my mother is very tired every day. I understand things better now and I'm more forgiving. I feel sorry for her and want to be better for her." (LT3_102).

The abilities to communicate with others, to form positive relationships, to control one's emotions and be cooperative are crucial for students when they are growing up and facing the challenge of becoming independent from their parents (Hurrelmann et al. 2014: 76), and these social competencies can only be acquired in practice (Boer 2014: 24–26). Students had this practice during their internships, when they had to deal with different kinds of social relationships. The months spent in a company were an essential part of their education and the importance of social skills for professional development should not be underated. In their empirical study with university students in Germany, Anders et al. (2014) have shown that these soft competencies positively influence technical performance as well. With the ongoing automation of factories, traditional work stations are being integrated, hierarchies become flatter and workers are required to communicate more with each other (Lappe 2006: 80). Technical skills needed for a specific job are changing with the technical development and the ability to learn and develop with it has become a key for everybody. In their working lives, the students will have to rely on their ability to communicate, ask questions and engage with their environments. According to their self-assessment, students are prepared for this challenge.

6.3.1 Improvement of *Suzhi*?

The Chinese term *suzhi* (素质) refers to 'human quality' but there exists no clear definition of the term. It includes physical and cultural aspects, as well as IQ and education level. People can develop or have *suzhi* in five aspects: moral (*de* 德), intellectual (*zhi* 智), physical (*ti* 体), aesthetics (*mei* 美), and manual dexterity (*lao* 劳). Some *suzhi* qualities are inherited while other aspects can be improved during life. Generally, *Han* Chinese and people born in economically developed cities are considered to have higher *suzhi* than minorities or people from the countryside (Yan 2003: 496–497, 505, 507; Lin 2011: 322). Since the Communist Party cannot provide welfare, nor can it guarantee employment and health care for all people, it started using this concept to legitimize itself and to motivate the people to take care of themselves. Individuals are encouraged, for example, to improve their *suzhi* through further education, and thereby, become competitive in the labour market. Likewise, the birth control policy was promoted with the argument that parents are responsible for improving their offspring's *suzhi* and should therefore concentrate their resources on only one child. While on the one hand the concept of human quality allows the party to retreat from people's lives, it also, on the other hand, enables the party to intervene in and influence their lives (Murphy 1999: 4–5, 19) and the most important measure is probably 'education for quality' (*suzhi jiaoyu* 素质教育).

Since the 1980s, education in China has had the goal of enhancing the quality of its subjects (Kipnis 2011b: 291). The term *suzhi jiaoyu* is the answer to the oft-criticized exam orientation (*yingshi jiaoyu* 应试教育) and has been a political priority for many years. It aims to develop social responsibility, good morals, soft skills and physical abilities. It tries to introduce more creativity and activity into the classroom while easing the study pressure. Therefore, it is relevant for educational content as well as for teaching methods (Fong 2004: 122; Murphy 1999: 4).

Schools develop different measures to implement *suzhi jiaoyu*. Lin (2011: 325–328) took a primary school in Xiamen as an example, where children are encouraged to read 60 chosen books during their six years of primary school education. Additionally, they track their own improvements in a diary where they also set their own goals, and former prime minister Zhou Enlai has been established as a role model to teach desired behaviors such as social responsibility. Kipnis (2001: 12–13) analyzed measures taken in Zouping County, Shandong Province, where new teaching materials and broader curricula have been introduced to answer the call for *suzhi jiaoyu*. Students have less homework, fewer class hours and teachers are urged to use more interactive teaching methods. Additionally, regulations for entering lower and higher middle school have been adjusted to minimize the importance of exams. The effectiveness of the implemented *suzhi jiaoyu* measures has been criticized. Kipnis and Hansen both pointed out that teachers are not qualified to employ the required teaching methods and parents are afraid that fewer hours spent in classrooms, less homework and more creative, art-related lessons will interfere with students' chances to succeed in the *gaokao*. (Kipnis 2001: 15–18; Hansen 2013b: 173). The concept itself has also been criticized as being too vague (Kipnis 2011b: 294; Hansen 2012a: 4).

For vocational education, *suzhi jiaoyu* has long been less relevant, but in 2015 the Shanghai government published two documents on the evaluation of vocational education students and their human quality. The goal is to broaden the general knowledge of vocational education students and to train their comprehensive abilities and enable them to deal with new, complicated technical tasks. Social competences are also becoming more important (Dong 2015: C2). In the future, schools will have to assess students' development by creating a dossier for every student with yearly reports. Later this dossier will be available for tertiary education institutions and companies in order to facilitate their enrolment and hiring decisions (Shanghai Education Commission 2015).

The students in this study finished their vocational education before these new measures were implemented and they did not mention *suzhi jiaoyu*. The discourse was not relevant for the recipients of education. The answer to the question of whether vocational education raises students' *suzhi* has to be yes and no. Students learn to adjust to social rules, they gain empathy, a sense of responsibility and self-control – all of these traits represent good *suzhi*. At the same time, in Chinese society their *suzhi* will be considered low because they will be manual workers with a relatively low education level, at least by Shanghai standards; their *suzhi* will therefore be inferior compared with white collar workers and university graduates no matter how noble their personalities. It is clear that, with this inherent belief in play, even if the schools manage to implement ideal *suzhi jiaoyu* – and it is not even clear what this would look like – they could increase their students' *suzhi* only to a limited extent.

This exemplifies the dilemma of *suzhi jiaoyu* in China. Besides urban *hukou*, the most recognized indicator for *suzhi* is university education, but this can only be attained by passing the important exams. Vocational schools are completely excluded from this and their students both arrive and leave with low *suzhi*. For other schools too, the concept cannot work. By emphasizing creative content, reducing homework and trying out new teaching methods while reducing the importance of exams, *suzhi jiaoyu*, the education for quality, actually reduces students' chances to succeed in the university entrance exam and thereby attain higher quality. As long as the understanding of *suzhi* within society is not adjusted, *suzhi jiaoyu* is destined to be a failure. Either it fails to decrease the focus on exams and increase creativity, or it interferes with students' *suzhi* prospects. Under these circumstances, the students in the sample did improve their *suzhi* within the possible range: they improved their behavior and started to become self-reliant.

6.4 Conclusion

Vocational education in China is usually analyzed either from a technical perspective, focusing on vocational skills in which students train, or it is analyzed from a social perspective, exploring opinions in society. Hardly ever, though, are the voices of the students themselves in focus as they were in the present chapter.

It is evident that vocational education was not a preferred choice for the students. According to the questionnaires, 80% were forced to leave general education because they were either migrants in Shanghai and therefore not allowed to enter an academic middle school, or they had failed the lower middle school exam which left them with vocational education as the only option for further education. This finding is of great significance. While it seems logical that only poorly performing students entered the very ordinary Nanjing schools where Woronov (2016) did her research, with their inadequately qualified teachers and the poor equipment, it is distressing that key schools in Shanghai cannot attract students who are genuinely interested in technical subjects either. It shows how deeply rooted the assumption that vocational education is of lesser value than academic education actually is when not even these kind of schools are attractive enough to be considered a good choice.

Parents and teachers played an important role when it came to choosing a school and a training course. The location of the school and the usefulness of the course were the major considerations when making a decision. The personal interests of the students were rarely considered and only a few of them had the chance to be an active agent. The panel design which sets this study apart from other research in this field proves undoubtedly how important it is to allow students to have a say when it comes to educational choices. The more influence students had, the more likely they were to have positive experiences later on. This certainly has implications for tertiary education as well, where study courses are chosen according to *gaokao* results rather than interests. Students in academic higher middle schools do not even bother to think about what they would want to study since they will not be able to make a free choice anyway, according to Hansen (2015: 81–82). Giving students the chance to follow their interests would likely lead to a big positive change in students' motivation and success.

Nonetheless, this chapter also confirmed the results of the fifth chapter: students overall had positive experiences once they entered their vocational school. This supports the theory that students who are forced to enter a less desirable school form due to poor grades develop a positive outlook and regain self-esteem once they are among students with similar school performances. The vocational education students enjoyed the fact that they had less homework and new courses which focused on practical skills; their grades improved. Students were very receptive to teachers and other people telling them about the high employment rate among vocational education graduates and the lack of technicians in China. Vocational education was accepted as a new start. Male and Fengxian School students, who alternate between school and company in particular shared positive attitudes in the questionnaires.

The interviews showed that all these mostly positive attitudes were accompanied by a contradictory feeling of inferiority and preference for general education. Although it was not evident on the surface, students were influenced by negative opinions of vocational education in society. They were aware that they were considered bad students of low quality. As a result, students were happier in vocational education than they were in lower middle school while they at the same time wished they would have been able to enter an academic higher middle school.

According to the students themselves, social and self-competencies were the most important skills imparted to them during their education. They learned how to communicate with strangers and with older and higher ranking people; they learned to adhere to rules set by others and how to behave, and they gained empathy. Technical skills seemed to be of lesser importance for the students, and further research should clarify if these competencies were secondary because social skills mattered more to the students, or because they did not learn profound technical skills. Either way, it cannot be forgotten that social and self-competencies are of great value because they are the basis for acquiring new professional skills and adapting to a changing work environment.

Within the framework of *suzhi jiaoyu*, it had to be noted that the fundamental dilemma of the concept is that it tries to enhance *suzhi* through a departure from exam-oriented education while at the same time university education – which requires an entrance exam – is the most important, acquired *suzhi* indicator. Since *suzhi jiaoyu* does not focus on preparing students for the university entrance exam, it is to some extent counterproductive. Vocational education, which does not prepare for university at all, can improve students' *suzhi* only in personality and behavioral aspects. Although the concept of *suzhi jiaoyu* was not relevant for students' self-perceptions, their description of their changes in behavior and their better understanding of their social environment indicate that their *suzhi* did indeed increase, but due to their low education degree and their manual qualifications, it will always be considered low by wider society.

This chapter has established that the internship which students did as part of their training had a profound influence on their attitudes and led to a change in how students' viewed their education and also in their plans for their professional future. The following chapter will take a closer look at how students experienced work during and after their training.

7 Experiencing Work

Previous analyzes indicated that students' experiences during their internships were less positive than in school and that this leads to a change in students' attitudes. The present chapter will take a closer look at why and how these changes occur. During the internship, students leave school for the first time and enter a work environment. The first part of this chapter focuses on the challenges students were facing during this time, while dealing with social relations outside of school. It lists benefits as well as deficits of the internships. Most students spent their days doing monotonous tasks. Not being able to improve their technical skills was a common complaint which left students frustrated. Yet, student experiences were not all negative. Many interviewees reported that they trained their communication skills and subsequently became proud of their ability to handle social interactions.

The second part concerns students' jobs after graduation and the beginning of their lives as professionals. Difficulties and opportunities students encounter in the labour market influence how they evaluate vocational education in hindsight. After looking at students' expectations and career plans during their education, their methods of finding a job and their experiences with work will be analyzed. This chapter is concerned with the question of whether vocational education was able to prepare students for the unregulated labour market, and which resources were available to the students. It turned out that interviewees found jobs relatively easily after graduation but certainly not all of them were satisfied with their employment situation. Also, many students came to realize that getting a tertiary education degree was a far less realistic option than they had thought.

7.1 Being an Intern

Internship placements in companies, where students get to apply their knowledge in a real-life environment, are an integral part of vocational education in China. In Qingpu School, students spent the last year of their education in a company doing their internships. In Fengxian School, students alternated in eight-week blocks between school and a company, starting in the second year. Both schools had agreements with companies who employed interns. Fengxian School had several German-Chinese joint ventures as partners; otherwise the companies were domestic. Schools and companies selected students while, in theory, students were also allowed to choose their company. As a result, better students got to go to companies with better reputations. During their internships, many students stayed in the company dormitories with regular workers.

A frequent criticism was that the work during the internship was not related to electrical engineering. One student, for example, was sent to a hotel for his internship, and another one was working in a company's office supply department. In Qingpu School, several students did not do an internship but found a job themselves. This practice was tolerated by the school.

For most students, this was the first time that they entered a paid work environment. They had a smaller work load than regular workers but were often given monotonous, simple and tiring tasks with little benefit to their education. These kinds of inadequate internship placements and the lack of training, is a well-known deficit in Chinese vocational education (Woronov 2016: 118–123; Dettmer 2017: 204). Many students spent their whole internship assembling the same product on the conveyor belt, and their original expectations – that they would be applying their theoretical knowledge in practice and learning new techniques – were only partly met, or were not met at all. The long hours and the tiring work left students disillusioned about their own career prospects. Many focused on getting a higher education degree, starting their own small business or trying to get an office job to avoid being stuck at a conveyor belt for the rest of their working lives. At the same time, they gained a better understanding for their parents, many of whom were working in similar environments. In general, students preferred going to school over doing their internships since school was more relaxed, they were together with their peers and they felt that they learned more.

7.1.1 Social Relations during the Internship

Before students entered the companies, teachers had prepared them for their new environments. Students learned that rules in companies were much stricter than in school. Behaviors they could get away with in school, such as being late, playing with their mobile phones or taking sick days, were not tolerated in companies. The majority of the students were able to cope but during an informal talk with a Fengxian School internship management teacher, it became clear that complaints about the students engaging in bad behavior or staying away unexcused were nothing unusual.

Relationships and behavioral rules in the companies were very different from what students were used to in school. Their teachers were an authority but at the same time they were very forgiving when students made mistakes, and it was their duty to teach and repeat content until everybody understood. During their internships, students came to realize that mistakes led to actual costs in production and superiors did not forgive them easily. Students learned that they needed to ask if they did not understand something, because not asking could lead to serious consequences. The ability to communicate was crucial while students tried to adjust to the working environment. Wen Qing (1_F/F3) described:

> While maintaining the speed, one also has to guarantee the quality. Here, they do not say that you cannot make mistakes but you have to minimize them. [...] When you encounter difficulties, you have to use the brakes and communicate with the tutor. In this way, you can avoid repeating mistakes. (WQ1_2)

Li An (2_F/F2) agreed:

> What I learned during the internship is [...] you have to communicate. If you are not well you have to say it. If you just stay quiet people will not know and nobody will ask you. We have a saying in Chinese which expresses this well: a child who cannot scream will have no milk (*buhui jiao de haizi mei nai chi* 不会叫的孩子没奶吃). (LA2_56)

Zhao Jing (3_M/F3) is an example for how the failure to communicate appropriately can lead to an overall failure. He made his superior angry because, according to his own account, he talked too much. In the end, Zhao Jing was sent back to school. He summed it up in a short but enlightening statement: "With my boss, it [the relationship] was not good, because I did not know how to talk with him." (ZJ3_62).

Although students worked, ate and often slept in the same quarters with the other workers, they were aware of their different status in the company. They did not have the work load of a regular worker, and their relationships with other workers were mixed. Some students got along well with their older colleagues; others spoke about having to do tasks for them in the evening, or about having a basic lack of understanding. Li An (3_F/FG) explained that interns were like passing guests who were treated politely but without any deeper connection. Han Feng (1_M/F3) felt childish and not trained enough because the other workers saw a student in him. Wen Qing (3_F/F3) realized that people in society were selfish. She did not have a very good relationship with the other workers. Thus, the majority of the students were able to handle social relationships during their internship well, but they did not become an equal part of the workforce.

For further guidance, students were assigned a tutor who introduced them to their tasks. The tutor was often an older worker who had been in the company for many years. Both tutors I spoke to during my research had grown very fond of their interns and treated them as friends and equals. "She [the intern] is about as old as my daughter. Sometimes I treat her as a child and sometimes as a friend, on one level. I do not need to give her a senior or superior attitude." (ZWN1_24). "Besides work, we also talk about life. We have common interests and hobbies. This brought us very close together." (XYK1_51). The fact that both of these tutors were female workers taking care of female students probably facilitated their communication and the development of a positive relationship. Zeng Weina stressed the similarities to her own daughter who also went to a vocational school, and Xu Yingke stressed the common interests and joint after-work activities such as having dinner. These positive tutor-student relationships are probably not the norm. The aforementioned Fengxian School teacher explained that tutors themselves often lack communication skills and behave in an authoritarian manner. During our informal conversation, he recounted that he even had to get one tutor dismissed after violent behavior towards students.

7.1.2 Benefits of the Internship

According to the students, communication was the most important skill they learned during their internship. First, they had to learn how to deal with superiors and older people who were neither family nor teachers, and who were generally less forgiving than either. Second, since students had to do simple tasks and did not learn a lot of new technical skills, communication and social skills became more important. Wen Qing (3_F/F3) summed it up:

> Actually, I do not think you can learn anything during the internship because you are a student and the company will not let you do difficult tasks. You will only do simple, simple work. [...] I feel that dealing with the people here [in the company] is different from dealing with my classmates in school; I feel that it is very difficult. [...] In school, you can learn basic knowledge but in the company you just do the same work and do not learn anything. You just learn how to deal with people. (WQ3_58)

If the internship was completely unrelated to the vocational training course, social skills became even more relevant. When Lei Qiang (2_M/F3) complained about a non-matching internship placement, his teacher told him to learn how to deal with society and how to obey rules and complete tasks.

Students also started to understand what hard work felt like and how difficult it was to earn money. They admired their parents for having worked all their lives. They became eager to relieve their parents' burden and sole responsibility for the family, and students became more empathetic, trying to avoid conflicts. Qingpu School student Xue Mei (1_F/Q4) recounted her experiences:

> Benefit, how to say... Knowing how hard our parents worked; this was a big realization. How they raised us. Before, I did not understand and fought with my parents. I did not know how hard they worked - now I know it. Then what else: well, working is much, much harder than studying, and there's this pressure. (XM1_10)

Very similar is Fengxian School student Li An's (1_F/F2) statement:

> Advantage: I think letting [vocational education interns] experience the hardships of life is not bad; and letting them understand how hard their parents worked. Look, parents leave early and come back late, how hard. Like myself, I want to help my parents at home. I want to let them have a rest because they do not have much time off. So hard! If we are naughty then they have it very hard, very tiring. (LA1_8)

The internship certainly contributed to students growing up, becoming more understanding, and learning important social skills which will have been valuable after their graduation – and which also set them apart from their peers in an academic higher middle school.

Therefore, the main benefit of the internship was less the improvement of technical skills but the training of social skills. Herein lies an advantage of vocational education over academic education: students are brought closer to the working environment via their internships. By the time they graduate, they have a much more precise idea about what their work life will be like than a graduate from an academic higher middle school, or even some university graduates. Fengxian School teacher Zheng Lina summed up the benefits of the internship:

> When they get to the factory, some children do not know what society is like, society is an unrealistic idea (konglong louge 空中楼阁) to them. After they get to the company, they know what it is like there. [...] It is very important, that they know how hard their parents work for their money. The experience in society makes them cherish the study opportunity in school; this is also very important. They can also use the things they learned in school – although in school there is also the chance to practice, but it is limited. In the company, students broaden their hori-

zon, see more things, learn things they cannot learn in school and one other important thing: they change their environment. How to communicate with the company, how to communicate with the superiors and the colleagues and also with their classmates, there is a new communication environment. The social communication is very important. (ZLN1_52)

The internship is without doubt an important part of vocational education, setting it apart from general education.

7.1.3 The Concept of 'Entering Society'

Students described their school as a closed, safe space and contrasted it with society. De Hua (3_M/Q3): "If you make a mistake in school, the teacher will forgive you, excuse you, because school and society are not the same." (DH3_28). Society is the world beyond school and during their internships students entered society for the first time. They had to deal with the 'outside', where not everybody is as understanding, well-disposed or supportive as their teachers and parents. Wen Qing (3_F/F3) complained: "I think in society people are all selfish. The classmates in school all help each other but everybody in the company is very selfish." (WQ3_62). The words 'society' and 'company' were used interchangeably. The internship was a way to get in touch with and to train for society. Lei Qiang (3_M/FA) described vocational education as a process of becoming a part of society and the above-mentioned student De Hua explained: "School is one place and the internship in the company, in society, is a road. From the place, school, one is assigned a road which one always keeps following." (DH3_8).

The early contact with society was one of the advantages students saw in vocational education. They were confident that this would help them find work after their graduation and that it was an asset students in academic higher middle schools did not have. Relating to his upcoming internship, De Hua (1_M/Q1) in his first year of study explained:

> For example social relations... they are different from school. Simply said, if a higher middle school student studies, I think they are immature. They do not have much time to enter society. If you do an internship you gain individual experience. (DH1_14)

The schools took measures to facilitate the transition between school and society. Both schools had lessons on society, which included behavior advice and drafting career plans. There were job fairs in both schools close to graduation, and the internship itself was seen as training for society, where students learned to obey rules and to complete their tasks independently.

There are, as the philosopher Michel Foucault pointed out, striking similarities between schools and prisons. Schools are disciplinary institutions which prepare students for society just like prisons prepare inmates for their release. In school and in prison the days are structured. There are clothing rules, hierarchies and individual development is influenced and controlled (Eigenmann, Rieger-Ladich 2008: 228). This parallel is emphasized by the fact that students see their school as a closed place. After Fengxian School moved to Minhang district, the campus was indeed closed off and Wen Qing (2_F/F2) described the atmosphere: "[...] there are cameras everywhere [...] although I feel monitored by someone, I also feel very safe." (WQ2_35). This description of surveillance has a striking resemblance to the supervision in a panopticon prison, where cells are situated in a way that the inmates can be seen from outside without allowing them to see anybody else (Eigenmann, Rieger-Ladich 2008: 230). However, even without moving to such a campus, Qingpu school students still saw themselves 'inside' despite being able to leave and go home.

Schools and prisons aim to form individuals in the desired way, for example making them disciplined, diligent and so forth, through means like reward and punishment (Rose 1992: 144). Students are subject to disciplinary education, and, just like a prisoner after their term, they are released into society after their graduation and from then on have to function according to social rules without having further guidance. Certainly, none of the students themselves would have drawn a parallel between prison and school but they were very aware that they were in a special institution where the goal was to train and prepare them for society.

Foucault's parallel prison-school is especially relevant for vocational schools despite the fact that academic middle schools have even longer days following an even stricter timetable. Vocational schools specifically aim to train social skills. They send their students to companies to guarantee a smooth transition from school to the labour market. Vocational education students are often considered difficult, problematic and less disciplined. Besides learning and applying technical skills, vocational education students are taught the rules in companies and in society, and how to become more diligent, well-behaved and disciplined. Whereas academic middle school students stay in their safe place – the classroom – and prepare for university, vocational education students are sent out earlier and prepared for their 'release' into society.

7.1.4 Encountering Reality

Apart from all of the positive effects of the internships, there was also a negative effect: several students became disillusioned and lost the desire to work in their field of study. Students realized that their education was only qualifying them for tiring and monotonous tasks on the conveyor belt. Li An (3_F/FG) spoke about how she experienced this kind of work:

> It is a big challenge. I felt as if I was breaking apart because I was so tired... My hands were so tired, everything was tired. We were standing the whole day. ... I felt as if I could not go on, but I had to. The biggest challenge is to keep going. (LA2_62)

Whereas Li An struggled with the physical challenges, Li Qing (1_M/Q3) was disappointed by the simplicity of his tasks:

> In the beginning, I thought that I could learn many technical things in the factory but then I realized that things are pretty simple and do not involve a lot of technique. Then every day was very dull [...]. (LQ1_76)

At this point Li Qing still said that he would look for a job which matches his training but none of the jobs he had in the two years after his graduation were related to electrical engineering and he was not the only one who did not work in his field of training. For example, two years after his graduation, Wang Yuan (1_M/QG) remembers:

> My first employer [his internship company] was a mechanical engineering company where I worked as a sales assistant. It was an internship for one year and then I graduated. This work was too dull and the management was problematic, so I left. (WY1_16)

Wang Yuan started to work for a Taiwanese coating company and hasn't changed jobs since. His internship placement was in an electrical engineering related company but his tasks as an assistant in the sales department were neither related to his training nor enjoyable enough to stay – another example for an internship which did not contribute to education and instead drove the student away from electrical-engineering related jobs.

Essentially, interviewees had no interest in poorly paid factory jobs and therefore began to focus on other options, such as getting a tertiary education degree in order to be qualified for an office job, or starting their own business to enjoy the freedom of being one's own boss, or entering the service industry because it promised lighter and better paid work. Finding a job in the field of their training was not important anymore. Three out of four interviewed teachers confirmed that at least some students undergo this kind of development and Isabel Dettmer (2017) reached a similar conclusion after interviewing students, workers and employers in the hotel industry: repetitive, simple and physically challenging tasks during the internship are one of the main reasons why hotel business students will often avoid this industry after their graduation (Dettmer 2017: 204). The fact that vocational education graduates choose not to work in their field of study further aggravates the problem of training enough skilled workers to meet the demand of the economy – and if vocational education fails to provide skilled workers for the industry it fails to fulfill its purpose.

7.2 Entering the Labour Market

Vocational education students enter the labour market at an early age. In addition to the internship, some students in the sample had part-time jobs or worked occasionally to earn some money. After graduation, they found jobs through internet websites or by word of mouth. Other students stayed with their internship companies, took up jobs allocated by the school, entered family businesses or worked for their parents' friends and acquaintances. Students changed jobs frequently, jumped from one opportunity to the next and most migrant students returned to their hometown after some time or, at least, were planning to return one day.

During their education, very few students had regular part-time jobs to finance their studies; others worked occasionally. Li Qing (1_M/Q3), for example, worked for a fast food chain and financed his education himself. Some students worked during their holidays in factories, and others worked for people who needed a job done whenever they had the opportunity. Distribution of flyers or other advertising material was a common job for students. Usually the work was not very attractive and not beneficial for students' education. Wen Qing (3_F/F3), for example, was a migrant student in Fengxian School who lived alone with her father and described her family's financial assets as moderate but poor compared to Shanghainese families. During her vocational education, she spent both of her summer holidays working in a factory which produced toy balls. Each day, Wen Qing worked between 10–13 hours at the conveyor belt. In the second year, the factory ran out of orders after 20 days and she had to leave, which she regretted. Earning her school fees and relieving her father's burden was her motivation. During long shifts, she realized how difficult it can be to earn money.

Having a part-time job was so attractive for students that they put up with hard, unregulated and unreliable work situations. They were proud to have their own income. Having funds let them contribute to the family income and also gave them more independence when it came to going out or buying goods for themselves. At the same time, they knew that their part-time job was only a temporary employment situation and they believed that they would have a better, easier job after graduation. Parents, on the other hand, seemed to be more reluctant to let students work. Two students said that they wanted to have a part-time job but their parents wanted them to focus on their studies.

At the same time, in the third year of their education, some Qingpu School students did not go to their assigned internship companies and looked for jobs instead. They argued that they would not learn anything during the internship and would have a higher income if they went to a company as a worker and not as an intern.

7.2.1 The Concept of 'Good Work'

When it came to their future jobs, two factors mattered the most for the students: income, and matching their interests. Most students would have liked to become rich quickly but they were aware that their income would be low in the beginning of their working lives. The goal therefore was to have an income high enough to live on their own or with a spouse, and to provide for their parents. Lei Qiang (3_M/FG), for example, described good work as an employment situation in which he would be able to save some money and the employer would pay for insurance and old age security. During the interviews, students said that they were willing to start on a low salary if they had the prospect of getting a higher income later. Concerning their interests, Wang Ming (1_M/F2) argued: "Good work: you have to look at what you like, [...]. If it does not fit and you're not happy [...], I guess it will not work out then." (WM1_54).

Additionally, students mentioned several other factors which would be important to them when looking for a job. At the start was that work should not be too tiring and it should match their skill set so that they could be good at what they would be doing and fulfill the company's requirements. Since most students considered themselves good communicators, the preferred jobs were also not necessarily in the field of electrical engineering. Matching their education was sometimes mentioned as an important aspect but it seemed to rank below the two other factors mentioned above. Additionally, further development and the opportunity to learn were important aspects for some students, as were a harmonious working atmosphere, a safe and friendly environment and a location close to home. The ideal form of work for many students was white collar work and some planned to study and develop until they could work as a low-level manager in a company. Often, foreign companies were preferred because they were considered cleaner, safer and were supposed to have more efficient management. Being one's own boss and owning a small business was even more attractive than office work. Many students aspired to become professionally independent but did not have concrete ideas of how to fulfill their plan or what kind of business might be a success. More realistic and still attractive were commission-based sales jobs. They suited students' communication skills and promised the opportunity to earn money quickly. Also, commission-based jobs usually allowed workers to decide themselves when and for how many hours they worked. Agency was important for the students and they changed jobs quickly if they thought something else would be more interesting or lucrative.

To check how similar job-seeking preferences were, the questionnaire asked students to agree or disagree with the importance of different factors. There was a high agreement rate for all items with 'Matching one's interest', 'Matching one's abilities' and 'Social networking resources' being top priorities. 'Financial income' and 'Company reputation' mattered significantly more to female students, which is in line with the fact that female students appeared to be more career oriented whereas male students were more family oriented (also see Chapter 8.1.1). Despite 4.1 still being a high agreement rate, 'Matching one's education' was of lesser importance than the rest of the factors. The prediction that students would in consequence be open to take jobs that do not match their education could be confirmed with the graduated students in the interview sample, of whom the majority were not working in a training-related field (see Table 7.1).

In order to identify latent variables, a principal axis factor analysis was conducted on these ten items with oblique rotation (direct oblimin). The Kaiser-Meyer-Olkin measure verified the sampling adequacy (KMO = 0.89), and all KMO values for individual items were greater than 0.83, which is considered a good value (Field 2013: 706). An initial analysis was run to obtain eigenvalues for each factor in the data. Two factors had eigenvalues over Kaiser's criterion of 1, and in combination explained 51% of the variance. Therefore, two factors were retained. Both factors had high reliabilities, with factors 1 and 2 having Cronbach's α of 0.9 and 0.8 respectively. The items 'Matching one's education' and 'Stable profession' were not represented in any factor. Factor scores were obtained by computing the means of all items loading ≥ 0.4 on one factor (see Table 7.2).

Table 7.1: Questionnaire A – What Matters When Looking for a Job.

Questionnaire A (First, third and fourth year electrical engineering, second year Mechatronic Company Class)		Mean	Standard deviation
Important when looking for a job		Mean	Standard deviation
Matching one's interest		4.5	0.8
Matching one's abilities		4.6	0.7
Matching one's education		4.1	1.2
Stable profession		4.4	0.9
Promotion opportunities		4.4	0.9
Financial income		4.4	0.9
Financial income	Male students	4.4*	0.9
	Female students	4.7*	0.6
Further training		4.2	1.0
Company reputation		4.3	1.0
Company reputation	Male students	4.2*	1.0
	Female students	4.5*	0.8
Social status		4.1	1.0
Networking resources		4.5	0.8

Notes: * = sign .05; Likert Scale 1 = 'Do not agree at all' – 5 = 'Totally agree'

Source: Author's own survey 2014, 2015

Table 7.2: Questionnaire A – What Matters When Looking for a Job Factor Analysis I.

Questionnaire A (First, third and fourth year electrical engineering, second year Mechatronic Company Class)		
Important when looking for a job	Pattern Matrix	
	Factor 1 'Career'	Factor 2 'Suitability'
Further training	.808	
Social status	.758	
Company reputation	.695	
Promotion opportunities	.625	
Financial income	.518	
Social networking resources	.477	
Matching one's abilities		.947
Matching one's interest		.661
Stable profession	.332	.398
Matching one's education		.345

Notes: Extraction Method: Principal Axis Factoring; Rotation Method: Oblimin with Kaiser Normalization

Source: Author's own survey 2014, 2015

The items that cluster on factor 1 suggest that students were looking for career and development opportunities. Further training, promotion opportunities, social status, company reputation, networking resources, and income, are all part of this factor. These items concern the company and the employment situation; none of them say anything about the job itself or the daily tasks. Consequently, factor 1 describes the general conditions of employment. Factor 2, on the other hand, relates to the work itself: a job should match the interests and abilities of the employee. Students with a high factor loading on factor 1 cared about their development and their status, whereas students with a high factor loading on factor 2 sought satisfaction through their work. They wanted to find a job which would be enjoyable, suiting their skills and where they would do well.

Factor 1 and 2 are not mutually exclusive and it is not surprising that students in the sample generally had a high factor loading for both of them, meaning that students cared about their employment situation and career prospects as well as their tasks and how much they enjoyed doing them. The average agreement rate stayed very much the same for different years of study and there was no difference between *hukou* either. The only differences were between male and female students, where the latter cared slightly more about their career as well as the suitability of the job, and between Fengxian and Qingpu School students where the latter cared slightly more about career. In summary, students were seeking jobs which matched their interests and abilities while also offering career prospects. The least important aspect was finding a job which also matched their education. As long as students had the skill set to do a job well they did not care if it was related to their vocational education or not (see Table 7.3).

Students' preferences, as they came to the fore during the interviews and in the questionnaires, match the results of other empirical research in China. Amy Hanser's young urban interviewees in northern and north-eastern Chinese cities also looked for jobs which would match their skill set, and they also cared about work environment, career options, income and work hours. (Hanser 2002b: 152). For Lisa Hoffman's sample of interviewees in north-eastern Dalian, matching one's education and being able to develop one's skills were important factors. Her participants liked the idea of being self-employed as well, and they felt pressured to find a good job (Hoffman 2008: 174–175). Both studies were based on qualitative methods.

Hanser's interviewees were between 19 and 29 years old by the time they were interviewed in 1998, and their education level varied between high school and three years of graduate study (Hanser 2002a: 191). Hoffman's interviewees, meanwhile, were holding a university degree when they were interviewed in 2003 (Hoffman 2008: 168). The interviewees in this present sample, however, were considerably younger and had a lower education level; they were additionally living in Shanghai, which is considered more developed and more competitive than the northern and north-eastern parts of China, and the interviews were conducted more than ten years after Hoffman's and more than 15 years after Hanser's. Yet, despite these differences – and particularly the time span – all of the interviewees generally agreed about which factors would be important when looking for a job. The only difference seems to be that Hoffman's university graduates were looking for jobs matching their education, whereas, this criteria was not relevant, neither in the present sample nor in Hanser's sample which also included youth with a relatively low education level. Having a degree which only qualifies for (rather simple) manual work, reduces the desire to find a job related to the education. Consequently, lower qualified interviewees care more about career options and work environment. In China, there is a popular

expression for this phenomenon: 'High eyes and low hand' (*yan gao shou di* 眼
高手低)[22], meaning that expectations are higher than actual skills.

Table 7.3: Questionnaire A – What Matters When Looking for a Job Factor Analysis II.

Questionnaire A (First, third and fourth year electrical engineering, second year Mechatronic Company Class)	Important when looking for a job – Career (Standard deviation)	Important when looking for a job – Suitability (Standard deviation)
All students	4.3 (0.7)	4.6 (0.7)
Fengxian School students	4.2 (0.7)	4.6 (0.7)
Qingpu School students	4.4 (0.7)	4.6 (0.7)
Male students	4.3 (0.7)	4.5 (0.7)
Female students	4.5 (0.7)	4.7 (0.7)

Notes: Factor scores 1 = very low – 5 = very high

Source: Author's own survey 2014, 2015

7.2.2 Professional Plans and Work after Graduation

In the past, jobs were assigned by the government and after entering the labour
market the individual became part of a work unit, a *danwei* (单位), where they
stayed for the rest of their working life. Food and housing were provided as well.
The individual had no choice but at the same time there was nothing to worry
about. After labour market reforms in the 1990s, employment became a case of
mutual choice. Today, employer and applicant both make a decision. The individual faces the risk of unemployment but at the same time has the opportunity
to choose where, in which industry, and for which employer to work. Instead of
staying at one level for the rest of their lives, people in China can now become
rich or poor and influence their future with their own actions. This can be a big
motivation – but it can also lead to a lot of pressure for the individual. Changing jobs has become a way to push development and career (Hanser 2002a:

---

[22]   This expression was used by a Fengxian School teacher during an informal talk, referring to
students' expectations concerning their internships.

191–195). Additionally, forms of employment have changed. There is higher mobility and short term contracts have become common (Yang 1998: 290).

As Ulrich Beck pointed out in 2002, and as we have noticed earlier, the modern Chinese labour market shares several similarities with the employment conditions in the Western second modernity – one of Beck's focuses of research. With the end of the 'iron rice bowl' system, people, for the first time, face the risk of unemployment and in order to avoid this, they have to take their lives in their own hands (Beck, Beck-Gernsheim 2002: 1). With each job change individuals have to re-enter the labour market. Increased competition forces individuals to be very flexible when it comes to location and type of job and also to work on their qualifications – higher education degrees are often expected even for simple positions in China (Shieh et al. 2008).

This kind of labour market furthers individualization in society (Beck 1994: 47–48). The profession is no longer the basis on which individuals form their identity. A predetermined career and job security have been replaced with the chance to choose a job and quit an undesirable employment situation. The individual in China eventually lost stability in life and gained control. These are characteristics of individualization as Beck described it (Beck 1986: 206–207). With the reform of the labour market and the introduction of mutual choice between employer and employee, choice not only became an option but also a necessity – which is another parallel to individualization in Western European societies. The individual always has to choose whether they want to take a job or not. It is important to remember that not every choice is a desired one. If vocational education students have the choice either to finish their education after lower middle school or to enter a vocational school, they *chose* vocational education – but this by no means says that it was a desired choice (Beck, Beck-Gernsheim 1993: 181–182). After their graduation, students need to choose a strategy for how to find employment. They need to decide what kind of job they want to look for. They need to get information on open positions. They need to compete against other applicants and once they are employed they need to decide how long they'll stay with one employer. This requires a level of activity and decision making that none of the students had faced before in their lives.

When asked in the interviews about future plans, students saw three options: working for a company, starting their own business or continuing with further education. The questionnaires made clear that further education was the most popular option, closely followed by doing business. Working in a factory, which is the kind of work environment students will be trained for, was by far the least popular choice. Further education was significantly more attractive for Shanghainese students, which has already been explained in Chapter 5.1.1. Doing business was significantly more attractive for migrant students, which could be a hint that these students are more entrepreneurial, but could also be the result of migrant students' limited further education opportunities due to financial and other constraints (see also Chapter 7.2.2.3).

After graduation, students have the option to get a job through their school because the school is the intermediary between students and employer (Hanser 2002b: 146). The fact that schools arrange employment was a relevant factor for many students and their parents when choosing the school. Presumably, parents thought about their own parents, who were still working in the old labour system with assigned jobs, and saw the advantages of avoiding the competition in the labour market they themselves had to face. In fact, Cliff (2015: 157) found, during his research in a state-owned oil company in Xinjiang, that *danwei* style employment, i.e. secure and stable jobs, are an employment form people still value and aspire to. During the first and second year of this present study, many students planned to take up such a school-referred job. They did not have clear ideas about the kinds of jobs to which their education could lead, and they also did not know how they would look for a job themselves. Therefore, relying on their school was a convenient and secure alternative.

Table 7.4: Questionnaire A – Professional Plans After Graduation.

Questionnaire A (First, third and fourth year electrical engineering, second year Mechatronic Company Class)		Mean	Standard deviation
After vocational education, I want to get a higher education degree.		3.7	1.4
After vocational education, I want to get a higher education degree.	Shanghainese students	4.1**	1.3
	Migrant students	3.2**	1.4
Later, I want to work in a factory.		2.9	1.4
Later, I want to work in a factory.	Male students	2.9**	1.4
	Female students	2.4**	1.4
Later, I want to do business.		3.5	1.3
Later, I want to do business.	Shanghainese students	3.3*	1.4
	Migrant students	3.7*	1.2

Notes: * = sign .05, ** = sign .01; Likert Scale 1 = 'Do not agree at all' – 5 = 'Totally agree'

Source: Author's own survey 2014, 2015

In the third year and after graduation, however, more and more students decided to go looking for a job themselves. This development was certainly related to students' experiences during their internships, and the realization that the jobs their school had to offer might not be very attractive. At the same time, students had a broader knowledge of how to find jobs and were better prepared for both the job market and society in general. Students still attended the job fairs which both schools organized; these events were generally considered helpful because students got an idea of which companies were hiring and what the job conditions were like. In the end, though, most students found a job through online portals or through friends, relatives and acquaintances. A detailed analysis of the different job hunt methods follows below.

7.2.2.1 Job Hunt and Guanxi

Following socioeconomic changes in China in general and in the labour market in particular, there is an ongoing debate about the importance of *guanxi*, personal relationships. Hanser (2002b: 137–161) argues that with the recent changes in the labour market, where jobs are no longer allocated and a high mobility is required from employees, *guanxi,* defined as social ties including trust, reciprocity and obligation, lose their importance. During her empirical research in northern China in 1998, she realized that higher mobility reduced available *guanxi* because employees moved without their network. Also, specific skill sets which come with a higher education level would require a *guanxi* network in a specific field. Most of Hanser's interviewees did not have this kind of connections and therefore had to rely on their merits to get a suitable job. Hanser additionally argued that companies nowadays have more freedom in the hiring process while being under bigger pressure to perform well economically, resulting in more merit based hiring procedures. She admits though, that for lesser skilled people such as middle school or vocational middle school graduates who do not have marketable skills, *guanxi* is still important to avoid exploitable or very poorly paid jobs. The difficulty, of course, is that newly graduated vocational middle school students without work experience cannot compete in the labour market, but they also do not have a personal *guanxi* network and therefore need to rely on their parents, who might not be locals either, or on friends when looking for a job. This means that the people who are still the most likely to depend on *guanxi* are also the ones least likely to have it. Overall, Hanser concluded that *guanxi* is still used but that other methods are becoming more important and popular.

Bian (2002: 117–133) on the other hand, rejected the idea that *guanxi* was losing its significance in China's labour market. After conducting 100 interviews in six Chinese cities between 1997 and 1998, Bian confirmed the persisting relevance of *guanxi*. A significant number of his interviewees relied on *guanxi*, defined in this case as strong ties including mutual trust, frequent interaction and intimacy, to get a job. Bian argues that China did not undergo a smooth transition from planned to market economy, which would have been accompanied by the diminishing importance of strong ties, and an increasing importance in information networks in the hiring process. Instead there are institutional holes in the system which lead to the persistence of strong ties. Jobs are no longer allocated; employer and future employee need to find each other, but at the same time there is a lack of market institutions which would regulate the job finding and hiring process. Job seekers and employers rely on *guanxi* to obtain information, to build trust and strengthen mutual obligations. With an additional survey in five Chinese cities[23], Bian, together with Huang (2015: 326), strengthens his argument. The use of ties to gain information and influence, and especially the use of strong ties, has been increasing since the opening reforms. Bian and Huang once again disprove the idea that the labour market reforms have led to a decline of *guanxi* use.

Hasmath (2011: 189–201) focused on the experiences of migrant workers in the labour market in Beijing. He drew on the 2000 census and complemented this data set with his own interviews with employees and employers, as well as observations of hiring practices in six companies between 2006 and 2008. Hasmath did not provide a definition for *guanxi* except for it being a social connection but he agreed with Bian that it is still very important when looking for a job. He also pointed out that this is the case because job agencies and job advertisements are not popular, and therefore companies and job seekers prefer informal channels when it comes to getting information and applying for jobs. *Guanxi* fills the institutional holes. It turned out that Hasmath's subjects, ethnic minority workers in Beijing, were disadvantaged in the labour market because they lacked the important connections, *guanxi*, which *Han* Chinese have. This is certainly a problem since minority workers who come from other provinces often will not be able to compete with the education levels of the average Beijing population, and are therefore more dependent on social capital.

Whereas Bian and Hasmath argue that *guanxi* are important to fill institutional holes, Hanser argues the opposite: formal application and job distribution procedures are becoming more important because of the holes in the *guanxi* network, as Hanser had pointed out herself (Hanser 2002b: 160–161).

---

[23] Changchun, Tianjin, Shanghai, Xiamen, Guangzhou.

Additionally though, these authors differ on the definition of *guanxi*. For Hanser, *guanxi* means strong ties including, among others, a strong obligation which would mean that if someone uses his uncle as a *guanxi* connection to get a job, the uncle would have to be the hiring manager or somehow have an influence big enough to guarantee a successful hiring. Bian defines *guanxi* 'just' as strong ties. With this definition, an introduction through an uncle to the hiring manager – while the latter still chooses whom to hire by himself – would be considered using *guanxi* in Bian's understanding. Hasmath, who has not provided a definition in his article, seems to have the broadest understanding of *guanxi*, where the mere passing of information already qualifies as a use of *guanxi*. The different understanding of *guanxi* makes the debate imprecise since empirical proof for the use of *guanxi* by one author might be used as empirical prove for the lacking use of *guanxi* by another. Additionally, there is a continuum between weak and strong ties and *guanxi*; the quality of a relationship can change over time. Empirically, the differences are not always unambiguous even if a common definition would be used.

In summary, the research done by all three authors suggests that if there is the opportunity, strong ties, understood as *guanxi* or not, are being used to secure a job. The current labour market situation is defined by an unsatisfactory information distribution system, where only low paid jobs with poor work conditions are publicly advertised and information on attractive jobs is distributed through informal channels. At the same time, high mobility especially in the big cities – and a lack of experience, reduces the likelihood of young job seekers having useful *guanxi* or strong ties available. In reality, people have to, and also do, rely on a mix of methods when looking for a job but, as the above mentioned authors pointed out, the lower the education level, the more important *guanxi* become. It follows that the students of the present study find themselves in a difficult situation: their education level is low *and* they are unlikely to have *guanxi* or useful connections of their own since they are too young to have established them. They might be able to use their parents' networks but otherwise all they have is the school referring jobs or friends pointing out opportunities.

During the interviews, two students explicitly mentioned that they might or did use their families' *guanxi* network. One student chose electrical engineering because his uncle could then employ him in his company, and another student secured a job in a company through his fathers' network. This student, Qian Qin (3_M/Q3), confirmed what had been pointed out before: "Work is easy to find, but finding good work is hard." (QQ3_140). Asked how he would look for work, he said: "I rely on my parents; what kind of work would I be able to find?!" (QQ3_142). Li Qing (2_M/QG) said that in the beginning work was not easy to find because vocational education graduates do not have any experiences. He found his first job with the help of a friend. Ming Ming (1_F/FG) agreed that companies look for experiences which vocational education students do not yet have. Lei Qiang (3_M/FG), who was getting a higher vocational education degree at the time of the interview, explained the situation:

> In China, there is a problem: social relations (*renji guanxi* 人际关系). Social relations are being paid a lot of attention. If somebody in your family knows someone or has good *guanxi* then you can enter a company very easily, but when you do not know anybody then the requirements are very strict. There is this problem in China. (LQ3_28)

As did several interviewees in Hanser's study, Lei Qiang described *guanxi* in a negative way (Hanser 2002b: 156–157), but looking at the questionnaires, 'Social networking resources' were considered one of the most important factors when looking for a job.[24] It is safe to say that when entering the labour market the students in the sample would use *guanxi* if they were able to, because they do not have anything else to offer which would set them positively apart from the millions of job seekers with higher education degrees. Yet, most of the students did not have *guanxi* and therefore relied on their luck or on ties, weak and strong, which helped them by passing on information or securing an interview for a desired job.

It turned out that in the case of low qualified individuals who enter the labour market for the first time, the present study confirmed both theories: the persisting *and* the diminishing relevance of *guanxi*. The lower the qualification level of a job seeker, the more important *guanxi*/strong ties become to compete with higher qualified individuals and job seekers will actively try to use them in order to secure a good job. In practice, though, most graduates with twelve years of schooling have no useful connections available and have to fall back on weak ties passing on information or job advertisements. Therefore, *guanxi* is of great importance for the students and at the same time are used only by a very small percentage of them.

Interestingly, Dettmer (2017) came to a different conclusion. She analyzed quantitative and qualitative data gathered from employers and employees in the hotel business and concluded that *guanxi* are not used for filling low or entry-level positions, and are also considered less important by employees with lower education levels.[25] Yet, Dettmer did not make a distinction between employees

---

[24] Mean 4.5, standard deviation 0.8; Questionnaire A (First, third and fourth year electrical engineering, second year Mechatronic Company Class), Likert Scale 1 = 'Do not agree at all' – 5 = 'Totally agree'.

[25] In her study *guanxi* were found to be relevant for higher positions and higher education levels.

in different age cohorts and only included informants who were already in one specific industry. In comparison, all graduated interviewees in the present study were in their early twenties and not determined to work in one specific sector or industry. Therefore, further research needs to clarify if at all and if yes, to what extent, the length of work experience of employees with low education levels correlates with the importance ascribed to *guanxi*.

7.2.2.2 Employment after Graduation

After their graduation, most students did not work in fields matching their education and they changed jobs frequently. This was contrary to statistics for 2014 published by the Shanghai Education Commission, in which 87.31% of the 2014 vocational education graduate cohort worked in the field matching – or basically matching – their training (Shanghai Education Commission 2015). The dean of Qingpu School electrical engineering department confirmed during an informal talk that most students do not work in a field related to their training after they graduate and a Fengxian School teacher pointed out that there was no definition for which job would match which training course. Many jobs used electrical appliances so they could all qualify as matching an electrical engineering education.

Following are some examples which highlight graduates' experiences with the labour market and the development of their careers in the first years after graduation. Han Feng (2_M/FG) was a common example of a student changing jobs frequently, pursuing his own freedom while trying to maximize his income. Wang Yuan (1_M/QG) had the same goals but he found a position in a company that allowed him to get close to or reach these goals without changing jobs. Ming Ming (1_F/FG) went to a higher vocational school and, just as many of her peers, she took a part-time job. Ai Wu (1_M/FG) was an unusual example. He is included here to illustrate that secondary vocational education graduates can be loyal to one company and make their career if they receive company support.

Han Feng did his internship with Electronics Minhang, a German company with a good reputation. After graduation, he stayed with the company because the work there was comfortable and included better working hours than other companies. After one year, though, he left and took up a job with a call center, but it turned out that the center was not licensed and in order to avoid trouble, Han Feng quit after his first day. At the time of the interview, one year after his graduation, he worked for a real estate agent where he liked the flexible hours. Han Feng was confident that real estate was a good business since most people in China buy an apartment before they get married. When looking for work, he looked for development opportunities and a good salary, and made sure that the work was suitable for him. In 2015, Han Feng said that in general he does not have high goals or the urge to become very rich, but one year earlier he had spoken about the fact that people are never satisfied and that he will proceed step by step.

After his graduation, Wang Yuan began to work for a Taiwanese varnishing company – a job which was unrelated to his education. By 2015, he had been with the company for two years and was very satisfied. Work allowed him to travel freely around the city and Wang Yuan liked his independence as well as the contact with customers. The only downside was that since his graduation, he experienced more pressure than in school, but he admitted that that pressure not only came from work but also from himself and his desire to improve. Also, rising prices and financial dependence on his parents created pressure for him. Development opportunities were important for Wang Yuan, especially since salaries were not high for young people after their graduation. In his current job, development opportunities depended on diligence and luck, which made him confident that he could reach his goals there.

Ming Ming continued on to get a higher vocational education degree after she finished vocational middle school. She was studying to become a kindergarten teacher – something completely unrelated to electrical engineering and a choice which, in hindsight, she regretted. Ming Ming also had a part-time job. After her graduation, she had looked at online job postings and went to interviews but finding a job was not easy. As discussed above, companies were looking for people with work experience which was even more important for them than a degree. Ming Ming complained that vocational education students did not have work experience, because their internships were not related to their training courses. At the time of the interview, she had been doing various jobs in a restaurant for two years. She was, for example, helping out in the kitchen, collecting money or taking care of deliveries. Ming Ming did not like this job because her income was low and the work environment was difficult for her; she needed a lot of patience and sometimes had problems communicating with customers. A good job, in her opinion, would not be too tiring and would be in an air-conditioned office. Ming Ming's ideals and her actual life choices did not match up. She enrolled in a kindergarten teaching course while liking office work, and realized later it would have been better to get a stable job first and then continue her electrical engineering education. At the time of the interview, these were merely 'pipe dreams' and her actual goal was to finish her higher vocational education degree and to start working in a kindergarten.

Whereas the three aforementioned students were 20 or had just turned 21, the fourth graduate, Ai Wu, was already 38 and had been working as a promotion manager with Electronics Minhang ever since his graduation 18 years ago. Due to his career, he was a 'model' former student for the German-influenced Fengxian School and was occasionally invited to talk to current students about their future prospects. After he graduated, Ai Wu joined Electronics Minhang, where he had done his internship. The company saw his potential and financed him to do a part-time German course for two years. In 2015, he thought about changes in life; he would have liked to change his position, learn more, face new challenges and own his own company. A good job for Ai Wu would be challenging and allowing for personal development and the improvement of self-value. His current restlessness, despite having already climbed the career ladder, proved that for some people a good job needed to offer constant development opportunities of all levels. This is contrary to Cliff (2015: 157) who concluded that stability was valued more than upward mobility but he conducted his research in the western province of Xinjiang which is a completely different setting from Shanghai, where the pressure to succeed and not to be left behind is felt more acutely by individuals. In this context migrant student Zhang Hua (2_F/FG) described her feelings: "If you don't have progress and just stay where you are, then other people will get ahead of you and you will be eliminated (*taotai* 淘汰)." (ZH2_35)

This brief look at four graduated students illustrates that the school is the most important and often the only *guanxi* students have when they graduate. Staying with their internship company is an option available to most students, and the school is also able to refer students a job in a different company, which facilitates the transition from school to employment.

The example of these students also shows that although statistics confirm that job hopping is a common practice among young employees, they were willing to stay with one employer if the work lived up to their expectations concerning income, everyday tasks, work environment, development opportunities, and so forth. Yet, students did not feel obliged to be loyal to one employer; instead they felt obliged to further their development. As soon as they got a better offer, they would change jobs. Vocational education graduates were not threatened by unemployment, since there were plenty of jobs available for technical workers or in the service industry. When it came to attractive jobs though, they had to face high competition from their peers and job seekers with a higher education degree. Offering a concrete plan for development while paying a fair salary might be a good start for companies who want to keep their employees. Ai Wu is, without a doubt, the best example – his education did not stop once he began working; in a way it only just started then.

7.2.2.3 Further Education

As we have seen, not all students started to work after their graduation – further education was a popular alternative frequently mentioned throughout the interviews. In the questionnaires it turned out to be more popular than doing business or working in a factory. Enrolling in a tertiary vocational education institution became an option after a recent reform in Shanghai which was widely advertised to make vocational middle school education more attractive. In the third year of their education, many students enrolled in extra-curricular classes which prepared them for the *gaofu* (高复) exam, which – when passed successfully – would then allow them to enter tertiary vocational education. According to statistics published by the Shanghai Education Commission, 97.9% of the students who graduated from a vocational middle school in Shanghai in 2014 either started to work or continued to study, with 44.0% of them doing the latter (Shanghai Education Commission 2015).[26]

Although all students can participate in the *gaofu* exam in order to continue their studies, chances to do so are not spread equally. Migrant students graduating from vocational middle schools in Shanghai in 2014 had an activity rate of 98.8%, which was even higher than the overall activity rate, but only 23.4% of them continued to study (Shanghai Education Commission 2015). This was confirmed in the questionnaires, in which Shanghainese students had a significantly higher agreement rate than migrant students with the statement 'After vocational education, I want to pursue further studies'.

Compared to Shanghainese students, migrant students were without doubt less likely to continue their education beyond vocational middle school. The underlying reason was the financial constraint migrant families face in Shanghai. *Gaofu* preparation classes are private and cost money, and once graduated from vocational middle school the family is often not able to support their children any longer. Li An (3_F/FG), a migrant student who studied in the Mechatronics Company class and then decided to continue with further education, felt that she was a burden for her family because she was not working yet. Her former classmate migrant student Wang Ming (3_M/FG) also continued to study but he enrolled in a part-time program that allowed him to get his degree while working. Wen Qing (3_F/F3) did not have the opportunity to continue to study. She explained the situation:

> Most students take *gaofu* classes, local students. Migrant students are getting ready to start working, [...] because their financial situation at

---

26 The article does not say what the 2.1% of graduates who neither start to work nor continue to study do but it can be assumed that they are unemployed.

home is much worse compared to Shanghainese families. The *gaofu* classes are expensive and, of course, some students do not want to continue studying. [...] In my case, my family's finances aren't good enough. I would like to study but my family's situation does not allow it. I can only start working and quickly help relieving the financial pressure. (WQ3_46, 48, 50)

Here we also find the explanation for the slightly higher activity rate among migrant students. As pointed out before, finding a job is not difficult for the students, the challenge is finding a good job. Whereas Shanghainese students might be able to live on their parents' money for some months and wait for a good offer, most migrant students cannot afford to be unemployed and without an income.

Table 7.5: Questionnaire A – 'After vocational education, I want to get a higher education degree'.

Questionnaire A		
(First, third and fourth year electrical engineering, second year Mechatronic Company Class)		
After vocational education, I want to get a higher education degree.	Mean	Standard deviation
All students	3.7	1.4
Shanghainese students	4.1**	1.3
Migrant students	3.2**	1.4

Notes: ** = sign .01; Likert Scale 1 = 'Do not agree at all' – 5 = 'Totally agree'

Source: Author's own survey 2014, 2015

7.3 Conclusion

School is an institution which prepares students for their adult lives. They are being trained for society and shaped in a desired way. In China, students are trained to be self-reliant and self-responsible, while contributing to the nation (Hansen 2015: 176–179).

Michel Foucault pointed out the similarities between prison and school, and indeed, students considered themselves as being 'inside' when being in school and 'outside' after graduation or during their internships. School was a safe place where mistakes were easily forgiven and where communication happened in an uncomplicated fashion since peers were friends and teachers were friendly. During their education, students left school for their internship and 'entered society'. In the beginning, this was an exciting and new experience and students were proud to earn their first money. Later, students became disillusioned because they realized that their future work was likely to be dull and poorly paid. At the same time, students gained a better understanding of the hardship their parents surmounted in order to feed their family.

The internship was often unrelated to students' training courses and the tasks were simple. As a result, the training of relevant technical skills was limited. The biggest benefit for the students was the training of communication and social skills. Among their co-workers, students were for the first time facing people who were neither related nor responsible for them. Students learned that they needed to ask questions in order to avoid costly mistakes; they learned how to speak with older and/or superior people, and how to deal with criticism. Additionally, students realized that behavior they could get away with in school would have serious consequences on the job. They learned to stick to rules and not to give up. Students took responsibility, did what was expected of them and became more pro-active. They gained empathy and began to feel more grown-up. A disadvantage was that students realized that their education would lead to undesirable jobs in factories. Some of the students not only lost their interest in finding a job related to their education, they also lost their positive attitude towards vocational education, with extreme cases considering vocational education a waste of time.

Students wanted to have interesting, well-paid work which also offered development opportunities. Factories were unattractive employers since the work was likely to be monotonous and, therefore, neither interesting nor well-paid, nor development enhancing. Students hoped to work in a healthy, friendly environment ideally as white collar workers, or they aspired to own businesses, although these ideas were not very specific. Further education was also an attractive option for students who were hoping to qualify themselves for better-paid office jobs. In reality though, most migrant students had difficulties financing the *gaofu* classes which prepared students for the entrance exam. In the end, most students started to work in a field unrelated to their education, and changed jobs as soon as another job offered better conditions, in order to further their development and better their circumstances. Commission-based sales jobs were popular since they promised more money and more personal freedom than factory positions. The interviewees used their agency to switch jobs whenever there was a better employment opportunity. However, the example of Wang Yuan and Ai Wu revealed that students would be willing to stay with one employer if they were given agency and development opportunities.

Among the graduated students interviewed for the present study, only one student did not start working or proceed to higher education. Instead he stayed with his parents for a few months until his mother told him to find a job which he subsequently did. The *ken lao* (啃老 = to chew the old) phenomenon which describes young adults who are depending on their parents, either financially or for labour assistance, and which has become an important topic in China, was not present among the students of my study. Liu (2017a) described four different cases of *ken lao* adults and their parents in Shanghai which can explain why this phenomenon was not found in my sample. In two cases the parents-child arrangement was endorsed by both generations. These were families who were financially well-off and could afford to have members staying at home. In the other two cases, the situation caused conflict among the family members. Parents had financial worries and also did not approve of their child's life style.[27] As became clear during the interviews, none of the families in my sample would have the financial background allowing a *ken lao* life without compromising parents' retirement options and the strong filial obligations felt by students (see next chapter) prevented them from aspiring to a *ken lao* life when this would create difficulties for their parents. Therefore, none of them stayed at home for long.

Finding a job was not difficult for the students but it was difficult to find attractive jobs. Students were lacking experience and most of them did not have *guanxi* of their own or in their families, which would have helped them find a better paid job or a better working environment. Therefore, they had to rely on online advertisements despite advertised jobs being considered to be the kind of jobs nobody wants. Additionally, students tried to employ their own network which consisted of ties of varying strengths. As Amy Hanser pointed out, there are currently holes in labour market institutions as well as in the *guanxi* system. The vocational education graduates in the sample were facing both holes: they had no *guanxi* network of their own and no qualifications to compete for good jobs. Further research is needed to find out if former students who have already gained experiences and established a work related social network rely on ties or merits when looking for a job.

Remembering the two responsibilities of vocational education in China – contributing to building a harmonious, stable society by enabling Chinese people to make a living, and contributing to the country's economic development by providing skilled workers – we can draw the following conclusions. Vocational education successfully prepared students for the job market, and the high

---

[27] A daughter was divorced with two children, a son was a bachelor concentrating on his career as an artist.

activity rate proves that students were well-equipped to find employment if they chose not to proceed with further studies. Vocational education enabled the students to integrate in society and to make a living and, therefore, contributed to social stability in China. Yet, vocational education did not provide the skilled workers needed in the Chinese economy because a considerable number of students did not enter the vocational field they had been qualified for and their technical skills did not benefit the industry.

While the previous three chapters introduced students' environment and their experiences with vocational education and work, the next two chapters will turn to students' inner lives, i.e. their values, personalities and identities. It will be explored how individualization in society and the experience of being a vocational education student shape the individuals and further examination will illustrate into what kinds of members of society they develop.

8 Values and Responsibility

The previous chapters have provided an in-depth analysis of students' educa-tion related attitudes, their experiences and their environment. The present chapter now turns to students' inner lives, exploring their value systems and discussing their ideas of personal responsibility. Students adhere to collective as well as individual values and it will become clear that what appears to be a con-tradiction at first is a system where individual values are functionally dependent on collective values. A similar phenomenon was found in relation to money. Financial assets mattered to the students but they were not, as I will argue, a value by itself.

During the interviews and the questionnaires, it became clear that students had strong feelings of personal responsibility. This kind of attitude is one of the defining features of individualization. This chapter will discuss the consequenc-es and implications of students' perceived responsibility and thereby reveal how individualization manifests itself among the young Chinese in the sample. Ex-amples will show that some students were very similar to the 'enterprising self' as Nicolas Rose has described it. Finally, it will be seen that students saw only one way to influence their fate and live up to their responsibility, and that was by learning.

8.1 Values

In order to find out with which values students agree, they were asked to rate the importance of several value-related items in the questionnaire. A principal axis factor analysis was conducted on ten items which might be important to them with oblique rotation (direct oblimin). The Kaiser-Meyer-Olkin measure verified the sampling adequacy (KMO = .854).

An initial analysis was run to obtain the eigenvalues for each factor in the data. Three factors had eigenvalues over Kaiser's criterion of 1 and in combina-tion explained 54.3% of the variance. These three factors were retained. The table shows the factor loadings after rotation with a loading >= 0.4. The items which cluster on the same factor suggest that factor 1 represents 'Good Life is Important', factor 2 represents 'I am Important' and factor 3 represents 'Other People's Opinions are Important'. Concerning liabilities, factor 1 has a Cron-bach's Alpha = 0.799, factor 2 = 0.866 and factor 3 = 0.585. The last factor has a relatively low liability which can be explained by the fact that it is created by only two items. Nonetheless, this factor is unambiguous and allows further insights into students' value systems. To get factor scores for each case, the mean of sum scores of all items loading >= 0.4 on factors were computed.

Table 8.1: Questionnaire A – 'Important for me' Factor Analysis I.

Questionnaire A	Pattern Matrix		
(First, third and fourth year electrical engineering, second year Mechatronic Company Class)	Factor 1 'Good Life is Important'	Factor 2 'I am Important'	Factor 3 'Other People's Opinions are Important'
Important for me_Harmonious living environment	.790		
Important for me_Personal development	.665		
Important for me_Sense of security	.639		
Important for me_Sense of success	.594		
Important for me_Independent life			
Important for me_Contributing to society		-.911	
Important for me_Contributing to the state		-.849	
Important for me_Helping others		-.601	
Important for me_Consumer goods			.640
Important for me_Face			.578

Notes: Extraction Method: Principal Axis Factoring; Rotation Method: Oblimin with Kaiser Normalization

Source: Author's own survey 2014, 2015

Overall, students agreed highly with 'Good Life is Important'. There was an agreement with 'Other People's Opinions are Important' but it was far less strong than the agreement with factor 1. Finally, students disagreed with 'I am Important'. It became clear that students cared about their own life and things that concern themselves directly most. Caring for society and impressing others came second and third. When looking at school, *hukou* and sex, the only significant difference was between the schools. Students studying in the alternating system in Fengxian School agreed more with 'I am Important' than Qingpu School students who studied in the 2+1 system. This would suggest that Fengxian School students were more egoistic but there is also another aspect that should not be overlooked. Contributing to state and society are ideals propagated and demanded by the Chinese Communist Party (CCP). Students in Fengxian School get, at least to some extent, in touch with German culture. Some of them have the opportunity to participate in a students exchange with Germany and many of their teachers participated in training run by German experts. Further research would be necessary to prove that these influences resulted in a certain neglect of the mentioned party ideals.

Table 8.2: Questionnaire A – 'Important for me' Factor Analysis II.

Questionnaire A (First, third and fourth year electrical engineering, second year Mechatronic Company Class)		Factor 1 'Good Life is Important'	Factor 2 'I am Important'	Factor 3 'Other People's Opinions are Important'
All students		4.5	1.9	3.5
Students' school	Fengxian School	4.4	2.1**	3.4
	Qingpu School	4.5	1.8**	3.5

Notes: ** = sign .01; Factor scores 1 = very low – 5 = very high

Source: Author's own survey 2014, 2015

When directly asked about values, most students struggled with an answer because the concept was too abstract. Nationalism only came up in one interview, when a student said that she would support Chinese Mangas despite preferring Japanese ones. Moral campaigns such as *Lei Feng* were not mentioned by the students. Agreement rates with 'Contributing to society' and 'Contributing to the state' were with 4.0 on a five point Likert scale, lower than the agreement rates with all the items constituting factor 1, 'Good Life is Important' (harmonious living environment, personal development, sense of security and sense of success). Therefore, students overall did not prioritize values which can be directly linked to government campaigns.

As explained above: students cared about things which concerned them directly and were part of their own lives. Within this broad sphere were common ideals which students valued and pursued. These were family and independence. Family was the most prominent value, with students sharing a sense of obligation and respect towards their parents, and wanting to have their own families. This traditional piety and family life ideal was complemented by an almost contradictory value: independence. Independence, however, was mostly understood in a financial sense. This, along with the fact that income and property were seen as necessary preconditions to making a family, led to money being something that students valued and aspired to having as well. Additionally, students tried to internalize what they considered good behavior. However, ideas on good behavior were vague and highly influenced by what students were taught, and they were in the process of becoming able to listen to their inner feelings when judging how to act properly.

8.1.1 Collectivism

Historically, China is a group-oriented culture with collectivistic values. Individuals are tied to their groups and define their identities in relation to their group (Chen et al. 2004: 129). Consequently, the family was the most important institution in Chinese society and used to be at the center of an individuals' life (Hu, Scott 2016: 1268). Yet, social changes since the opening reforms also led to changes in the family structure. Today, families are smaller, and co-residence with multiple generations is less common. At the same time, divorce rates are increasing and other non-traditional family forms – such as single motherhood or couples without children – have started to appear. Some researchers took this as an indication of the disappearance of traditional family values (Hu, Scott 2016: 1268). Yunxiang Yan (2010) for example argues that the individual is put above the family and Hansen and Pang (2008) found that family and freedom both matter to young people. Hu and Scott (2016) on the other hand supported the view that traditional family values and filial piety in particular are still dominant in society, and so did Fuligni and Zhang (2004), who found among 708 high school students in Shandong a strong sense of obligation to support, assist and respect their family. Also worth mentioning is Liu (2017b) who analysed several large-scale surveys and concluded that young people are still filial and that more and more children are supporting their parents financially. The present study supports these latter views: family turned out to be central in students' lives.

Family was a support, an obligation and an overall goal for the students. They were being supported by their parents financially and emotionally, and students felt obliged to repay their parents and wanted to have their own family in the future, which pushed them to work harder in order to ensure an income high enough to meet those obligations and goals.

Students connected family with positive feelings. Zhang Hua (1_F/F3) described family as a 'harbor', and in the questionnaires students strongly agreed with the statement 'Family is my harbor'. With 4.3 this statement had the highest agreement rate of the five family related items in questionnaire A.[28] Family gives a sense of security, so Lei Qiang (1_M/F1) said during an interview, and the questionnaires confirmed that 'Sense of security' was important for the students as a group. When asked about the word 'jia' (家), students thought about 'happiness', 'warmth' and 'harmony'; some students relied on their parents to find a job or a partner or to get an apartment. Students agreed with the statement that 'My parents love me' (4.3)[29]; there was also a high agreement rate with 'I have a good relationship with my parents.' (4.2) and a low agreement rate with 'I often fight with my parents.' (2.3).[30] Also, parents were considered the biggest influence on students' lives. Students felt they were going on their way because their parents enabled them to do so.

Yet, students did not want to stay on the receiving end forever; they wanted to 'repay' their parents by providing for them after retirement. Explaining why they felt the need to take care of their parents, students recounted how they realized, while working during their internship, that their parents had had a 'bitter' (ku 苦) life which involved working long hours and doing tiring work. They wanted to ease parents' pressure by providing financial support. This was something they worried about since it would not be easy for them to make enough money.

Hearing how convinced students were about taking care of their parents one has to keep in mind that the Chinese constitution requires children to take care of their parents in old age (Fong 2004: 129), and parents rely on their offspring to support them after retirement. Since the One-Child Policy, daughters are also required to provide for their parents (Hansen, Pang 2008: 85) and since

---

[28] First, third and fourth year electrical engineering, second year Mechatronic Company Class, Likert Scale 1 = 'Do not agree at all' – 5 = 'Totally agree'.

[29] Questionnaire B (Second year electrical engineering), Likert Scale 1 = 'Do not agree at all' – 5 = 'Totally agree'.

[30] Questionnaire A (First, third and fourth year electrical engineering, second year Mechatronic Company Class), Likert Scale 1 = 'Do not agree at all' – 5 = 'Totally agree'.

2013, a revision of the *Law of the People's Republic of China on Protection of the Rights and Interests of the Elderly* (*Zhonghua Renmin Gonghe Guo Laoren Quanyi Baozhang Fa* 中华人民共和国老人权益保障法) further specifies this obligation: children are obliged to care for their parents financially and to visit them regularly (Standing Committee of the National People's Congress 2012). Therefore, students were not only following some moral ideas. Although the fact that law requires them to provide for their parents was never mentioned, it is likely to have influenced how students felt since the revision was accompanied by a broad popular debate. The statement 'Later, I will care for my parents' had a high agreement rate of 4.6 overall,[31] and there were no significant differences between male and female, Shanghainese and migrant students, or between the schools or the year of study. The agreement rate with this statement was constant.

The question about filial piety among the younger generations in modern China is heavily debated with some authors arguing that changes in society such as decreasing family size, new forms of cohabitation and higher geographical mobility lead to less filial piety while others have found evidence for the persistence of it (Jiang, Tang 2007: 25–26; Yan 2010a: 21; Hu, Scott 2016: 1286–1288). The traditional concept consists of two different parts: *xiao* (孝) and *shun* (顺).[32] The first part refers to children's duty to take care of their parents materially and the second part refers to the respect and obedience with which children are expected to treat their parents (Hu, Scott 2016: 1270).

Hu and Scott (2016: 1279, 1286–1288) analyzed the 3050 cases in the China General Social Survey from 2006 and found that traditional attitudes towards family values generally prevail especially when it comes to filial piety. There were no gender differences and the younger generations supported traditional attitudes towards the *xiao* part of filial piety even more than older cohorts. Also, better educated individuals and employed women showed strong support. The same argument appeared in Liu Fengshu (2008b: 425–426): the young generation supports filial values. While there is little difference between gender or socio-economic background, only-children feel that they are under bigger pressure to fulfill their filial duties because they do not have any siblings who could take over the responsibility which suggests that the generation who grew up under the One-Child Policy would be more filial than older cohorts.

After conducting several interviews with Chinese youth, Yunxiang Yan (2011) developed a different idea. He found that children were still filial but that

---

[31]   Questionnaire A (First, third and fourth year electrical engineering, second year Mechatronic Company Class), Likert Scale 1 = 'Do not agree at all' – 5 = 'Totally agree'.

[32]   *Xiaoshun* (孝顺) means filial piety.

the term itself was understood in a different way in modern China: children considered it their obligation to live happily because their parents wanted them to be happy. Students' concern with their parents' well-being in the present study proved that they supported filial piety in the traditional sense and not in Yan's new understanding. According to students' statements the *xiao* part of filial piety was what concerned them most, whereas *shun* – obedience – was mentioned only occasionally. Students felt that their parents suffered for them and, in consequence, they felt guilty when not living up to parents' expectations and felt obliged to provide for their parents later. Lei Qiang (1_M/F1), as an example, said in 2013: "They [his parents] work only for me, very hard." (LQ1_61). Da Ming (2_M/Q2) was another example: "My parents worked so hard to let me go to school and become a good person. I certainly have to repay them, repay them with some results." (DM2_87). The same ideas were found by Vanessa Fong (2004: 143–144) during her study on only-children in northern Dalian in the 1990s, and by Hansen and Pang (2010: 53–55) during their study on young Chinese in Fujian and Shaanxi province in the 2000s.

Questionnaire B further proved students' filial attitudes. They agreed strongly with the statement that 'I respect my parents' (4.4) and 'I am a dutiful child of my parents' (4.2).[33] If they felt and acted according to what they said, students were filial in a traditional sense. This insight strengthens Hu and Yang's conclusion that filial piety is still strong with the younger generations and the urban population. The fact that the *xiao* part of filial piety is a must for young people with a low education level as well adds to their finding that better educated people strongly support filial piety.

Thinking about their own future, most students described a family life that involved having a spouse and a child while caring for their parents. They agreed in questionnaire B with the statement that 'Family is the foundation of happiness' (4.0). Most students in the third year of their education have had some relationship experiences. Towards the end of the third year and after graduation, male students became worried if they had not found a girlfriend yet. They saw a difficulty acquiring the financial assets required to establish a family. Even if they were already in a relationship, the problem persisted. Lei Qiang (3_M/FA) who by 2016 had been with his girlfriend for six years, wanted to wait until his life was more stable. His parents were going to provide an apartment but Lei Qiang was not happy with having to accept this and would have preferred to be

---

[33] Fengxian School students agreed more with 'I respect my parents' (Fengxian School: 4.7, Qing-pu School: 4.2, sign .05).

able to provide for himself. Family life, understood as husband and wife living together in their own apartment, is the lifestyle to which students aspired.

Having their own family is a wish mentioned throughout the interviews, but the questionnaires revealed an interesting insight: fewer than half of the female students wanted to have children, while a higher proportion of male students wanted have traditional families. When comparing the answers of the first and third year students, it can be seen that the difference was more pronounced in the first year, while in the third year both groups became more similar. Considering the importance of family and offspring in China, the answers of the female students come as a surprise. Fong (2007: 93) who also found in her survey among Chinese youth in Shandong province that a higher proportion of girls wanted to stay unmarried, concluded that they might have realized that family-related responsibilities are especially heavy for women.

Table 8.3: Questionnaire A – Getting Married and Having Children.

Questionnaire A (First, third and fourth year electrical engineering, second year Mechatronic Company Class)			
'Later, I want to get married'	All students Valid percent (cases)	First year Valid percent (cases)	Third year Valid percent (cases)
Female students	54.8% (34)	51.6% (16)	56.3% (9)
Male students	67.7% (189)	69.5% (107)	65.2% (58)
'Later, I want to have children'	All students Valid percent (cases)	First year Valid percent (cases)	Third year Valid percent (cases)
Female students	41.9%* (26)	41.9% (13)	43.8% (7)
Male students	58.1%* (162)	59.1% (91)	57.3% (51)

Notes: * = sign .05

Source: Author's own survey 2014, 2015

In China, owning an apartment is often considered a necessary precondition for marriage. According to a survey conducted by the Committee of Match-Making Service Industries of China Association of Social Workers and Baihe website in 2011, 70% of women agreed that men should own an apartment before getting married (Wu 2012). Students' agreement with the statement that 'Without an apartment one cannot find a wife' in questionnaire B was relatively low, however, with an average of 3.0, meaning they neither agreed nor disagreed. Shanghainese students and male students agreed significantly more with this statement, which proved that they felt the need to buy an apartment in order to get married more than female and migrant students. In the first year of their education, 66% of these students wanted to buy an apartment, with a significantly higher proportion of Fengxian School students wanting to buy property (see Table 8.4). In the first year, there was no significant difference between Shanghainese and migrant students concerning this question. During the interviews, most male students confirmed that they will buy an apartment but migrant students usually planned to invest in their home provinces. Students also mentioned that they will have to wait until they have a stable job and a regular income which is in line with the survey cited above where 92% of the women considered a stable income necessary in order to get married (Wu 2012).

Students' focus on nuclear families – their parents and themselves in the present, and themselves with a married partner and one child in the future – reveals which aspects of Chinese society have changed with the individualization and which aspects stayed the same. Individuals are still rooted in their families, the group-orientation is still at the core but the group itself has become smaller and precarious. Meeting the conditions to get married, such as having a stable income, maybe owning an apartment and then finding a suitable partner, has become more difficult. Additionally, since family has been reduced to parents and one child, adolescents in modern China face the risk of being separated from their parents because of their work situation, or a divorce which would leave them without their most important social group.

Students who did not live with intact families described a more negative picture of family life. They had the ideal of a harmonious family but were much less confident of being able to live this ideal themselves. Wen Qing (1_F/F1) said that a family is harmony and happiness in theory, but in reality parents often fight. Zhao Jing (1_M/F1) also said that there is no love in a marriage and that men destroy women's lives. Han Feng (1_M/F3) said that feelings are not relevant for a marriage and that women only marry men who own an apartment, yet he still considered family the most important thing in life. All of these students' parents were divorced. Growing up with divorced parents did not impact the idea that family is very important and valuable, but students were more likely to question the actual existence of a truly harmonious family.

Table 8.4: Questionnaire A + B – Marriage and Apartment.

'Without an apartment one cannot find a wife'		
Questionnaire B (Panel Data – Second Year)		Mean
All students		3.1
Students' sex	Male students	3.2*
	Female students	2.5*
Students' hukou	Shanghainese students	3.6*
	Migrant students	2.8*
Students' school	Fengxian School	3.6
	Qingpu School	2.9
'Wish for the future – buying an apartment'		
Questionnaire A (Panel Data – Second Year)		Valid percent (cases)
All students		66% (105)
Students' school	Fengxian School	87.1%* (27)
	Qingpu School	60,9%* (78)

Notes: * = sign .05; Likert Scale 1 = 'Do not agree at all' – 5 = 'Totally agree'

Source: Author's own survey 2014, 2015

8.1.2 Individualism

The emergence of a Chinese variety of second modernity raises the question of whether individualization is a consequence and, if so, wether collective values will become secondary or disappear altogether? The analysis above already made clear that the family is still the central unit in Chinese society and the importance of filial piety is not diminishing at all. At the same time, several scholars discussed the rise of the individual and a new focus on the self and individualistic values in China (Hansen, Svarverud 2010; Yan 2010a; Griffiths

2013). Independence as a value was also found by Larry Nelson and Chen Xin-yin (2004) during their survey among university students. For these students, independence meant not only financial independence from parents but also the ability to make independent decisions and develop their own value systems. This, Nelson and Chen concluded, was evidence for a new focus on self among young adults in China.

The debate on collectivistic versus individualistic values has already developed to a point where both concepts are not seen as mutually exclusive anymore (Tamis-LeMonda et al. 2007: 184; Huang et al. 2013: 1–2). The findings of the present study not only confirm this view but actually suggest a hierarchy where individualistic values are pursued in order to support overarching collectivistic values.

During the interviews in the present study, it became clear that independence was also something to which vocational education students aspire. For the most part the term was used in the context of being financially independent from parents, not having to rely on them and not being a burden anymore. Related to the concept of independence (*duli* 独立) was the term freedom (*ziyou* 自由) which was used to describe a work situation many students preferred – being self-employed and not having to listen to others. The same idea also appears in Hansen (2015), where students in an academic middle school in Zhejiang expressed perceptions of choice and behavior options with the notion of freedom (Hansen 2015: 84). Interviewees in Hansen's and the present sample shared a similar understanding of freedom meaning to act the way they wanted to act without other people's interference. Students in the present study also used the term self-reliance (*kao ziji* 靠自己), but this was not something they aspired to out of their own will but rather something they had to achieve. Both concepts were closely related: independence was an ideal because self-reliance was a necessity. The latter will be discussed in Chapter 8.2.

Vocational education enabled the students to become independent from their parents. During the internship, students, often for the first time in their lives, had their own income, and after their graduation they had a skill that enabled them to find work. Bai Wei (1_M/Q3) explained:

> The advantage [of vocational education] is that everybody learns working manually, relying on oneself, and when one does not have to rely on the family, one does not rely on them but helps them relieve the burden. (BW1_86)

The prospect of learning a skill which would enable them to make a living on their own was one of the big advantages seen in vocational education.

Already during their education and especially after graduation, students became more and more independent from their parents. In the beginning, some students lived in the schools' dormitories but still returned home during the weekends. A minority, four out of 17 students interviewed in 2013, had parents living in other provinces and, therefore, only returned home during holidays. The rest of the students lived with their parents. In the second year, at 17 or 18 years old, several students took up part-time jobs. During the internship, many students had to live in company dormitories due to the distance between school, home and company. After graduation, when most students were between 18 and 19 years old, they moved out of the dormitories and their parents' homes. Only students who found a job close to their parents stayed with their families; otherwise, renting an apartment with friends was common. Being able to earn their own money, and with that move out of their parents' homes, reduce parents' financial burden and leave them more space was an accomplishment which made students proud.

These developments are certainly new in China, where the individual used to exist only in relation to the collective (Mühlhahn 2010: 229), but students' reasons why they wanted to live independently were still group-related. This finding contradicts Yunxiang Yan, who suggested that personal happiness and individual fulfilment have become the primary goals for young Chinese, and that in consequence individual-oriented values have become dominant in Chinese society (Yan 2010a: 2). While most scholars agree that individualistic values are on the rise in China, few would support Yan's opinion that they are paramount. In his ethnographic study conducted in Liaoning province, Griffiths (2013) also detected a new "selfishness" among his participants some of whom felt morally obliged to fulfill their own needs and desires. At the same time, Griffiths found that some people had developed what he called an "altruistic deferent" where they did not only focus on their own network of family and friends but also wanted to contribute to society in general. Finally, he found that the "proximity law", meaning that individuals were morally obliged to their own network, was still valid for his participants as well.

Griffiths does not specify if his sample included individuals who represented two or all three of these orientations. However, it is important to remember that collectivistic and individualistic values are not mutually exclusive. A large-scale study on collectivistic and individualistic values among different cultures including a sample of Chinese households in Nanjing concluded that value systems in China are changing with the transition from a planned towards a market economy, and that parents in Nanjing supported collectivistic as well as individualistic values when it came to educating their children. The two value systems were seen as additive and parents strengthened their children's feelings of relatedness and autonomy at the same time (Tamis-LeMonda et al. 2007: 195–201). Encountering the same phenomena among young people aged between 16 and 28 years, Hansen and Pang concluded: "The individualism they exhibited was to a large extent indistinguishable from their concern with collective family interests." (Hansen, Pang 2010: 61). Taking this into consideration, it is not surprising that students' aspiration to independence does not contradict their family values. They wanted to gain independence and move out in order to do something good for their parents and reduce parents' financial pressure. Independence did not equal independent thinking, or a focus on the self at the expense of the collective – the family. On the contrary, independence would support and strengthen the family. This means that students' value systems were not additive, as suggested by the large-scale Nanjing study and Hansen and Pang, but functionally dependent: being able to live an independent life benefits the family because it relieves financial pressure (Tamis-LeMonda et al. 2007: 189–194). Differing from the above mentioned authors, I argue that students display what can be labeled as 'collectivism with individual characteristics', suggesting a hierarchy in which individual values support the overarching collective values.

The interviews with Li An (3_F/FG) exemplified how dependence on parents can be a strain for students. In 2013, Li An described the tiring working life her parents had and how she tried to help them with the household chores during the weekends when she returned home from school. One year later, she said that she was the only one in the family who was not working yet and, therefore, tried to help at home as much as she could. In 2015, Li An had graduated from Fengxian School and was studying at a higher vocational school. Her parents had returned to their home province and she was living in her school's dormitory. Her next goal was to find a part time job, so that she finally could become financially independent from her parents and stop being a financial burden. Independence was not something she aspired to for herself; instead she aspired to independence for her parents. Also, Wen Qing (3_F/F3) took pride in being able to contribute to her school fees by working during the holidays and, hereby, relieving her father's financial burden a little bit. She would have liked to have a weekend job but her father, same as Lei Qiang's (3_M/FA) parents, stopped her by telling her to focus on her grades instead.

Very few students focused on independence as a personal accomplishment, a goal they needed to reach in order to be considered grown-up. In his first interview, Li Qing (1_M/Q3), for example, asserted immediately that he was already a grown-up and independent. He had his own income thanks to a part time job with KFC, and his older sister, with whom he was living in Shanghai at that time, had educated him to be independent. His urge to make his own decisions and do things in his way did not disappear in the following years. Li Qing was one of the students who decided to work and earn more money instead of doing an internship in the third year of his education, and one year later he had his own small business. Also Zhang Hua (2_F/FA) saw independence as a personal accomplishment. After her graduation, she explained that her goal was to become independent and stop relying on other people. While she was talking, she realized that she had already reached this goal since she was paying for her own apartment, and paying her own bills and food. Both students were very self-aware and able to reflect on themselves more than others, proving that among vocational education students there might be a few exceptions who strive for independence in a more self-focused way than the majority of their collective-driven peers. Both students' attitudes will be further discussed in Chapter 8.2.1.

There was a high level of agreement in questionnaire A throughout the classes that an independent life is important. Looking at the schools, having an independent life was more important for Qingpu School students. Migrant students felt a little bit more strongly about it than Shanghainese students, yet the difference was not significant. Therefore, the preference for an independent life among Qingpu school students appeared to be related to the school's education.

Table 8.5: Questionnaire A – 'Important for me – Independent life'.

'Important for me – Independent life'			
Questionnaire A (First, third and fourth year electrical engineering, second year Mechatronic Company Class)		Mean	Standard deviation
All students		4.2	1.1
Students' school	Fengxian School	4.0*	1.0
	Qingpu School	4.3*	1.0
Students' hukou	Shanghainese students	4.1	1.1
	Migrant students	4.3	0.9

Notes: * = sign .05; Likert Scale 1 = 'Do not agree at all' – 5 = 'Totally agree'

Source: Author's own survey 2014, 2015

8.1.2.1 Workplace Independence

Apart from independence from their parents, some students also sought independence at work. This independence was understood as not having to listen to anybody else and was considered very attractive. The easiest way to be independent at work was being self-employed, an employment form which some students knew because their parents sold goods. Also, the labour market in Shanghai offers plenty of commission based work where employees basically decide themselves how many hours and how many days per week they want to work. Independence provides agency, which is an important value for the students. Hansen and Pang (2010: 51–53) who interviewed young people – mostly with nine years of schooling or fewer – also discovered that independence at work was important. Their interviewees stressed the option of being able to quit a job and move between cities without constraints such as labour contracts.

The agreement rate with the statement that 'Later, I want to do business.' was considerably higher than with the statement that 'Later, I want to work in a factory.' When looking at the Panel Data, differences between the first and second year only become obvious once the data is divided by schools. Although, there was no significant correlation between students' school and their attitude towards these statements, Fengxian School students were more willing to work in a factory or to do business in the second year than they were in the first year, whereas, for Qingpu School students agreement rates with both statements were lower in the second year. This is conforming to Fengxian School students generally showing a higher motivation (see Chapter 9.3). It is also important to keep in mind that Fengxian School students already started their internships in the second year and, consequently, had a more precise idea of what working in a factory meant. Ultimately though, doing business is more popular with all students in every stage of their education. It became even more obvious when looking at the students in their last year of education, where the preference for doing business is most pronounced. This was in line with the *Report on Development and Employment of Secondary Vocational Education Students in China* published by the Chinese Society of Vocational and Technical Education in 2012. According to the report, 81% of secondary vocational education students think about starting a business after their graduation (Da 2013: 1).

According to my questionnaires, female students were less willing to work in a factory than male students and migrant students were keener to do business than Shanghainese students. One third of the graduated students whom I interviewed and who had started to work were working in sales. Their work was mainly commission-based and they were able to schedule their work time themselves. Pressure was mentioned in that context, but also the opportunity to earn money quickly and the freedom that comes with such an employment situation.

Table 8.6: Questionnaire A + B – Factory vs. Doing Business.

Questionnaire A + B		'Later, I want to work in a factory'	'Later, I want to do business'
Questionnaire A (First, third and fourth year electrical engineering, second year Mechatronic Company Class)		2.9	3.5
Panel Data	First year	2.9	3.5
	Second year	2.8	3.3
Panel Data – Fengxian School	First year	2.7	3.2
	Second year	3.2	3.4
Panel Data – Qingpu School	First year	3.0	3.6
	Second year	2.6	3.3
Questionnaire A – Qingpu School	Third and fourth year	2.9	3.6
Questionnaire A – Fengxian School	Third year	2.6	3.7
Questionnaire A (First, third and fourth year electrical engineering, second year Mechatronic Company Class) – Students' sex	Male students	2.9**	3.5
	Female students	2.4**	3.4
Questionnaire A (First, third and fourth year electrical engineering, second year Mechatronic Company Class) – Students' hukou	Shanghainese students	2.9	3.3*
	Migrant students	2.8	3.7*

Notes: * = sign .05, ** = sign .01; Likert Scale 1 = 'Do not agree at all' – 5 = 'Totally agree'

Source: Author's own survey 2014, 2015

Independence at work was also an antidote to working at the conveyor belt. Students' feedback on their tasks during their internship was often negative and, in consequence, these students decided that they did not want this kind of work. Wang Ming (3_M/FA), for example, who was a student in the Mechatronic Company class, decided after his internship that he would not want to start working for Mechatronic Company after his graduation. Also Li An (3_F/FA) did not have positive things to say about the work during the internship with Mechatronic Company and decided just like Wang Ming to pursue further education. My request to visit the class during their internship was declined by Mechatronic Company but Li An described students assembling microwave doors on the conveyor belt while standing the whole day. Deciding themselves when and how long to work, and earning their own (and potentially a lot of) money seemed to be far more attractive than working within the strict timeframes and rules of a factory. Therefore, students sought independence at work.

The authors in Kleinman's anthology on Chinese people adjusting to modern China encountered similar phenomena. The current generation in China pursues freedom, prosperity and happiness. This is a departure from the collective and state-oriented life goals of the past (Kleinman et al. 2011: 16). The students did not want to live the way they saw their parents' lives: boring, old-fashioned and hard. The younger generation is striving for development, said Li Qing (1_M/Q3). Students strove for independence in order to be able to cater to their desires and follow their own goals without having to rely on their parents' support or having to follow other people's orders. Nevertheless, behind these individualistic desires was still the very traditional wish to relieve the parents of their burden of child-rearing. Individualism and collectivism, the desire for independence along with close family ties, are by no means mutually exclusive.

8.1.3 Materialism

Several surveys detected strong materialistic attitudes in Chinese society. The Ipsos Global Trends Survey published in 2017 found that among the 23 participating countries the Chinese sample had the strongest agreement rate with the statement that 'I measure my success by the things I own'. 70% of the approximately 1000 Chinese people surveyed agreed with this (Ipsos 2017: 2). A survey conducted by the Communist Youth League and National Students Federation in Guangdong showed that becoming a billionaire was the first choice among 1780 participating students, followed by becoming the boss of a multinational corporation. During another survey on university students in Shandong, 71% of the participants agreed that the ability to make money was at least one standard for determining a person's value; 6% said that it was the only determining factor (Rosen 2004: 7–12).

These kinds of quantitative surveys which draw wide ranging conclusions from one or two statements have been rightly criticized (Morrissey 2016: 1–2). Nonetheless, as Stanley Rosen (2004) pointed out: money has become very important for success in many aspects of life, including education, career and marriage (Rosen 2004: 7–12). The CCP who, after the opening reforms, promoted the rise of materialism among the people, is now trying to strengthen traditional morals, such as contributions to the collective, but, according to Rosen, the success of these campaigns is very limited (Rosen 2004: 46–47).

The students of the present study did care about money and their financial situation but, as I will argue below, this cannot automatically lead to the conclusion that they were materialistic. The development of society, explained Zhang Hua (1_F/F3), has created more needs and desires. The younger generation is spending a lot, said Bai Wei (1_M/Q3), and Xue Mei (1_F/Q4) explained that her generation likes to go out eating and shopping. Li Qing (1_M/Q3) complained that things were becoming more expensive and Han Feng (1_M/F3) mentioned the big financial pressure he felt. Providing for parents, which as I explained earlier is a must, was always understood as providing financial support. Students also helped with household chores in order to relieve parents' burden, but ultimately only financial support will enable parents to retire. Not surprisingly, the most cited factor students consider when looking for a job was the salary. Income was not the only criteria that mattered; learning and development opportunities were also mentioned regularly, but income was something every student considered at least to some extent before taking up a job. This is in line with a survey conducted in 2001 among urban and rural youth in Shanxi: all of the young people wanted higher salaries and the opportunity to develop their skills in order to better their social status (Rosen 2004: 13–14).

In questionnaire A, financial income turned out to be less important for students when they were looking for a job than 'Matching one's interests', 'Matching one's abilities' and 'Social networking resources'. When looking at the Panel Data, the importance of financial income had risen in the second year, but only with Fengxian School students. Although there was a rise for Shanghainese students as well within the panel, there was almost no rise (0.1) for Shanghainese students in Qingpu School. The rise occurred solely in Fengxian School where the students started to alternate between school and company in their second year of training. There were no differences in the Panel Data between male and female students. In conclusion, financial income, together with networking resources, had developed into the most important factors for Fengxian School students thinking about looking for a job.

According to the Panel Data, 80.5% of the first year students wanted to improve their financial situation in the future; the only item rated higher in the 'Wish for the future' section was the wish for health (81.1%). There was a significant difference between the schools within the first year Panel Data, with 96.8% of Fengxian School students, basically the whole electrical engineering cohort, wanting to improve their financial situation and 74% of Qingpu School students. Although this difference is less obvious when comparing the answers of students in their last year of education, there is nonetheless a significant difference between the schools. There was also a difference between male and female students with more of the latter wanting to improve their financial situation. This difference is significant for the first year of the Panel Data and also exists within the students who were about to graduate. This fits in with the fact that a higher percentage of male students in my sample wanted to get married and have children, whereas female students were more ambitious. They wanted to buy an apartment, go abroad and experience social approval. One possible explanation for this difference is the fact that women in Shanghai are expected to contribute to the family income and support their parents. There were no relevant differences between *hukou* for this item.

Students appeared to have a materialistic outlook because financial assets mattered to them. When asked what kind of person he would want to be, De Hua said: "I want to be a rich person." (DH2_54). He described the lack of money as one of the difficulties in his life. Consequently, salary was an important factor when looking for work but his aspirations were not high. According to De Hua, the income should be high enough to make a living, to have enough to eat. When asked about what motivated him, he talked about his dream of buying two apartments in his hometown, one for his parents and one for himself so that he could get married. Money was important for De Hua, something he aspired to but money was a means to be able to make a living and take care of his family. Han Feng (1_M/F1) also explained that an income is necessary if one wants to start a family which was something very important for him. Students did not want money itself or money to buy luxury goods. Students wanted money for survival and their families. Again, collectivism – family as a value – lies beneath the materialistic surface of students' value systems.

Table 8.7: Questionnaire A + B – Materialism.

'Important when looking for a job – Financial income'		Mean (Standard deviation)
Panel Data – Qingpu School	First year	4.5 (0.8)
	Second year	4.4 (1.0)
Panel Data – Fengxian School	First year	4.3* (0.9)
	Second year	4.7* (0.6)
'Wish for the future – Improving financial situation'		Valid percent (cases)
Panel Data first year		80.5% (128)
Panel Data first year – Students' school	Fengxian School	96.8%* (30)
	Qingpu School	76.6%* (98)
Panel Data first year – Students' sex	Male students	81.6% (102)
	Female students	85.2% (23)
Questionnaire A (Third and fourth year)		71.5% (93)
Questionnaire A (Third and fourth year) – Students' school	Fengxian School	73.5% (25)
	Qingpu School	70.8% (68)
Questionnaire A (Third and fourth year) – Students' sex	Male students	68.6% (70)
	Female students	86.4% (19)
Questionnaire A (First, third and fourth year electrical engineering, second year Mechatronic Company Class) – Students' school	Fengxian School	86.6%* (110)
	Qingpu School	73.9%* (167)

Notes: * = sign .05; Likert Scale 1 = 'Do not agree at all' – 5 = 'Totally agree'

Source: Author's own survey 2014, 2015

Li Qing (2_M/QA), who was already 21 years old when I interviewed him in 2014, most drastically represented the phenomenon of students who were forced to adopt a materialistic outlook without sharing materialistic values. Li Qing said that he has his own value: "salary" (LQ2_48). In 2015, he reaffirmed his opinion saying that his goal is "*money*" (using the English word). "It's not about [which industry] I like or not like. It's all about existence, earning money and not about liking or not liking." (LQ3_18). Then, Li Qing's explanation highlighted the interesting aspect: He admitted that he would not choose money as his goal but without money he could not buy anything to eat, drink and live (LQ3_126). Despite Li Qing saying so, money was not a value in itself but a means to acquire other things in life which are not materialistic.

Therefore, I argue that the students in my sample were not materialistic. They wished to have a high income in order to be able to make a living, start a family and provide for their parents. Money was not the goal itself but the means to an end. It is important to keep in mind that these students came from relatively poor families compared to the Shanghai average. Their parents worked hard and long hours in order to feed the family and cope with the rising costs of living. Students therefore wished for an easier job with more money, and to have an easier life, but they did not aspire to having high-end luxury goods. In the section 'What is important for me', the item 'Consumer goods' had, with 3.2, the lowest score, with the highest scores going to 'Harmonious living environment', 'Personal development' and 'Sense of security' (scores of 4.5). There were no significant differences between school, *hukou*, sex and year of study. Also, students agreed more with the statement that 'The purpose of work is to realize one's value.' than with 'The purpose of work is to earn money.' (4.1 compared to 3.8).[34]

These findings match Isabel Dettmer's study on workers in the hotel industry across 18 Chinese cities. Workers were seeking well-paying jobs not so much because they wanted to become wealthier, but simply because the average wage of a frontline hotel position in a first or second tier city in China is too low to make a family. Dettmer came to the same conclusion: what looks like materialistic aspirations are actually profound family values (Dettmer 2017: 166). At the same time, Rosen (2004) proclaiming the "victory of materialism" in China must be questioned and when interpreting quantitative data it is important to keep in mind that questionnaires cannot capture the underlying values and desires such as education, family life or filial piety that young people have in mind when they agree that a high income is their most important goal.

---

[34]   Questionnaire A (First, third and fourth year electrical engineering, second year Mechatronic Company Class), Likert Scale 1 = 'Do not agree at all' – 5 = 'Totally agree'.

8.1.4 Good Behavior

After the examination of students' value systems, we turn to the question of what kinds' of behaviors they learn and perform. Students recognized the importance of good behavior and tried to act accordingly. As per their feedback, they learned good or proper behavior in school. The terms used were 'how to behave' or the 'morality of behavior' (*zenmeyang zuoren* 怎么样做人 / *zuoren de daode* 做人的道德). They struggled when asked what this concept actually means besides not doing anything wrong and not making people angry. Traits mentioned were being honest, helping others, respecting private space, being considerate when correcting other people, trying very hard, matching actions and words, and good conduct. Few students said that good behavior was more important than educational achievement and skills.

In the questionnaires, students described themselves in positive ways: being polite and being a dutiful child to their parents had the highest agreement rates, both 4.3.[35] These, of course, are socially desired answers and might not say a lot about students' actual behavior.

Students were in the process of learning what good behavior is. They started out from being told how to behave and then developed an inner feeling for what is right and what is wrong. Lei Qiang (2_M/F3) and Han Feng (1_M/F3) shared the point of view that what is good is defined by others. Good behavior, according to Lei Qiang, is not doing things that are considered bad and, according to Han Feng, doing what the collective has defined as good. For Lei Qiang, good behavior was additionally already connected to his inner feeling, which is doing what the heart says is right. A year later, Han Feng shared a similar opinion concerning professional ethics: as long as one is at ease at heart, it is OK. Wang Ming (2_M/F2) agreed, saying that one needs to know, according to their heart, what to do and what not to do. Yet, for most students this feeling was still rudimentary, and the main goal of behaving in a certain way towards others was not to provoke conflicts or negative judgement from them. As a result several students spoke about their attempts to be less impulsive. Migrant student Wen Qing (2_F/F2) described her behavior-related problem: "I am quite straightforward. If I have something to say, I just say it. However, I think that people like me have it difficult in society because some people do not want to hear the truth…" (WQ2_51). One year later she had developed: "Before, I said out loud what came to my mind, I had told you this last year… now, I will consider if I will hurt the other person or if I will create a disadvantage for myself…"

---

[35] Questionnaire A (First, third and fourth year electrical engineering, second year Mechatronic Company Class), Likert Scale 1 = 'Do not agree at all' – 5 = 'Totally agree'.

(WQ3_94). Li An (3_F/FA), another migrant student, underwent a similar process. According to her, she did not understand things in lower middle school and only during her vocational education did she stop making other people angry and communicated better with her parents. Students learned that good behavior is what is accepted in their environment – which is in school, at home and, later, in their place of work.

In professional life, responsibility and a diligent working attitude were the values acquired by the students throughout their education. Students were told to adhere to the rules, to care about quality and to fulfill their tasks. During their internships, students learned that many things they could get away with in school were not possible in a company: e.g. being late, taking days off, or playing with their mobile phones. Zhao Jing (3_M/F3) was a student who failed at appropriate conduct during his internship. He made his superior angry and, in the end, was sent back to school. Other students were challenged by the rules in a company and the code of conduct when dealing with superiors but they were able to adjust. They learned that in a company the accepted behavior was being diligent, following the rules and doing one's best.

When asked about their idols, many students said that they did not have any. Some of the reasons they gave were that they would not know who would be suitable, or that famous people were only human beings as well. Other students did mention singers or actors as their idols, usually because of their songs or movies and also because of their happy, funny, determined or good personalities. Few students named one of their parents as idols, for example Wen Qing (2_F/F2), mentioned above, or Lei Qiang (2_M/F2) who admired his dad's meticulous way of doing things. Students generally agreed that teachers were role models (4.0).[36] They did not mention any political idols or role models such as *Lei Feng*.

In summary: Teachers and families were the biggest influences in students' lives and, therefore, the ideas of good behavior could be traced back to parental and school education. Media and political campaigns did not seem to be a relevant influence on student behavior, or at least were not perceived as influential by the students. They had a shallow understanding of good behavior and professional ethics in particular. It basically came down to doing everything the way it was expected, sticking to the rules, being diligent and meticulous and not doing anything that was considered bad or would make other people angry. Additionally, some students were able to use their intuition to decide what was good and what was bad.

---

[36] Questionnaire A (First, third and fourth year electrical engineering, second year Mechatronic Company Class), Likert Scale 1 = 'Do not agree at all' – 5 = 'Totally agree'.

8.2 Personal Responsibility

Looking at students' value systems, it became clear that they did not set out to find values by themselves; instead they absorbed what surrounded them. Family, being the environment in which students had lived in the longest, had turned out to be the most important value and also, at least partly, the value beneath the quest for money and independence. School, as the second immediate environment, was the major influence when it came to shaping ideas and behavior. It would be wrong though to conclude that students attribute their destiny and future to their family and school thereby handing responsibility over to their environment. On the contrary, students felt personally responsible for their fate.

In the questionnaires, they agreed that success and failure depended on their own efforts (4.4) and affirmed this position during interviews: "If [I am] diligent, [I am] leaning more towards being a winner" (DW3_120).[37] The feeling of being responsible arose when students answered the question of why they went to a vocational school. They considered it their own fault because they did not learn well enough in lower middle school. Even some of the migrant students who were not allowed to go to a general higher middle school in Shanghai mentioned that they were not good students. There was a relatively high agreement rate with the statement that 'With diligence one can reach all goals.' (3.8).[38] In comparison, the agreement rate with 'I don't have a big influence on my life' in the same questionnaire was relatively low (2.8).[39] Only Wen Qing (1_F/F1) explained in the interview that she had been in a migrant children's class in lower middle school in Shanghai, and teachers neglected the class since they knew that none of the students would be allowed to enter an academic higher middle school in Shanghai. Wen Qing also admitted that she was not interested in studying.

This feeling of personal responsibility has been detected by other authors as well (Hanser 2002a: 190; Hansen, Pang 2008: 97–98, 2010: 60–61; Hansen 2015: 150). Hansen (2015) in particular suggested that the curriculum teaches students to take over responsibility. Moreover, Craig (1999) pointed out the risks that come with feeling responsible for failures. In his study on the relations

---

[37]   Questionnaire A (First, third and fourth year electrical engineering, second year Mechatronic Company Class), Likert Scale 1 = 'Do not agree at all' – 5 = 'Totally agree'.

[38]   This is especially true for Fengxian School (Fengxian School: 4.2, Qingpu School: 3.6, sign .05). There is also a significant difference between the schools for the statement that 'If I'm diligent my grades will be good' (Fengxian School: 4.2, Qingpu School: 3.5, sign .01). Questionnaire B Panel Data – Second Year, Likert Scale 1 = 'Do not agree at all' – 5 = 'Totally agree'.

[39]   Questionnaire B Panel Data – Second Year, Likert Scale 1 = 'Do not agree at all' – 5 = 'Totally agree'.

between attributional styles and depression and loneliness among Chinese and American university students, Craig found that maladaptive attributional style – attributing bad outcomes to internal causes (self-blame) and good outcomes to external, uncontrollable causes – contributed to depression and loneliness in both cultures. He also brought to the fore that his Chinese participants made more ability attributions to failure than to success compared to the American participants, and they showed higher levels of loneliness and depression, which were at least partially caused by their attributional styles. While the students in the present sample believed in their ability to become successful, and therefore did not have maladaptive attributional styles in general, their self-blame for failing in school must have put them at risk of developing depression, loneliness and feelings of guilt.

Interestingly, students found themselves in a situation Beck has described in relation to risk society: They felt responsible for their lives but lacked influence. They did not recognize that the reasons for failing the lower middle school exam might not be solely connected with their own learning ability and diligence but also with their circumstances of growing up and their family situations. Beck as well pointed out the psychological risks these attitudes can cause (Beck 1986: 216–218).

Giddens described how the individual in times of high modernity might stop assessing every risk encountered and might trust in fate instead. Thus, Giddens sees Machiavelli's Fortuna becoming relevant again (Giddens 1991: 182–183). Fortuna leaves 50% up to the people and 50% depending on fate. If one makes an effort, one can influence the future but sometimes even the biggest effort is not enough (Giddens 1991: 110). The students in my sample did not even hand parts of the responsibility for their lives over to fate. Furlong and Cartmel developed a metaphor which is quite fitting: in modern society fate is no longer determined by given factors such as class, sex, and so forth. Now, everybody has to master their own individual fate just like a driver in a car. Each turn has to be decided by the driver. What cannot be forgotten though, is the fact that the car itself has a crucial influence whether the driver will reach his/her destination and how fast he or she will get there (Furlong, Cartmel 1997: 6–7). In our case, the students failed to recognize that on the highway of life they are driving a Santana and not a Ferrari. One example was the oft-mentioned opportunity to get a higher education degree after vocational education. The schools did not tell the students that being able to take the preparation classes was highly dependent on their families' financial situation. Students were made to believe that they alone controlled Fortuna. Only in the third year were students confronted with the reality that they might not be able to get a higher education degree and still, some tried to make themselves and others believe that it was down to their own decision. During the last interview with Wen Qing (3_F/F3), she said that she was not taking the higher education entrance exam classes because she preferred to go to work sooner. Later, she mentioned that most Shanghainese students took *gaofu* classes, whereas migrant students prepared to enter the job market because of financial constraints in their families. When asked directly, she admitted that she would have prefered to study more but was unable to do so because of the financial situation in her family.

8.2.1 The 'Enterprising Self'

The perceived responsibility for their lives forces students to become active agents so that they can achieve success and avoid failure. Individuals who take their lives in their hands and shape their biographies in order to become successful have been described by Nicolas Rose as 'enterprising selves': "The enterprising self will make a venture of its life, project itself a future and seek to shape itself in order to become that which it wishes to be. The enterprising self is thus a calculating self, a self that calculates about itself and that works upon itself in order to better itself." (Rose 1992: 146).

The 'enterprising self' is understood to be the result of a neoliberal government which retreats from society and leaves it up to the individuals to provide for themselves. The individuals need to be self-reliant, self-responsible and striving. Since the state gives up its responsibilities, success and failure depend on individual efforts and individuals need to be proactive in order to reach personal satisfaction. The state does not interfere directly anymore but governs from afar while the individuals govern themselves within the goals of the state (Hanser 2002a: 190–191; Ong, Zhang 2008: 3).

The fact that a neoliberal government produces enterprising, self-reliant individuals striving for personal satisfaction does not make the concept look relevant for Chinese society, in which the CCP still influences and governs many aspects of private life including place of living and number of children. Nonetheless, current Chinese politics aim to produce enterprising individuals. With the closing of state-owned companies and big lay-offs in the 1990s, the state found itself unable to provide for its people the way it used to. As a result, unemployed and laid-off workers were pushed to become more proactive (Won 2004: 72). Individuals who found work on their own initiative were portrayed as 'model' workers. Usually, they found their way back to reemployment after a difficult phase and through their own effort while being self-reliant. Today, the

Chinese government is pushing all people to become more competitive and entrepreneurial, more self-driven and self-reliant (Won 2004: 82; Yan 2011: 69–70). This new reality does not leave the 'disembedded' individuals any choice but to take care of themselves, become self-responsible and develop into enterprising selves (Yan 2010b: 495–505). Despite using neoliberal technologies, the government did not change the nature of its state (Ong, Zhang 2008: 9–10). Modern China is characterized by a "highly liberal economic system based upon a neoliberal logic of the free market and a highly authoritarian political system under a one-Party leadership" (Liu 2008a: 196). This is why there seem to be neoliberal circumstances in China without liberal democracy.

Studies on Chinese society found characteristics of an enterprising self within Chinese youth, in that they consider themselves autonomous and they strive for development. Hoffman called the young people she interviewed during her field work "patriotic professionals", and argued that neoliberal governing techniques had been connected with nationalistic rules and values of pre-reform China. This mix had created young, professional people who were enterprising and patriotic at the same time (Hoffman 2008: 170–171). Also, several authors found that young people from disadvantaged families felt self-responsible and blamed failure or lack of professional success on themselves (Kleinman et al. 2011: 4). These traits were present as well within the student sample.

The feeling of being personally responsible led students to the conclusion that self-reliance was a must. "I reckon being grown-up, one cannot rely on parents, one has to rely on oneself, and only relying on oneself will work" (LQ1_73), said Lei Qiang (1_M/F1) and Xue Mei (1_F/Q4) emphasized: "Whatever aspect, one always needs to rely on oneself…in the end it has to be oneself" (XM1_168). Students learned a skill in order to be able to find a job, have their own income and build their lives. Wen Qing (2_F/F2): "If one has a skill, one does not have to starve" (WQ2_103). Students agreed more with the statement that 'The 1990s Generation has more chances than the 1970s and 1980s generations' than they agreed with 'The 1990s Generation has more difficulties than the 1970s and 1980s generations' and Shanghainese students agreed more with both statements than migrants. Overall, students shared a positive outlook, recognizing more that their chances are better than an increase in difficulties.

Table 8.8: Questionnaire A – Generations.

Questionnaire A (First, third and fourth year electrical engineering, second year Mechatronic Company Class)		Mean	Standard deviation
The 1990s Generation has more chances than the 1970s and 1980s generations.	Shanghainese students	4.0*	1.2
	Migrant students	3.7*	1.3
The 1990s Generation has more difficulties than the 1970s and 1980s generations.	Shanghainese students	3.7	1.4
	Migrant students	3.5	1.4

Notes: * = sign .05; Likert Scale 1 = 'Do not agree at all' – 5 = 'Totally agree'

Source: Author's own survey 2014

In order to be self-reliant, several students wanted to develop. Female student Zhang Hua (1_F/F3): "My ideal life is… when I can develop and better myself." (ZH1_54). Personal development was, together with 'Harmonious living environment', the item with the highest agreement rates in the 'What is important for me' item-battery (both 4.5).[40] There were no differences between school, sex and *hukou*.

Professional development did not rank very highly, with only 50.6% of the students claiming this as a wish for the future. It was more important for Fengxian School students. Migrant students agreed more with the statement that 'I always set strict demands on myself', whereas Shanghainese students agreed significantly more with 'I have no special aspirations; living a quiet life is good enough'. As noted earlier, female students were more career-oriented than male students. They were not only more likely to want to better their financial situation, to buy an apartment, go abroad and experience social approval than their male peers, but also, when looking for a job, income and company reputation were more important for female students (see Table 8.9). This contrasts with Hanser's findings. Based on her fieldwork in China's northeast in the late 1990s, she wrote that women were less enterprising than men because it was expected that they would have children and because of the challenges of combining family and work (Hanser 2002a: 200–201). Two decades later in Shanghai, young women were more ambitious than their male peers. Further research

---

40   Questionnaire A (First, third and fourth year electrical engineering, second year Mechatronic Company Class), Likert Scale 1 = 'Do not agree at all' – 5 = 'Totally agree'.

would have to see if these attitudes change once they reach their mid-twenties: the common age for Chinese women to have children.

When I met migrant student Zhang Hua (1_F/F3) in 2013, she was 21 years old and in the third year of her education. I met her at Electronics Minhang, a well-known German company with a factory in Minhang district, where she was doing her internship. Zhang Hua described the pressure she felt working at the conveyor belt: everything had to be fast but, more importantly, she could not make any mistakes. Seeing the regular workers managing a much bigger work load than what was required of her, she felt inferior but at the same time was motivated to better herself and catch up. The expression she used throughout the interview was "refining" herself (*zhuomo* 琢磨). Zhang Hua explained: "At least, I need to make a little progress because no progress means regress" (ZH1_12). She mentioned that she was more stable than her peers and, indeed, one year later, Zhang Hua had graduated from her vocational school and started working for Electronics Minhang. She still stressed how she was learning every day and relentlessly working on bettering herself. Zhang Hua described how she felt in society: "When one does not make any progress and just stays at the same level, [...] other people will overtake you and you will be eliminated. This is what I think." (ZH2_35). As had been pointed out by Liu Fengshu (2008a: 203), there is a great competition in the labour market among the one-child generation, and if they do not want to lose out, they cannot afford to rest – or as Michael Griffiths (2010: 9) quotes one of his interviewees, a migrant worker in Liaoning province who used the same expression as Zhang Hua: without work one will be 'eliminated' (*taotai* 淘汰).

Zhang Hua's feelings resemble what has been coined a 'slipping slope': a situation where the individual needs to make an effort to keep their current status, compared to a slippery slope where the effort is made to achieve upward mobility. During his qualitative research in China, some of Björn Alpermann's informants (2012: 8) shared the feeling of losing out if they do not fight for their current status. Reasons can be the diploma disease, where ever higher credentials are required or change in how certain assets are being seen, e.g. a foreign university degree is not necessarily the key to good employment anymore. For Zhang Hua the threat was more general. She feared that other people, be it better skilled workers or university graduates, might overtake her during the career race which in her case involved securing a good and stable job with decent working conditions.

Zhang Hua showed some of the traits that characterize an 'enterprising self': she was working on herself and trying to better herself in order to not lose out in the future. However, she was not an 'enterprising self' as far as her career was

Table 8.9: Questionnaire A – Future Aspirations.

Questionnaire A (First, third and fourth year electrical engineering, second year Mechatronic Company Class)		Valid percent (cases)/ Mean (standard deviation)
Wish for the future – Professional development	Fengxian School	59.1%* (75)
	Qingpu School	46.0%* (104)
I always set strict demands on myself.	Shanghainese students	3.3 (1.3)
	Migrant students	3.5 (1.2)
I have no special aspirations, living a quiet life is enough.	Shanghainese students	3.5** (1.5)
	Migrant students	3.0** (1.6)
Wish for the future – Improve financial situation	Female students	88.7%* (55)
	Male students	77.4%* (216)
Wish for the future – Buy an apartment	Female students	74.2% (46)
	Male students	63.4% (177)
Wish for the future – Going abroad	Female students	48.4% (30)
	Male students	35.1% (98)
Wish for the future – Social approval	Female students	58,1% (36)
	Male students	50.2% (140)
Important when choosing a job – Income	Female students	4.7*
	Male students	4.4*
Important when choosing a job – Company reputation	Female students	4.5*
	Male students	4.2*

Notes: * = sign .05, ** = sign .01; Likert Scale 1 = 'Do not agree at all' – 5 = 'Totally agree'

Source: Author's own survey 2014, 2015

concerned. In 2014, she told me how much she missed her parents and that in her ideal life she would be together with her parents who were living in her hometown. Zhang Hua said that she was longing for success and independence but she also said that she was easily satisfied. When I wanted to meet her again in 2015, it turned out that she had indeed returned to her hometown and her parents. In that regard, Zhang Hua did follow through and made her wish, being together with her parents, reality. She was an example of an 'enterprising self' as far as her personality goes.

Migrant student Li Qing (1_M/Q3) was an 'enterprising self' in as far as his career goes. He was 20 years old and in the third year of his education when I first met him. During the interview, he stressed his independent way of thinking. One year later, he was working in sales. A friend had introduced him to the job and he enjoyed it because it fit his lively personality and he was hoping to start a career in this job. Li Qing explained that with his skills he was generating profit for the company. He described himself as striving and dynamic and hoping for better development, higher salary and ultimately being able to own a business. The following year, Li Qing was indeed running his own business: a bubble tea stall in a shopping mall. By that point he had changed jobs four times since his graduation. Li Qing took pride in the fact that among his former classmates he was probably the one who made the most money but he also faced heavy pressure reaching the monthly sales target. Li Qing was the only student who from the beginning had a very clear idea about his professional future and followed through with it. He jumped at chances, changing jobs quickly in order to better his situation. At the same time he felt pressure and competition, comparing himself with his former classmates and worrying about how to make a living with constantly rising prices in Shanghai.

Both of these students stood out in my sample. They were talkative, reflected a lot and were able to answer more complicated and abstract questions. They both were considerably older than their classmates but their ability to reflect and talk was not only age related since I interviewed other graduated students who, while still answering more elaborately than students between 16 and 17 years, were not as eloquent as Li Qing and Zhang Hua. Zhang Hua went to Fengxian School and Li Qing to Qingpu School. Both were migrant students without their parents in Shanghai and both mentioned older sisters who were working in Shanghai. Besides one other student, these were the only migrant students in my interview sample who came without their parents, which is another reason why their personalities were more independent and why they were more concerned about their future than other students. There were few outward similarities when comparing these two students with Griffiths' interviewees – migrant workers in a restaurant in Liaoning province – who also emphasized that they were resourceful and striving, busily building their lives and aspiring to independence (Griffiths 2010: 32).

Returning to the sample as a whole, a majority of students appeared to have the mindset the state was trying to promote: self-reliant and competitive while not expecting anything from the state or, more relevant in their case, not wanting to rely on their parents (Won 2004: 82). With that in mind, it is not surprising that independence was one of the major values found in the student sample while, at the same time, students were feeling strong personal responsibility for their lives. In fact, the government successfully reduced its responsibility to care for the population and the individuals were ready to take over this task. This was true for the present sample of vocational education students in Shanghai and other research done in China (Kleinman et al. 2011: 4).

8.2.2 The Importance of Learning

Looking at their future and faced with their own perceived personal responsibility, students needed to find a way to master their fate and learning was the only means students had. Major events in their lives, such as not being able to go to an academic higher middle school, were influenced by learning, and in their vocational school they were told that all paths were still open if they only studied diligently. Throughout the interviews, students stressed the importance of learning. Wen Qing (2_F/F2): "I still think only if one learns and is diligent there will be a future" (WQ2_101). Shuang Shuang (1_F/QA): "Vocational education is important because learning is important for the career." (SS1_54). Zhang Hua (2_F/FA):

> Where do skills come from? One has to better oneself, and learn unremittingly. No matter where one goes, one can never give up learning or lose one's enterprising spirit. This is very important. If these two [learning and enterprising spirit] are gone, then there is no need to talk about success. (ZH2_61)

The questionnaires, as well, made it clear that learning was important. The statement 'Degree has no big influence on success' had a low agreement rate of 2.4. Also, the statements 'I study to fulfill my parents' expectations' and 'I study because I like to learn' had low agreement rates. Students neither agreed nor disagreed with the statement that 'I study because exam grades are important' but they did agree with the statement that 'I study for my future development'.

There was a significantly higher agreement rate with the latter statement among Fengxian School students who studied with the alternating system. They also believed more in the statement that 'If I'm diligent, my grades will be good' and they agreed less with the statement that 'Degree has no big influence on success' compared to Qingpu School students. There were similar tendencies between Shanghainese and migrant students. Shanghainese students agreed more with these statements, but the differences were not significant. They also agreed more with the statement that 'These days, society only looks at the degree and not at the overall ability of a person'.

When it comes to professional plans after graduation the statement that 'After vocational education, I want to get a higher education degree' had the highest agreement rate[41] and it was consistent over time. The agreement rate was higher with Fengxian School students as well as Shanghainese students overall, and the differences became more pronounced when looking at the Panel Data of the first and second year.

Learning turned out to be something all of the students and especially Fengxian School and Shanghainese students desired and considered necessary for their future. This opinion was formed by past experiences and by what they were told in school and, probably, also by their parents and wider society (see Table 8.10).

---

[41] 3.7 compared to 'Later, I want to do business' (3.5) and 'Later, I want to work in a factory' (2.8).

Table 8.10: Questionnaire A + B – Attitudes towards Learning.

Questionnaire B (Panel Data – Second Year)		Mean	Standard deviation
Degree has no big influence on success.		2.4	1.3
Degree has no big influence on success.	Fengxian School	1.9*	0.9
	Qingpu School	2.6*	1.4
I study to fulfill my parents' expectations.		2.7	1.3
I study because I like to learn.		2.8	1.3
I study because exam grades are important.		3.1	1.4
I study for my future development.		4.0	1.2
I study for my future development.	Fengxian School	4.6**	0.7
	Qingpu School	3.8**	1.3
If I'm diligent my grades will be good.		3.6	1.3
If I'm diligent my grades will be good.	Fengxian School	4.2**	1.0
	Qingpu School	3.5**	1.3
Questionnaire A (First, third and fourth year electrical engineering, second year Mechatronic Company Class)		Mean	Standard deviation
These days, society only looks at the degree and not at the overall abilities of a person.		3.6	1.4
These days, society only looks at the degree and not at the overall abilities of a person.	Shanghainese students	3.8*	1.3
	Migrant students	3.4*	1.5

Notes: * = sign .05, ** = sign .01; Likert Scale 1 = 'Do not agree at all' – 5 = 'Totally agree'

Source: Author's own survey 2014, 2015

Table 8.11: Questionnaire A + B – 'After vocational education, I want to get a higher education degree'.

After vocational education, I want to get a higher education degree.		Mean	Standard deviation
Questionnaire A (First, third and fourth year electrical engineering, second year Mechatronic Company Class)		3.7	1.4
Questionnaire A (First, third and fourth year electrical engineering, second year Mechatronic Company Class)	Fengxian School	3.9	1.2
	Qingpu School	3.6	1.5
	Shanghainese students	4.1**	1.3
	Migrant students	3.2**	1.4
Questionnaire A + B (Panel Data)	First year	3.6	1.4
	Second year	3.6	1.5
Questionnaire A (Panel Data – First Year)	Fengxian School	3.8	1.1
	Qingpu School	3.5	1.5
Questionnaire B (Panel Data – Second Year)	Fengxian School	4.1*	1.1
	Qingpu School	3.4*	1.5
Questionnaire A (Panel Data – First Year)	Shanghainese students	3.7	1.4
	Migrant students	3.3	1.5
Questionnaire B (Panel Data – Second Year)	Shanghainese students	4.0*	1.3
	Migrant students	3.4*	1.4

Notes: * = sign .05, ** = sign .01; Likert Scale 1 = 'Do not agree at all' – 5 = 'Totally agree'

Source: Author's own survey 2014, 2015

8.3 Conclusion

This chapter explored students' value systems and their idea of personal responsibility. The findings of the present study were similar to what Hansen and Pang concluded for rural Chinese youth in 2008: Family is important for young Chinese; they care about their parents but also want to have their independence. Ironically, despite lacking control, today's Chinese youth feels responsible for their own lives (Hansen, Pang 2008: 97–98). Students wanted to have their own families and to stop relying on their parents. They did not want to be a burden for their parents any more. The wish for independence did not contradict family as a value; it was another facet of it and functionally dependent: individualistic values supported the overarching collective values. Some students also desired professional agency and dreamed about being independent at work, and deciding themselves when and how many hours to work. Money was important for the students but it was neither the money itself nor luxury goods that mattered; money was important to make a living, achieve independence and set up a family. Again it had turned out that underneath the materialistic outlook, the family was the ultimate goal. The outcome of the analysis was: Students combined collective and individualistic traits in their value systems with collective traits 'producing' the individualistic ones. Students were filial towards their parents and wanted to live in traditional family structures while at the same time they wanted to be their own masters and not rely on their parents because being able to make a living will allow them to start a family.

In order to facilitate the integration of students in society, school and internship companies taught them what kinds of behaviors were expected and appropriate. The learned behavior included following the rules, not doing anything wrong and doing one's tasks in a meticulous way. Students relied mainly on outside authorities telling them what is right and what is wrong while also considering their own intuition. Even more important though was the fact that students took over responsibility for their lives.

Over the last 40 years, the Chinese government has stopped job and housing allocations, closed unprofitable state-companies and started to allow temporary migration to the cities because the government found itself unable to take care of people's employment and handed this responsibility over to the individuals. With neoliberal governing techniques, the authoritarian state aims to make people self-reliant and independent from state support, while at the same time motivating them to support the ruling party and to reach government goals such as economic development. Students' attitudes towards their own lives proved the success of the governments' policy and use of neoliberal techniques.

Students felt personally responsible for their own fates. They felt that they had to rely on themselves and that success and failure depended on their own actions. Some students strove for development, tried to better themselves and reach a better position compared to their peers and in society in general; they showed traits of what Rose described as the 'enterprising self'. For the students, the only method to master their fates was learning. In their mind, only learning enabled them to reach professional success, receive a higher income and find a stable job, which are the necessary pre-conditions for starting a family. These students took their own 'failure' in lower middle school – which resulted in becoming vocational education students – as a proof of how much learning matters. They ignored the limitations of their own agency and the pre-existing inequalities in their backgrounds. As Beck has described, this is a risky state of mind: "In consequence, social problems turn into psychological conditions: into personal insufficiency, feelings of guilt, anxieties, conflicts and neuroses"[42] (Beck 1986: 158). In this regard, students are at risk of developing mental health problems. Therefore the following chapter will look at students' self-assessments, how they managed their 'vocational education' stigma and if they, in the end, considered themselves to be winners or losers.

---

[42] Author's own translation, original: „In der Konsequenz schlagen gesellschaftliche Probleme unmittelbar um in psychische Dispositionen: in persönliches Ungenügen, Schuldgefühle, Ängste, Konflikte und Neurosen".

9 Students' Personalities and Identities

Having analyzed students' family background, their attitudes to vocational education, their experiences with working life and their values, it is time to look at students' personalities. It was pointed out in Chapter 3.2 that not only vocational education has a negative reputation, but the students in these schools are also considered to have inferior quality. If students take these negative assumptions for granted and view themselves in the same way, they will likely become a frustrated social group with a high risk of developing psychological problems which would influence their ability to make a living and impact on society in general. Therefore, the present study again takes students' perspectives as focal point. In the first part, their self-assessments give an insight into how they see themselves, how confident they are and where they see personal shortcomings. Questionnaire and interview results are reviewed separately, and the panel data makes it possible to expose changes over time. Students were able to mention positive and negative traits in their personalities and reported balanced pictures of themselves. Their self-assessments were by no means similar to society's opinions of vocational education students; rather, students were able to see themselves in a more nuanced way – a surprising result considering that other studies indicated that students would adopt negative opinions (Hansen, Woronov 2013: 249).

The next part of this chapter focuses on development and changes during vocational education, followed by a detailed analysis of students' motivations and influencing factors. It turned out that students shared what Deci and Ryan (2000) described as a stable form of external motivation. They were understanding that learning would positively influence their future. Hence, students did not need to rely on other motivational factors, such as rewards and punishments by teachers or parents; instead they were able to study because they understood the long-term consequences. Again, a surprising outcome as the majority of the students did not study well in lower middle school.

Subsection 'Gender Identities' focuses on female students' experiences with technical education and the question of how prevalent gender stereotypes were among the students. The results are in line with Liu Fengshu (2006): parents have strong gender-specific expectations when raising their children. Consequently, the female students enrolled in electrical engineering had to face the fact that they were qualified in a profession considered unsuitable for women.

Following are two chapter sections where students' understandings of 'growing-up' and their ideas about their generation are explained, and in the final part, this chapter draws on Erwin Goffman's theories on stigma and identity. Students' social identities as vocational education students are summarized, and their differing techniques for managing the stigma attached to this identity are analyzed. The very last sub-chapter gives students the opportunity to themselves answer one of the initial research questions: do they see themselves as winners – coming from top vocational schools in a country which lacks skilled workers – or do they see themselves as losers – having left the academic education system and being stigmatized by their vocational education. Here it turns out that the positive self-assessment was indeed in conflict with society's prejudices and students were unable to resolve this contradiction. The chapter explains the different methods students employed to manage their contradicting feelings.

9.1 Self-Assessment

9.1.1 In Their Own Words

When students described themselves during the interviews, 'open and optimistic' (*kailang* 开朗) was the adjective used most frequently. In the questionnaires, too, students agreed that they were open and optimistic (see next subchapter). As observed in one Moral Education lesson in Fengxian School, students were advised to work on themselves in order to be neither too extroverted nor too introverted. This appears to be a new development. Traditionally shyness and sensitivity were considered positive traits. Chen et al. (2004) compared the self-perception of young teenagers in five countries and while shyness turned out to be negatively associated with self-perception in Brazil, Canada and Italy, the relation in China was not significant. Further insights have been gained by Nelson et al. (2007) who researched perceptions and values of Chinese university students and found that the shyness and sensitivity which used to be considered positive values are now considered negative. The authors suggested that similar research among non-university students should be done. Chen et al. (2013) did another study, with primary school children in Beijing, on the relationship between shyness and academic performance. This time they found that shyness was associated with later loneliness, depression and other problems, especially among low-achieving children. The present study can add to this body of work with the insight that while shyness has indeed lost its purely positive association, being too extrovert is not considered ideal either. Students were told to find a balance between being too outgoing or too quiet. Some of the interviews gave further proof to how students were trying to find a middle path.

Wen Qing (3_F/F3), for example, struggled with being too extroverted. In 2013, she admitted that she couldn't control her behavior. One year later, she said that she had become more mature but still risked causing problems with her direct manner. Her idol in this regard was one of her teachers, who told the students to act in a slick and sly way. In 2015, Wen Qing was still aspiring to becoming a person who is considerate towards other people's feelings and popular because of her manners. Lei Qiang (3_M/FG) also used to get into trouble in the past, but then he learned from his teacher to calm down and control his impulsiveness. While these two students were working on themselves to control their actions, De Hua (3_M/Q3) was working on himself to become more outgoing. He admitted that he was a poor communicator and an introvert and, as a result, had difficulties finding friends.

In China, self-evaluation and criticism are encouraged because this facilitates the integration of the individual into the group (Chen et al. 2004: 130) and during the interviews students did not have difficulties with being self-critical; several of them admitted that they were short-tempered and impatient, or started fights with their parents despite knowing better. On the other hand, most students had a generally positive opinion of themselves, recognizing that they were quite alright in the overall scheme of things. They were neither arrogant, bragging about their high morals, nor did they put themselves down by listing personal failures. Over the years, students kept working on themselves and detected improvements in their behavior: such as becoming more mature, less naïve and becoming more understanding towards their parents. They were self-aware and realistic regarding their self-assessments. These findings contradict the prevalent opinion in Chinese society that vocational education students are problematic (Renmin Ribao 2013: 1).

Students' assessed their own skills similarly to how they assessed their personalities. They were aware of their strong points but also pointed out deficits. Wang Ming (2_M/F3) praised his own practical skills and his quick reactions, but he admitted that he sometimes was not thinking enough. During his last year of study, Han Feng (1_M/F3) felt that he was not trained enough for society and that his colleagues in his internship company would look down on him. Also Zhang Hua (1_F/F3) did not believe that she was as good as the other workers. Li Miao (1_F/Q2) had a more positive view: although she did not like manual labour, she still thought that it was one of her strengths. Zhao Jing (1_M/F1) also considered himself a practical person with good social skills.

Thus it was clear that students saw their strong points in how they were able to deal with work and social situations.

As was discussed in Chapter 7.2.1, students were not interested in doing hard manual labour after their graduation and were aware of their limited ability to endure hard labour permanently. Wen Qing (1_F/F1) described this as follows: "When it comes to working, I can take some hardship. Being able to work hard and train is probably good but I also do not want it [future work] to be too tiring. If it's too tiring, I probably would not last long." (WQ1_64) This is similar to Zhang Hua's statement (1_F/F3) in which she stressed that she had never been lazy when working but admitted that she cannot endure as much hardship as her parents' generation had.

9.1.2 Common Personality Traits

During the survey, students were asked to assess their personality through 28 different items. What stood out were the high agreement rates with the statements that 'I am a dutiful child to my parents' and 'I am polite', which both had a low standard deviation as well. Certainly, these statements were considered socially desirable, but so were other statements in this item battery. There was also a high agreement rate with 'I like interaction with other people', and very low agreement rates with 'I am gloomy' and 'I am lonely'. Students indicated that they were social and seemed to have sufficient contact with peers in their daily life. Most surprising was probably the high agreement rate with the statement that 'I often think about the future'. There was a higher agreement with this statement and with 'I am lonely' and 'I am gloomy' among male students, whereas female students agreed more with 'I like interaction with other people', 'I am polite' and 'I am a filial child to my parents' – though none of these differences were significant. Qingpu School students agreed significantly more with 'I am polite' than Fengxian School students, and migrant students agreed significantly more with 'I am a dutiful child to my parents' than Shanghainese students.

Table 9.1a: Questionnaire A – Self-Assessment.

Questionnaire A (First, third and fourth year electrical engineering, second year Mechatronic Company Class)	Mean	Standard deviation
I am good at manual work.	3.7	1.2
My ability to think is strong.	3.7	1.2
I am a good communicator.	3.6	1.2
I am a good team worker.	3.8	1.2
I like interaction with other people.	4.1	1.1
I like challenges.	3.8	1.3
I always set strict demands on myself.	3.5	1.3
To make no progress is to regress.	3.6	1.4
I often feel that I am inferior to other people.	3.3	1.4
I often think about the future.	4.1	1.2
I have no special aspirations; living a quiet life is good enough.	3.3	1.6
I am introvert.	3.1	1.5
I am extrovert.	3.3	1.5
I am open and optimistic.	3.9	1.2
I am quiet.	3.5	1.4
I am irritable.	2.7	1.5
I am shy.	3.3	1.4
I am honest and simple.	3.8	1.2
I am strict.	3.6	1.2
I am self-confident.	3.7	1.2
I am lazy.	2.9	1.4
I am gloomy.	2.5	1.4

Notes: Likert Scale 1 = 'Do not agree at all' – 5 = 'Totally agree'

Source: Author's own survey 2014, 2015

Table 9.1b: Questionnaire A – Self-Assessment.

Questionnaire A (First, third and fourth year electrical engineering, second year Mechatronic Company Class)	Mean	Standard deviation
I am lonely.	2.5	1.4
I am different from other people.	3.1	1.4
I am underestimated.	2.7	1.4
I am traditional.	3.0	1.4
I am a dutiful child to my parents.	4.2	1.0
I am polite.	4.2	0.9

Notes: Likert Scale 1 = 'Do not agree at all' – 5 = 'Totally agree'

Source: Author's own survey 2014, 2015

In order to reduce the data set and to identify latent variables, a principal axis factor analysis was conducted on these 28 items with oblique rotation (direct oblimin). The Kaiser-Meyer-Olkin measure verified the sampling adequacy for the analysis, KMO = .84 which is considered a good value (Field 2013: 706). The KMO values for individual items were all over .72 which again is a good value. During an initial analysis, six factors with an eigenvalue of >1 were retained but the scree plot strongly suggested retaining only four factors. These four factors together explained 40.2% of the variation. All factors had relatively high reliabilities with a Cronbach's α = .823 for factor 1, α = .735 for factor 2, α = 676 for factor 3 and α = .696 for factor 4. It turned out that when leaving out the item 'I am shy' in factor 4, Cronbach's α would rise to .731. Since this is a better value, and from an interpretive perspective 'I am shy' does not fit very well with the rest of the items in this factor, it was excluded from the analysis. Factor scores were obtained by computing the mean of all items loading on one factor > .4.

Table 9.2a: Questionnaire A – Personality Traits Factor Analysis I.

Questionnaire A	Pattern Matrix			
(First, third and fourth year electrical engineering, second year Mechatronic Company Class)	Factor 1 'Professional Confidence'	Factor 2 'Depressive Tendencies'	Factor 3 'Open Personality'	Factor 4 'Good Manners'
My ability to think is strong.	.841			
I am good at manual work.	.764			
I am a good team worker.	.675			
I like challenges.	.608			
I am a good communicator.	.593			
I always set strict demands on myself.	.507			
I am different from other people.	.337			
I am lonely.		.637		
I am irritable.		.618		
I am gloomy.		.610		
I am underestimated.		.608		
I am lazy.		.569		
I often feel that I´m inferior to other people.		.491		

Notes: Extraction Method: Principal Axis Factoring; Rotation Method: Oblimin with Kaiser Normalization

Source: Author's own survey 2014, 2015

Table 9.2b: Questionnaire A – Personality Traits Factor Analysis I.

Questionnaire A	Pattern Matrix			
(First, third and fourth year electrical engineering, second year Mechatronic Company Class)	Factor 1 'Professional Confidence'	Factor 2 'Depressive Tendencies'	Factor 3 'Open Personality'	Factor 4 'Good Manners'
I am traditional.		.472		
I have no special aspirations; living a quiet life is good enough.		.320		
To make no progress is to regress.				
I am extrovert.			.752	
I am introvert.			-.637	
I am open and optimistic.			.506	
I am polite.				.685
I am honest and simple.				.667
I am a dutiful child to my parents.				.634
I am shy.				.423*
I am self-confident.	.310			.404
I am strict.	.308			.400
I often think about the future.				.352
I like interaction with other people.				.338
I am quiet.				.332

Notes: Extraction Method: Principal Axis Factoring; Rotation Method: Oblimin with Kaiser Normalization; *Excluded from factor in order to improve Cronbach's α

Source: Author's own survey 2014, 2015

The items which cluster on factor 1 suggested that students with a high score were confident about their abilities. They trusted in their ability to think and to work manually. They considered themselves good team workers and communicators. They liked challenges and set strict demands on themselves. Factor 1 therefore represents 'Professional Confidence'. Items clustering on factor 2 described a person who feels low and unhappy. Students with a high score for factor 2 felt lonely, gloomy and inferior. They were irritable and considered themselves lazy, underestimated and traditional. Factor 2 therefore represents 'Depressive Tendencies'. Items clustering on factor 3 described someone who is not introverted but extroverted, open and optimistic – someone with an 'Open Personality'. Items clustering on factor 4 suggested that students with a high score cared about manners. They considered themselves polite, honest and simple. They were dutiful to their parents and strict, as well as, self-confident. Factor 4 represents 'Good Manners'.

Factor scores for 'Good Manners' were high, which was certainly influenced by the fact that these were socially 'correct' answers. Scores for 'Depressive Tendencies' were low; students on average did not agree with these items. 'Open Personality' had a score just above average, and 'Professional Confidence' was a little bit higher than 'Open Personality' but not as high as 'Good Manners'. There were no significant differences between Shanghainese and migrant students, but for factor 4, 'Good Manners', Qingpu and female students scored higher than Fengxian and male students. Female students also had significantly higher scores for 'Open Personality', compared to their male peers. Male students on the other side were more professionally confident while also showing more depressive tendencies than female students – although these differences were not significant. Looking at the year of study, third and fourth year students had significantly higher scores for 'Professional Confidence', while the score for 'Depressive Tendencies' was also higher among older students.

For the students in the Panel Data the average of the items clustering on 'Depressive Tendencies' stayed the same for the first and second year of study, with Fengxian School being an exception. Here students had an average of 2.5 in the first year and 2.7 in the second, with a standard deviation of 0.8 for both years, while Qingpu School students had an average of 2.7 for both years. This obviously could have many causes, such as the beginning of the internship in the second year in Fengxian School, and the pressure students felt while alternating between school and company. At the same time, the agreement rate with the items clustering on 'Professional Confidence' was rising among Fengxian School students from 3.4 to 3.8, while the same rate was slightly decreasing for Qingpu School. A similar development can be seen between male and female students. While the overall and male agreement rates for 'Professional Confi-

dence' related statements were slightly lower in the second year than they were
in the first year of study, the agreement rates went up among female students in
their second year compared to the first year.

Table 9.3a: Questionnaire A – Personality Traits Factor Analysis II.

Questionnaire A (First, third and fourth year electrical engineering, second year Mechatronic Company Class)			
Factor 1 'Professional Confidence'		Mean	Standard deviation
All students		3.7	0.9
Year of study	First year	3.6*	0.9
	Second year	3.5*	0.7
	Third year	3.9*	1.0
	Fourth year	3.8*	1.1
Students' sex	Male students	3.7	0.9
	Female students	3.5	1.0
Factor 2 'Depressive Tendencies'		Mean	Standard deviation
All students		2.8	0.9
Year of study	First year	2.7**	0.9
	Second year	2.7**	0.6
	Third year	2.9**	0.9
	Fourth year	3.5**	1.1
Students' sex	Male students	2.8	0.9
	Female students	2.6	0.9

Notes: * = sign .05, ** = sign .01; Factor scores 1 = very low – 5 = very high

Source: Author's own survey 2014, 2015

Table 9.3b: Questionnaire A – Personality Traits Factor Analysis II.

Questionnaire A (First, third and fourth year electrical engineering, second year Mechatronic Company Class)		
Factor 3 'Open Personality'	Mean	Standard deviation
All students	3.4	1.1
Students' sex — Male students	3.3**	1.1
Students' sex — Female students	3.8**	1.0
Factor 4 'Good Manners'	Mean	Standard deviation
All students	3.9	0.8
Students' sex — Male students	3.9*	0.8
Students' sex — Female students	4.1*	0.7
Students' school — Fengxian School	3.7**	0.7
Students' school — Qingpu School	4.0**	0.8

Notes: * = sign .05, ** = sign .01; Factor scores 1 = very low – 5 = very high

Source: Author's own survey 2014, 2015

Table 9.4: Questionnaire A + B – Personality Traits Factor Analysis III.

Questionnaire A + B (Panel Data)			
Factor 1 'Professional Confidence'		Mean	Standard deviation
Panel Data	First year	3.6	0.9
	Second year	3.5	0.9
Fengxian School	First year	3.4	0.8
	Second year	3.8	0.7
Qingpu School	First year	3.6	0.9
	Second year	3.5	0.9
Male students	First year	3.6	0.8
	Second year	3.5	0.8
Female students	First year	3.4	1.0
	Second year	3.8	1.1
Factor 2 'Depressive Tendencies'		Mean	Standard deviation
Panel Data	First year	2.7	0.9
	Second year	2.7	0.8
Fengxian School	First year	2.5	0.8
	Second year	2.7	0.8
Qingpu School	First year	2.7	0.9
	Second year	2.7	0.8

Notes: Factor scores 1 = very low – 5 = very high

Source: Author's own survey 2014, 2015

9.1.3 Summary

When students described themselves during the interviews, they made an over-all positive self-assessment but also mentioned weak points. In their opinions, they were 'normal' people, which meant that they did not have the potential to become a role model or moral hero but also that they would not do anything considered bad in society. Moral Education lessons in both schools were designed to improve students' behavior, and during the interviews, several students recounted how they were working on themselves. A few students said that they were either too introverted or too extroverted. Over the years students claimed that their behavior improved and that they became more considerate and understanding towards other people. In summary, students' self-assessment sounded reasonable and showed a level of self-awareness which must have been trained in school.

In the questionnaires, students generally agreed with positive aspects such as being polite and being filial, along with aspects which showed a certain level of self-confidence such as liking challenges, liking interaction with other people, being a good manual worker and having a strong ability to think. Besides these being socially desirable answers, they were in line with the self-descriptions given during the interviews, which were a more relaxed setting. Male students were showing a higher level of professional confidence but also more depressive tendencies compared to female students who were more open and also rated themselves as being more polite. Looking at differences between first and second year in the Panel Data, it became clear that female students were able to gain professional confidence, and in Fengxian School there was a rise in the agreement with statements being part of the factors 'Depressive Tendencies and 'Professional Confidence' while agreement rates in Qingpu School stayed the same. It is most likely that the changes in Fengxian School were related to the beginning of the alternating system in the second year.

9.2 Personal Development during Vocational Education

Personal development, which students described during the follow-up interviews can be summarized as becoming more mature, more empathetic and less naïve. Students understood that if they wanted to be treated well and avoid conflicts, they needed to be considerate and think about other people's feelings. For example, in his second year of study, Lei Qiang (1_M/F2) pointed out that he liked it when his mistakes were being corrected and that he was likewise very direct when he realizes other people's mistakes. Two years later, though, he said that he had learned that being too direct when pointing out mistakes makes it difficult to get along with people. Li Qing (2_M/QG) mentioned that he trained his personality in school. He became more patient and also more outgoing. One year later, he added that he became more experienced with society and better in dealing with social relations during his years in school. Students did not have a moral motivation to aspire towards good behavior; instead they saw good behavior as a tool which enabled them to become more popular in their environment and more successful in society in general.

For the majority of the students these positive developments were just a side effect of growing-up and some students hoped that their future jobs would trigger more development. Aforementioned Lei Qiang (1_M/F2), for example, thought he could achieve further development by finding a job in Germany. Zhang Hua (1-2_F/F3-G) who was working for Electronics Minhang during both interviews, first as an intern, then as an employee, actively focused on personal accomplishments she could reach in her daily (work) life. She wanted to charge herself with knowledge and learn as much as possible. She always tried to be better than before. "I always set strict demands on myself." (ZH1_84) 'Refinement' (*zhuomo* 琢磨) was a word she used frequently in 2013, as well as in 2014. Likewise, Zhang Hua also chose her reading material carefully in order to cultivate herself (*xiuxin yangxing* 修心养性). Her idea of an ideal life was being able to improve herself. Although Zhang Hua experienced pressure because she was afraid of losing out and not improving quickly enough, she had an overall positive outlook and believed in herself: "I cannot become a rich person and reach everything I want in this moment, but I can get there gradually. I think that I have a persistent personality. I am not afraid of difficulties. They do not matter; everybody has difficulties." (ZH2_65). Zhao Jing (1_M/F1) used a word similar to Zhang Hua's 'refinement' to describe how he planned to work on his personality in school: "I want to steel (*molian* 磨练) myself and train myself and thereby become more mature." (ZJ1_2) One year later, he said that he had studied diligently and become better but was still striving to be the best.

Although three students said that they did not experience any development between the different interviews, the majority were able to find some aspects of improvement either in their behavior or concerning their skills. Improvement was reached as a natural process of maturation, by learning good behavior in school, and sometimes by actively working on their personality. In other related studies, it turned out that having a story about endured personal hardship to tell enables the individual to claim and justify value, significance and improvement. With that, the question arises of whether this endurance of hardship was also a relevant concept when students explained themselves and their personal development.

After conducting several interviews with urban and rural population around Chengdu in central China, Griffiths and Zeuthen (2014) coined the term 'chi ku discourse' (*chi ku* 吃苦 = eating bitterness). This expression stands for enduring hardship and it was traditionally used in the context of heroes, such as Lei Feng, who sacrificed themselves for a higher goal. Griffiths and Zeuthen realized that their informants were using the term now in a new sense: to validate themselves, achieve self-awareness and express their individuality in their story. 'Eating bitterness' is recognized as a virtue and it is one of the few, if not the only, virtues low-skilled workers can claim for themselves – unlike the *suzhi* discourse, which discriminates workers and peasants with the idea of innate low *suzhi*. The concept additionally benefits the government as it calls for actively striving and productive individuals while implying that difficulties and suffering depend on themselves.

Many students in the present study spoke with appreciation about their parents' ability to 'eat bitterness' while admitting that they themselves were only able to endure hardship to a certain extent. All students used the term *chi ku* in a traditional sense – making a sacrifice for others – when relating to their parents by stressing that parents endured hardship for the family. Zhang Hua (1_F/F3) spoke with admiration about her parents and their generation:

> We cannot eat bitterness like our parents [...] Families treat us [my generation] very well. No matter what you want to eat, or want to wear, or do; they will satisfy all your demands and give you the best things. (ZH1_62, 64)

Zhang Hua also created an 'eating bitterness' story for herself by recounting how she and her classmates were working on their first products during a practice lessons. Pressure to concentrate and avoid mistakes, and blisters on the fingers, were followed by the feeling of success when the students were finally holding their own products in their hands (see also Chapter 6.2.4). Li An (1_F/F2) likewise recognized the difficult life of her parents and argued that 'eating bitterness' was a valuable lesson for her and her peers: "The advantage [of the alternating system] ... I think it is not bad to let them [students] experience the bitterness of life and help them understand the many difficulties their parents have." (LA1_8) During the internship, Li An went through her own 'eating bitterness' experience when she was working at the conveyor belt and was not allowed to sit down at all. She described how she felt like she would collapse and just wanted to give up. It took all her strength but in the end Li An kept going. Lei Qiang (1_M/F2) was hoping to have a similar opportunity to experience bitterness. He asked his teacher to send him to the "most difficult company" (LQ1_25) for his internship so that he could be challenged and develop his potential. With this he was an exception since most students mentioned that they would actively try to avoid hardship in their future. These students also stressed that they were 'average' people with no special aspirations. Compared to Griffiths and Zeuthen's subjects, the students of the present study were younger, and therefore, may not have been mature enough to gain self-awareness by employing the '*chi ku*' discourse; or it might turn out that they belong to a social stratum between the urban middle class who uses the discourse to justify their assets, and the rural migrant workers who use the discourse to justify their low level of education and their naivety. Further research would be necessary to gain insights into why 'eating bitterness' was not desirable for the students.

9.3 Motivation

Previous chapters have described personalities, values and what students aspire to in their lives. The analysis has shown with which skills students graduate and what kind of work they would like to find. Yet, there is another important factor closely connected to education in school, which influences how likely individuals reach their goals: motivation.

Richard M. Ryan and Edward L. Deci (2001b) have done extensive quantitative research on motivation and environments which support or hinder the development of motivation. They identified three universal psychological needs which support psychological well-being and motivation: competence, autonomy and relatedness. Through quantitative studies outside of the US, Ryan and Deci were able to prove that these needs also exist in other, non-Western cultures and they also appeared to be relevant for the students in the present study.

Generally, people can experience intrinsic motivation which is unrelated to external factors and triggered by interest and curiosity, and they can experience extrinsic motivation where the ultimate goal is not connected to the motivated action. Intrinsic motivation is more desirable since it is the most stable form of motivation. Through several meta-studies, Deci and Ryan found that tangible rewards have a negative influence on intrinsic motivation (Deci et al. 2001a: 9–13). Although these results sparked a debate with Judy Cameron and David Pierce, Deci and Ryan's conclusions have been accepted by the majority of researchers and have had a significant impact on teaching practices (Cameron et al. 2001; Deci et al. 2001c: 43–51). Yet, in reality individuals often have to do tasks where they feel no intrinsic motivation at all since the task itself is unattractive or boring. In these cases, Deci and Ryan distinguish different kinds of extrinsic motivation. Students might do their homework because they get financial rewards from their parents or because they realize how the homework will contribute to their later career or because they have the desire to be successful students. In the first case the motivation is caused by an external regulation and as soon as parents stop rewarding, the students will not do the task anymore. The second motivation is still extrinsic since the students have no interest in the task itself but it is a much more stable extrinsic motivation since they understand the value and the personal importance of doing homework (Rohlfs 2011: 97–99; Ryan, Deci 2000: 71). Deci and Ryan label this an identified extrinsic motivation, where the personal importance of a task has sunk in. The last example, where students want to be successful in their studies, stands for an integrated extrinsic motivation, where the task has been evaluated and integrated with one's values and needs. This kind of motivation comes closest to internal motivation and, consequently, is very stable. (Ryan, Deci 2000: 72–73).

As pointed out earlier, most students performed poorly in lower middle school and entered vocational school because they failed the final lower middle school exam or because they were migrants and not allowed to enter an academic higher middle school in Shanghai. Under these preconditions, it cannot be implied that the majority of students had any genuine interest in their education – and with that the question of their motivation to study arises.

After her empirical research at vocational schools in 2007 and 2008, Woronov (2011: 85–86) concluded that students enrolled in vocational education because they wanted a higher level of education and not because they wanted to learn a profession. In the present study, students were also not motivated by the prospect of acquiring a certain skill-set related to a profession which means that they did not have any intrinsic motivation but they were aware that good results in school would influence their future positively. With this reasoning, students showed an identified extrinsic motivation where they realized the personal importance and the value of studying. Few students explicitly mentioned how they gained this awareness after lower middle school. Often the parents were mentioned as a motivating factor, either because they told students that they had to learn, or because students were reminded that they later had to take care of them, or because they generally wanted to better their family's circumstances. Huang Gui (2_M/F2) regularly remembered his parents reasoning about how learning can influence his future life. Li Tao (2_F/F2) remembered how much her parents did for her and thus she wanted to do her share. Li Qing's (2_M/QG) motivation was his family surrounding and the idea of improving it. Likewise Wen Qing's (2_F/F2) motivation was the belief that with studying she would have the chance to improve her living circumstances, and she would be able to take care of her parents. Lei Qiang (2_M/F3), though, wanted to become independent from his parents and so this was his motivation.

During her research in a middle school in Zhejiang province, Hansen (2015: 140–141) witnessed how the school tried to motivate students by telling them to learn for their parents, and Naftali (2010) came across the same attitudes among the mothers she observed in Shanghai: parents expected their children to work hard in school and repay them for their care with good grades. Evidently the appeal to students' filial piety in order to make them study harder is a widespread phenomenon. While neither Hansen nor Naftali followed up with students or children to check the outcome, my study shows that filial piety does indeed motivate students. This is in line with Kipnis (2011: 299–300), who pointed out as well that parents' desire for educational success of their offspring and teachers' appeals to their students' filial piety both influence students' willingness to study. Yet, the goal of Kipnis' students was to make their parents proud of their educational achievement. Different from his study which was conducted in academic middle schools in Shandong province, for the students in the present sample educational achievement was just a means to reach another goal. Their aim was to repay their parents, take care of them and improve their family's living circumstances, and students were convinced that they needed to study to get a better-paid job. Fong (2004) found very similar results during her study on singletons, conducted in Dalian in the late 1990s. Children from low-income families, who had failed in school, had the intention to better their lives either by getting a higher education degree, starting their own business or by finding a well-paid job in a bigger city. It becomes clear that filial piety as a motivational factor works differently depending on families' economic situations and educational expectations. For students whose parents expect them to go to university and who do not have to worry (much) about their financial future, educational success is something these students aspire to in order to make their parents proud. For students from low-income families or students who have already dropped out of academic education, studying well becomes important because it increases their chances to generate a stable income which will allow them to take care of their parents and afford a better lifestyle for their families.

Returning to the motivation types, the interviews confirmed that a majority of students indeed did not have any intrinsic motivation but described an identified or even integrated kind of extrinsic motivation. These two kinds of extrinsic motivation are stable and do not rely on direct external incentives such as tangible rewards or punishments. Students motivated in these ways are able to focus and to study without external compulsion.

Still, students preferred it when their daily study motivation was assisted by their teachers' behaviors. They liked strict teachers who were able to control the class, and humorous teachers who presented the content in an amusing way. Other effective but extrinsic motivational factors were competition and ranking. Lei Qiang (3_M/FG) had been chosen by his teacher to participate in a vocational skills competition. To prepare for the competition, he moved from his parents' home to the school dormitory and spent all his free time in the workshop, preparing with a few other contestants. Two other students mentioned during the interviews that they wanted to be the best students in their class, or simply better than the others, and Xue Mei (1_Q/F4) wanted to be number one in running competitions. After training and making first place several times, coming in second would be a defeat, and she was therefore training even harder with the motivation to defend her first place.

The survey gave an idea of how common an identified external motivation was among the students overall and which factors influenced their motivation. Questionnaire B, which was completed by the second year students from both schools who had already completed questionnaire A when they were in their first year, asked students to assess their own motivations. The highest agreement rates with the lowest standard deviations were for the statements that 'I study for my future development' and 'Technical skills are the foundation of my future development', which supported the findings of the interview analysis: students were motivated to study because they understood the implications their current behavior had for their future. Consequently, the lowest agreement rates were for the statements 'What we learn is useless' and 'Degree has no big influence on success' (see Table 9.5).

As a first step, these items were clustered hierarchically using Ward method and squared Euclidian distance. The results indicated that two clusters would be ideal. These two clusters were produced with K-Means analysis.

Cluster 1 'Future-Oriented'

77 students (57.9%) belonged to cluster 1 'Future-Oriented'. They agreed more than the overall average of the sample with the statements that 'With diligence, I can reach all goals', 'If I'm diligent my grades will be good' and 'I often have a sense of success in vocational education'. They also agreed more that they studied because they liked to learn, that they liked to solve complicated problems in class and that they chose themselves what they wanted to study. These students had a slightly higher agreement with the statements that 'Technical skills are the foundation of my future development' and 'I study for my future development', as well as, 'I do not have a big influence on my own life'. While the last statement does not fit well with this cluster, students' average was neutral (3.0) and

deviated only slightly from the overall average, while the standard deviation was relatively high which implies that the group did not have a uniform opinion. Students agreed less with the statement that 'What we learn is useless', and slightly less with the statement that 'I study to fulfill my parents' expectations'.

Students belonging to this cluster believed in their ability to study and acquire new knowledge. They also believed that this would benefit them in the future. In this cluster we find the same motivation as in the interviews: students did not learn for the sake of learning but because they believed that learning now would be beneficial for their future. Students in this cluster showed identified and integrated extrinsic motivation. They understood the reason for schooling and they agreed with it because of the personal benefits they saw (see Table 9.6).

Table 9.5: Questionnaire B – Motivation.

Questionnaire B (Panel Data – Second Year)	Mean	Standard deviation
What we learn is useless.	2.4	1.3
Degree has not big influence on success.	2.4	1.3
With diligence one can reach all goals.	3.8	1.3
I like to solve complicated problems in class.	3.2	1.3
I study because I like to learn.	2.8	1.3
I study for my future development.	4.0	1.2
I study because exam grades are important.	3.1	1.4
I study to fulfill my parents' expectations.	2.7	1.3
I often have a sense of success in vocational education.	3.1	1.3
If I'm diligent, my grades will be good.	3.6	1.3
I choose myself what I want to study.	3.2	1.3
I do not have a big influence on my life.	2.8	1.3
Technical skills are the foundation of my future development.	3.9	1.2

Notes: Likert Scale 1 = 'Do not agree at all' – 5 = 'Totally agree'

Source: Author's own survey 2014, 2015

Cluster 2 'Listless'

56 students (42.1%) belonged to cluster 2, which was the antithesis of cluster 1. Students in this cluster agreed more than the overall average of the sample with the statement that 'What we study is useless' and they agreed slightly more with the statement that 'Degree has no big influence on success' and 'I study to fulfill my parents' expectations'. Students agreed less than the overall average with the statements that 'With diligence one can reach all goals', 'If I'm diligent my grades will be good' and 'Technical skills are the foundation for my future development'. They also agreed less than the overall average that they studied for their future development or because they liked to learn. They agreed less with the statement that 'I like to solve complicated problems in class', 'I often have a sense of success in vocational education' and 'I choose myself what I want to study'. Finally, students in this cluster agreed slightly less than the overall average of the sample with the statements that 'I study because grades are important' and 'I do not have a big influence on my life'.

Students belonging to this cluster generally lacked motivation. Their parents' expectations were given as the only motivating factor to study while students did not believe in their ability to study well and also did not believe in the benefits of studying well. Contrarily, they agreed that what they learn is useless. They were unable to see which consequences their current behavior would have in their future. These students needed external factors such as pressure, rewards and punishment on a daily basis in order to study which means that they either had no motivation at all – if there were none of these incentives – or that they had a very volatile, externally regulated extrinsic motivation.

Hukou and sex were not significantly correlated with the clusters but there were evident differences between the schools. Three quarters of the Fengxian School students who alternate between company and school belong to 'Future-Oriented' compared to only 52% of Qingpu School students who study in the 2+1 system. Fengxian School students had a better idea of how learning would influence their future (see Table 9.7a).

The two motivation clusters were significantly correlated with two of the clusters concerning experiences of vocational education. Students who were part of the cluster 'Future-Oriented' were more likely to also be part of the cluster 'Happy in School', and students in cluster 'Listless' were more likely to also be part of cluster 'Preferred Lower Middle School'. Logically, 'Future-Oriented' students had significantly higher agreement rates for statements concerning future plans and work aspirations, such as 'After vocational education, I want to get a higher education degree', 'Important when choosing a job – Matching one's interests', 'Matching one's education', and 'Further training', and they also assessed their personality and skills in a much more positive way by agreeing significantly more than 'Listless' students with statements such as 'My ability to think is strong', 'I am a good team worker', 'I like challenges', and 'I am self-confident. 'Future-Oriented' students had a stronger feeling of competence, one of Deci and Ryan's universal needs which supports motivation. There were also several highly significant correlations between the motivation clusters and students' relationships with their parents. Students belonging to cluster 'Future-Oriented' agreed significantly more that they have a good relationship with their parents, that they respect their parents, that their parents love them, that

Table 9.6: Questionnaire B – Motivation Cluster Analysis I.

Questionnaire B (Panel Data – Second Year)	All students Mean (standard deviation)	Cl. 1 'Future-Oriented' Mean (standard deviation)	Cl. 2 'Listless' Mean (standard deviation)
What we learn is useless.	2.4 (1.3)	2.0 (1.1)	2.9 (1.3)
Degree has not big influence on success.	2.4 (1.3)	2.4 (1.2)	2.6 (1.4)
With diligence one can reach all goals.	3.8 (1.3)	4.4 (0.9)	2.9 (1.4)
I like to solve complicated problems in class.	3.2 (1.3)	3.7 (1.1)	2.6 (1.3)
I study because I like to learn.	2.8 (1.3)	3.4 (1.1)	2.1 (1.1)
I study for my future development.	4.0 (1.2)	4.4 (0.9)	3.4 (1.4)
I study because exam grades are important.	3.1 (1.4)	3.2 (1.4)	2.8 (1.4)
I study to fulfill my parents' expectations.	2.7 (1.3)	2.4 (1.2)	3.1 (1.3)
I often have a sense of success in vocational education.	3.1 (1.3)	3.7 (1.1)	2.3 (1.1)
If I'm diligent, my grades will be good.	3.6 (1.3)	4.2 (0.8)	2.8 (1.3)
I choose myself what I want to study.	3.2 (1.3)	3.8 (1.1)	2.4 (1.2)
I do not have a big influence on my life.	2.8 (1.3)	3.0 (1.3)	2.5 (1.2)
Technical skills are the foundation of my future development.	3.9 (1.2)	4.3 (0.8)	3.3 (1.4)

Notes: Likert Scale 1 = 'Do not agree at all' – 5 = 'Totally agree'

Source: Author's own survey 2015

family is their harbor, that their parents are proud of them and that family is the foundation of happiness. Students belonging to 'Listless' agreed significantly more that their parents do not understand them, that their parents put big pressure on them, and that they disappoint their parents (see Table 9.7b+c). This, again, supports Deci and Ryan: relatedness – feeling supported and cared for by their family – strengthens students' motivation (Ryan, Deci 2000: 73). To summarize: Positive experiences in their education, motivation and good relationships with their parents were all significantly correlated, nothing exists without the other. Therefore, when trying to foster positive attitudes towards education in students, no corner of this triangle can be neglected.

Table 9.7a: Questionnaire B – Motivation Cluster Analysis II.

Questionnaire B (Panel Data – Second Year)	Cluster 1 'Future-Oriented' Valid percent (cases) / Mean (stand. deviation)	Cluster 2 'Listless' Valid percent (cases) / Mean (standard deviation)
All students	57.9% (77)	42.1% (56)
Fengxian School	77.4 %* (24)	22.6%* (7)
Qingpu School	52%* (53)	48%* (49)
Male students	58.9% (63)	41.1% (44)
Female students	50.0% (11)	50.0% (11)
Shanghainese students	56.7% (34)	43.3% (26)
Migrant students	62.7% (32)	37.3% (19)
Cluster 'Happy in School'	79.6%* (43)	20.4%* (11)
Cluster 'Preferred Lower Middle School'	34.6%* (9)	65.4% *(17)
After vocational education, I want to get a higher education degree.	4.0** (1.3)	3.1** (1.6)
Later, I want to work in a factory.	3.0* (1.3)	2.4* (1.4)
Later, I will care for my parents.	4.8** (0.5)	4.3** (1.2)
I want to become a party member.	3.7* (1.3)	3.2* (1.5)

Notes: * = sign .05, ** = sign .01; Likert Scale 1 = 'Do not agree at all' – 5 = 'Totally agree'

Source: Author's own survey 2014, 2015

Table 9.7b: Questionnaire B – Motivation Cluster Analysis II.

Questionnaire B (Panel Data – Second Year)	Cluster 1 'Future-Oriented' Valid percent (cases) / Mean (standard deviation)	Cluster 2 'Listless' Valid percent (cases) / Mean (standard deviation)
Important when choosing a job – Matching one's interest.	4.5** (0.8)	4.0** (1.5)
Important when choosing a job – Matching one's ability.	4.6* (0.7)	4.2* (1.2)
Important when choosing a job – Matching one's education.	4.4** (1.0)	3.6** (1.5)
Important when choosing a job – Stable profession.	4.5* (0.9)	4.1* (1.2)
Important when choosing a job – Financial income.	4.7* (0.6)	4.3* (1.2)
Important when choosing a job – Further training.	4.4** (1.0)	3.7** (1.4)
Important when choosing a job – Company reputation.	4.3** (0.8)	3.7** (1.3)
Important when choosing a job – Social networking resources.	4.6** (0.7)	4.0** (1.2)
I am good at manual work.	3.9** (1.1)	3.2** (1.3)
My ability to think is strong.	3.9** (1.1)	3.1** (1.3)
I am a good team worker.	3.9** (1.0)	3.2** (1.3)
I like interaction with other people.	4.2** (1.0)	3.4** (1.5)
I like challenges.	4.1** (1.1)	3.4** (1.4)

Notes: * = sign .05, ** = sign .01; Likert Scale 1 = 'Do not agree at all' – 5 = 'Totally agree'

Source: Author's own survey 2014, 2015

Table 9.7c: Questionnaire B – Motivation Cluster Analysis II.

Questionnaire B (Panel Data – Second Year)	Cluster 1 'Future-Oriented' Valid percent (cases) / Mean (standard deviation)	Cluster 2 'Listless' Valid percent (cases) / Mean (standard deviation)
I always set strict demands on myself.	3.5** (1.2)	2.9** (1.3)
To make no progress is to regress.	4.0** (1.1)	3.1** (1.5)
I often think about the future.	4.4** (0.8)	3.7** (1.4)
I am honest and simple.	4.1** (1.1)	3.3** (1.4)
I am strict.	3.8** (1.1)	3.2** (1.3)
I am self-confident.	3.8** (1.1)	3.0** (1.4)
I am traditional.	3.1* (1.3)	2.6* (1.4)
I am a dutiful child to my parents.	4.4* (0.8)	4.0* (1.2)
I am polite.	4.4* (0.8)	4.0* (1.1)
I have a good relationship with my parents.	4.4** (0.9)	3.7** (1.4)
My parents do not understand me.	2.5* (1.3)	3.1* (1.5)
Family is my harbor.	4.5** (0.8)	3.6** (1.6)
My parents love me.	4.6** (0.7)	4.0** (1.4)
I respect my parents.	4.7** (0.6)	3.9** (1.3)
My parents put big pressure on me.	2.5** (1.2)	3.2** (1.4)
My parents are proud of me.	3.8** (1.2)	3.0 ** (1.3)
I disappoint my parents.	2.2** (1.2)	3.1** (1.5)
Family is the foundation of happiness.	4.3** (1.1)	3.6** (1.5)

Notes: * = sign .05, ** = sign .01; Likert Scale 1 = 'Do not agree at all' – 5 = 'Totally agree'

Source: Author's own survey 2014, 2015

As in Chapter 6.2.2, we again use the real Panel Data to check if students' motivation can be predicted by certain factors. Although correlations in this data set were not significant, students who belonged to cluster 'Listless' in their second year of study scored below the average for factor 'Likes Vocational Education' in their first year. 'Future-Oriented' students scored slightly above the average. There were no differences between the clusters and factor 'Prefers General Education'.

Table 9.8: Questionnaire A + B – Motivation Cluster Analysis III.

Questionnaire A (Panel Data – First Year)	Factor 'Likes Vocational Education' Mean (standard deviation)	Factor 'Prefers General Education' Mean (standard deviation)
All students	3.8 (0.9)	2.9 (1.2)
Cluster 'Future-Oriented' N=52	4.2 (0.7)	3.0 (1.2)
Cluster 'Listless' N=37	3.4 (0.9)	2.8 (1.2)

Notes: Factor scores 1 = very low – 5 = very high

Source: Author's own survey 2014, 2015

A few interesting correlations between motivation clusters and students' reasons for choosing vocational education, school and training course further proved the validity of the clusters and gave interesting insights concerning factors fostering or curbing motivation.

The majority of 'Future-Oriented' students claimed that they chose vocational education because of their interest in technology. Still, half of them also admitted that they did not pass the lower middle school exam. The majority of 'Listless' students went to vocational education because they failed the exam. The second most common reason among them was a recommendation by others. Significantly few 'Listless' students chose vocational education because of the high employment rate and even fewer chose it out of interest. Clearly, students who were forced into vocational education had a higher risk of being demotivated at a later stage.

For both cluster groups, parents most commonly chose students' school. For 'Listless' students the second most common reason for choosing the school was the convenient location, whereas, 'Future-Oriented' students followed their intuition.

The most significant differences between 'Future-Oriented' and 'Listless' are in students' reasons for choosing their training course. The majority of 'Future-Oriented' students were active agents and chose their training course out of interest, whereas a significantly lower proportion of 'Listless' students quoted 'Interest' as a reason. The second most common reason among the 'Future-Oriented' was the usefulness of the course. Among 'Listless' students the most common answer was that their parents made the decision, followed by the fact that desired courses were already full. Both of these two answers indicate that students did not have any agency, and these answers were significantly less common among 'Future-Oriented' students (see Table 9.9).

These significant correlations between choosing a training course out of interest or being signed up for a training course by others, and students' motivation one year later support Deci and Ryan once more: the third universal need – autonomy – also strengthens motivation in the present student sample. As was already concluded in Chapter 6.1, when it comes to training courses, students should be provided with the necessary information and freedom to make an informed choice to ensure their motivation and support their willingness to work in their learned profession.

The relatively high percentage (42.1%) of students belonging to cluster 'Listless' meant that study success for almost half of the students depended on external factors such as pressure, reward and punishments coming from teachers and/or families. Looking at it positively, more than half of the students understood the impact studying has on their future and they believed that their behavior can have a positive influence on this future. They showed a mix of integrated and identified extrinsic motivations which were stable and did not rely on rewards and punishments.

Comparing these results to Carsten Rohlfs' study conducted in 2008 and 2009 in Germany among high school students, some similarities come to the fore. A total of 1,689 students in nine secondary schools in Bremen filled in a questionnaire concerning their family and social backgrounds, personalities, experiences in school and attitudes towards education. All schools were located in "disadvantaged areas" (Rohlfs 2011: 137), meaning that there was an unusually high proportion of students coming from migrant families as well as students from educationally disadvantaged families. Additionally, the schools themselves produced poor results and some of them had a history of conflict and drop outs.

Table 9.9: Questionnaire A + B – Motivation Cluster Analysis IV.

Most common reasons for:	Choosing vocational education	Choosing school	Choosing training course
Cluster 'Future-Oriented' N=52	51.9% 'Interested in technique'* 50% 'Did not pass the lower middle school exam'	38.5% 'Parents decided' 32.7% 'Personal intuition'	51.9% 'Interested in electrical engineering'* 36.5% 'Useful course'* 23.1% 'Other courses already full'* 19.2% 'Parents decision'*
Cluster 'Listless' N=37	59.5% 'Did not pass the lower middle school exam' 24.3% 'Recommended by others' 21.6% 'High employment rate'* 16.2% 'Interested in technique'*	43.2% 'Parents decided' 27% 'Close to home'	40.5% 'Parents decision'* 35.1% 'Other courses already full' 8.1% 'Interested in technique'*

Notes: * = sign .05

Source: Author's own survey 2014, 2015

Rohlfs administered an extensive questionnaire and with the results he computed five motivation-related clusters: pragmatic performance oriented, unsatisfied and bored, disinterested and frustrated, extrinsically motivated and adapted, and intrinsic motivated education enthusiasts. Pragmatic performance oriented students made up the biggest cluster with 60%. This group comes closest to 'Future-Oriented' in the current study. Intrinsic education enthusiasts were not represented in the two clusters formed with the data of the present study. Considering that the vocational education students had already 'lost' in the education system, it seemed unlikely that such a group would have a relevant size in the present sample. The last three of Rohlfs' clusters were all variations of 'Listless'. Together they include 28.4% of the students in Rohlfs' sample

– a smaller proportion than in the present sample. Also, female students had more positive attitudes in Rohlfs' study compared to the female students in the present study. Finally, there was a strong connection between parents and education attitudes in both studies. Rohlfs found that parents' educational aspirations influenced their children's attitudes towards education, and in the present study a strong connection between motivation, school experiences and relationship with parents could also be proven. The comparison with Rohlfs' study shows that despite the different questionnaires, and samples which differ substantially and the stark differences in terms of education system, there are common characteristics between the Bremen students and the students in Shanghai: schools with a bad reputation can produce positive attitudes among a majority of their students but, at the same time, relying on the school alone to shape students' attitudes will not be sufficient (Rohlfs 2011: 209, 342–343).

9.4 Gender Identities: Female Students and Technical Education

One of the consequences of the birth planning policies in China is that parents today not only rely on sons to care for them in old age but also on daughters and, consequently, they invest in their daughter's education as much as they would invest in a son's (Liu 2006: 492; Hansen, Pang 2008: 85). Some people argue that gender relations in Chinese society are changing towards equality of men and women in professional life (Blair, Madigan 2016: 5). Yet, after conducting 20 interviews with parents in Northern China, Liu Fengshu (2006: 495–502) came to the conclusion that family education in the interviewed families was very gender specific. She included families with higher and lower socio-economic statuses, and all families had only one child. All participants wanted their boys to develop traits associated with masculinity such as being extroverted, whereas girls needed to be gentle and feminine. Also, parents expected boys to be assessed according to their talent, and girls according to their beauty. Some occupations were considered suitable only for boys and others only for girls. Parents with a higher socio-economic status still adhered to gender differences, except that some of them hoped their girls would develop not only beauty and elegance, but additionally 'manly' traits such as being ambitious, strong and independent. Liu concluded that despite parents having equal educational aspirations for boys and girls, traditional gender expectations still existed, and the only change in the last decades was that women might be assessed by beauty and talent, while men are still assessed by talent alone. Fong et al. (2012) ob-

mother and saw that both mothers wanted their daughters to become inde-

served the childrearing practices of a low-income and a high-income urban mother and saw that both mothers wanted their daughters to become independent individuals while at the same time being worried about them becoming too independent which would be considered dangerous for a young woman (but not for a young man). As in Liu's study, there was an ambivalence in what was considered appropriate or desirable for women.

The present study focused on technical training courses, electrical engineering and mechatronics, and female students were a minority of 18.1% (62 cases) in the questionnaire sample.[43] Among the 21 interviewed students, eight were female. Previous analysis already showed that while male students were more likely to choose vocational education and their training course out of interest, female students were more likely to end up in their training course due to their parents' decision, or because other courses were already full. Consequently, female students also had significantly lower factor scores for 'Likes Vocational Education' than their male peers in their first year of training. These differences disappeared in the second year, which led to the conclusion that female students were able to adjust to their training courses, probably due to their open personalities. Male students showed higher professional confidence and had significantly higher agreement rates with 'Later, I want to work in a factory'. This seemed to confirm the gender stereotype that girls are not interested in technical skills and professions. More surprising were the value-related results, where it turned out that a higher percentage of male students than female students wanted to get married and have children, whereas female students agreed more that they wanted to improve their financial situation. Female students were more ambitious which is in line with them not aspiring to work in a factory. Liu (2006) had similar results: most parents prepared girls to have a career of their own instead of just being a mother and wife, but the career path should still be via a profession which is considered suitable for women.

The interviews confirmed that marriage was not a priority for most of the female students. When thinking about their future lives, most of them saw themselves with their parents, spoke about professional aspirations or dreamt about having the means to travel. The interviews also revealed how a gendered education, similar to what Liu Fengshu found in her sample, had affected female students. Li An (3_F/FG) entered a higher vocational school after her graduation and changed her subject from mechatronics to business management because: "I think... how can I say this... For women working with machines is too tiring. Their bodies are not like men's bodies. Studying business is better." (LA3_12). Other female students agreed that they will not be prepared

---

[43]   Questionnaire A (First, third and fourth year electrical engineering, second year mechatronics).

for suitable jobs with their technical training course. In her third year, Wen Qing (3_F/F3) had no idea what kind of work she could do after graduation:

> I really do not know what I will do later. It is very confusing when it comes to my training course because only boys take this course and later you are an electrician but there are no women doing this work. (WQ3_86)

Her teacher suggested an office job but the dilemma for Wen Qing was more complicated because she actually liked working with machines in production and described herself as: "crazy like a boy" (WQ1_36). In her second year of study, Wen Qing revealed that she would prefer to be a boy and gave several reasons:

> Boys can do difficult tasks. I think that girls will always be weak. If boys do something diligently they will always be better than girls. Their physical features are better. Their innate circumstances are better. I think it is very cool to be a boy. Being a girl is really annoying, so annoying. It is much simpler to be a boy. Also, my dad does not like girls; he likes boys, and boys carry on the family line. (WQ2_137)

During all three interviews, the complicated relationship between Wen Qing and her father, with whom she had lived since her mother left many years ago, came up frequently. Her father, who apparently would have preferred to have a son, often scolded Wen Qing for behaving too boyishly, e.g. being too loud or not sitting in a way appropriate for girls. As can be seen with her insecurity concerning her professional career, Wen Qing did not question these gender standards. Instead of father and daughter embracing her 'manly' personality which would allow her to enjoy manual work and to become strong and independent, her father was doubly unhappy for not having a son and not having a traditionally 'female' daughter. Wen Qing meanwhile worked on herself, trying to cause less trouble, doing things in a smarter way and speaking less directly. It was also a given for father and daughter that Wen Qing, as the woman in the house, would do the household chores when she returned home from school over the weekends. Li Miao (1_F/Q2) was another female student who lived with her father alone after her parents' divorce. Her experiences were similar to Wen Qing's except that Li Miao struggled far less with ascribed gender roles. She also did the housework and the cooking when she returned home over the weekends, but while Wen Qing did not complain and just took her chores as a given – without further emotions, Li Miao felt pity for her father who seemed to be lost without a wife, unable to take care of his own meals. Li Miao enjoyed her vocational education less than Wen Qing. Fitting in with the gender stereotype, she did not like manual work and preferred academic subjects such as English. It was her dad who had enrolled her in electrical engineering, hoping that Li Miao would be able to support herself and him financially after graduation. Concerning her own future, Li Miao wanted to buy an apartment herself instead of relying on getting married to a man with an apartment – a view which was untraditional and which she probably had not shared with her father.

Han Feng (1_M/F3) described from the male persepctive the difficulties of fixed gender roles. In order to find a wife, a man needs to provide an apartment – and with ever-rising real estate prices in Shanghai, this becomes an almost impossible task for the majority of people living in the city. He explained regarding marrying: "Here in China it is probably different from where you are from. Feelings do not matter much here. An apartment, a car, money – this is most important." (HF1_22). According to Han Feng, he, as the man, had the more difficult task – finding a well-paid job, saving money, buying an apartment and then, finally, finding a wife, whereas: "Women look at the men, their economic situation. Women are not checked liked that. To say it in an unpleasant way, women just need the looks." (HF1_100).

It became clear that the students in the sample were not only raised according to gender stereotypes, but that these stereotypes were never questioned. Women need to learn how to cook because "my parents said the woman needs to learn it, otherwise nobody will want her later" (XM4_104) and men needed to earn money to buy an apartment. This is in line with Xu (2017a: 170, 183) who cited a Survey on Women's Social Status in China conducted by the All-China Women's Federation and the National Bureau of Statistics in China in 2010 where a majority of respondents (58.2%) aged 18–64 agreed that men should be community-based and women should be family-oriented. After analyzing other employment-related data, Xu concluded that occupational gender segregation persists in China. The results on the present study show how the segregation influences professional aspirations of China's youth. Students who did not fit in worked on themselves, and all female students had to come to terms with the fact that they were being trained in a field considered unsuitable for women. Liu (2006) and Fong et al. (2012) have shown how parents' education of daughters is contradictory: training gender specific behavior while also stressing independence and educational attainment. The present study depicts the outcome of this parental education: female students wish for a job considered "suitable" for a woman and, on the other hand, they want their own life, achieve some independence and care for their parents, while making their own family is of lesser importance.

9.5 The Concept of Growing Up

As adolescents, the students were in the midst of growing up which signified a change in their way of living and in their relationships with their parents. Han Feng (2_M/FG) described the development: "When you are born, you are alone. Then, you are with your family. When you enter the school, it is you and the school. When you enter society, you have grown up." (HF2_102). Qian Qin (2_M/Q2) had a similar idea that being grown-up meant one is living alone and earning one's own money. Li An (2_F/F3) also stressed the aspect of independence – grown-ups do not need their parents anymore and are able to take care of themselves. Nelson and Chen (2007), who came across similar ideas among university students, took this as evidence for a focus on self among young people in China. Yet, for most students living alone, making their own decisions and being independent was not the gist of what it meant to be grown-up. Instead, the idea was still mainly defined in relation to the family, and the focus on self and individuality must be seen as an addition to traditional collectivist ideas instead of a substitution.

For the students, being grown-up came down to a reversal in the roles between them and their parents. It meant that their parents were old and needed care. Responsibility and sometimes pressure were linked to this concept. Zhang Hua (2_F/FG) explained her feelings:

> Being grown-up is a responsibility for me. Being grown-up means that your parents are becoming old. You have to respect them and make sure they have a good, comfortable life. [...] Growing up for me is something I'm looking forward to and something I'm afraid of. I'm looking forward to it because I will respect and care for my parents with my own means. [...]. I'm also afraid because I might not have these means to provide for my parents. (ZH2_81)

Although Zhang Hua was 22 years old at the time of the interview, had graduated and was working for Electronics Minhang, she did not yet consider herself grown-up. Shuang Shuang (1_F/QG), 19 years old and graduated as well, had very similar ideas to Zhang Hua, only that she already considered herself grown- up: "I used to think that it would be very good to be grown-up. You do not have to listen to your parents anymore and you can live your own life. But after I grew up, I realized that it is a responsibility. Your parents do not take care of you anymore – it is you who has to take care of your parents." (SS1_104).

Few students mentioned having a family of their own as part of being grown-up. Likewise, career and professional development were not related to being grown-up at all. Being grown-up was still mainly defined in relation to their own parents and, as can be seen with Zhang Hua and Shuang Shuang, only when the parents needed assistance and the student was able to help them – always referring to providing a better, more comfortable, less tiring life through financial assistance – would the students consider themselves grown-up. Filial values and the Confucian idea of paying respect to parents were not something students expected to put aside after adolescence. On the contrary, living these values in practice was a defining aspect of living as an adult. This idea of linking adulthood with taking care of one's parents appears to be common among Chinese youth. Nelson and Chen (2007: 87) quoted a study on university students in which 89% of the participants agreed that being able to support parents financially is necessary for adulthood. Also, 91% believed that it was their responsibility to support their parents financially. Badger et al. (2016) found in another quantitative study which compared American and Chinese university students' criteria for adulthood that the Chinese participants were more likely to promote family capacity such as financial support and the ability to run a household as important criteria, reflecting once again the importance of family obligations. Further long-term studies would be needed to check if the students still consider filial piety as quintessential for an adult way of living when they enter their 30s.

9.6 Talking About My Generation

Before we turn to the question which vocational education related identities the students have, a brief excursion will reveal how they view their generation. In China, generations are grouped together according to the decade in which they are born, and each generation is assigned certain characteristics in public discourse. The students who were part of this study were all born in the mid-90s and are therefore all members of the 1990s Generation (*90 hou* 90 后). According to surveys, they are more open and independent, and share a broader value set than their predecessors. They are also more aware of their rights (Yang 2013: 94–95), and more selfish and materialistic than previous generations (Tang, Chen 2013: 85). They are considered to be lazier than the 1980s Generation and less responsible (Dettmer 2017: 213–216).

These generation-based analyzes are to be read with caution. Firstly, people born in 1989 and people born in 1991 grew up in the same decade but in China they are considered to be members of different generations with different traits. Secondly, youth in Shanghai and youth in China's western provinces grow up in vastly different environments. Even though the internet – and with it new forms of communication, new options for passing free time and new media channels – were available everywhere in China for the 1990s Generation, omnipresent luxury products and the ideal of owning a centrally located apartment and a big car are much more an aspiration for city dwellers on the east coast than for people in third-and fourth tier cities in China's interior. Also, the 1990s Generation's self-assessments do not match the stereotypes (Dettmer 2017: 213–216). Nonetheless, decade-based generation analyzes are highly popular in China and, therefore, the questionnaire contained several rather typical statements about the 1990s Generation. Students' answers cannot describe the *90 hou* generation since the empirical existence of such a generation must be questioned, but they give insights into students' own experiences and what they perceive as the norm. These general statements also make it easier for students to admit bad traits compared to a statement referring to students or their class directly. Standard deviations for these statements were around 1.5, meaning students' answers differed, which also proves that there was no undebated concept of the 1990s Generation and students had different perceptions. They generally agreed that their generation is under heavy economic and psychological pressure, but they also agreed that their generation is happy and free. They did not agree that their generation is egoistic, living at the expenses of the older generation or worshipping foreign things. Male students, though, agreed significantly more than female students with the statement that 'The 1990s Generation is spoiled' and that 'The 1990s Generation spends too much time online and playing games'. It can be concluded that male students were more likely to be spoiled by their parents and, also, that they spent more time playing online games, a reality which a youth study sampling 600 students aged between 12 and 25 confirmed at least for mobile phone usage: male students use their mobile phones to play games whereas female students are more likely to use it as a chat tool (Meng, Liu 2014: 66).[44] Male students also agreed significantly more that their generation is superficial.

Looking at *hukou*, it turned out that Shanghainese students agreed more than migrant students that the 1990s Generation plays too many computer games. Additionally, they also agreed more that their generation has greater chances in life than their parents' generation. Shanghainese students perceived a bigger improvement in life compared to their parents' lives than migrant students which can be linked to Shanghai's rapid development in recent years.

Zhang Hua (1_F/F3), a female migrant student, explained the changes in her generation compared to her parents' generation:

---

[44]   The location of the study was not specified in the publication.

> Our 1990s Generation is much happier than the 1970s and 1980s Gen-
> erations. The old generation says we are spoiled, but in reality, being
> spoiled is what this decade gave us. Before, having enough to eat was
> good enough but now, there are many material needs that need to be
> satisfied after one has eaten enough. With development, people con-
> stantly develop new needs. This is the difference, and we cannot endure
> as much hardship as our parents. (ZH1_62)

Her statement also explained why students overall neither agreed nor disagreed with the statement that 'The 1990s Generation is spoiled'. Students may
view material desires and their satisfaction as an unavoidable necessity created
by their living circumstances.

It should be noted that students did not use the term 90 hou during the interviews unless it was used by the interviewer, but they still conveyed the idea of
common views and behaviors among adolescents their age. The students saw
themselves either as similar to this mainstream, or different from it. The comparison helped explain why they would think or act in a certain way. Some
students considered themselves part of a bigger group which freed them from
making decisions or forming opinions by themselves, because they adopted
what others did and, at the same time, it justified their own opinions by making
it a 'common view'. Students who considered themselves different also used this
separation to justify their opinions. Clarifying that they were different freed
them from the imperative of acting or thinking in ways associated with their
own generation. The 'similar-different' statements helped students place themselves in a perceived social circle when speaking to the interviewer, and it as-
sured them that their opinions were part of a bigger group, either the group of
individuals who did not agree with what they considered mainstream or the
group of their peers who were part of this mainstream.

Li Qing (3_M/QG) stressed how different his attitudes were compared to his
peers. He claimed to be influenced by his foreign brother-in-law, whose attitudes differed from general Chinese opinions. One example was his plan to get
married only after he had turned 30, a plan Li Qing later revised. He also pointed out that he was older than most of his classmates and already worked in a
fast-food chain besides going to school. Li Qing's further career choices, having
several sales jobs and finally opening a bubble-tea stall, proved that he not only
said he was different because it was convenient in the interview situation, but
because he was indeed different and followed his own ideas. Zhao Jing (1_M/F1)
also differentiated himself from his peers. He argued that he had a different way
of thinking and throughout the years he seemed to do things mainly on his own.
His background explained this behavior: his parents were divorced and were
living with new partners. Zhao Jing had to move from Shenzhen to Shanghai,

change schools, and was bullied by his classmates in lower middle school. Distancing himself from his peers allowed him to be 'different' without feeling inferior.

Table 9.10: Questionnaire A – Opinions on Generations.

Questionnaire A (First, third and fourth year electrical engineering, second year Mechatronic Company Class)		Mean	Standard deviation
The 1990s Generation is under heavy economic pressure.		3.5	1.4
The 1990s Generation is under heavy psychological pressure.		3.7	1.4
The 1990s Generation is free.		3.7	1.3
The 1990s Generation is happy.		3.8	1.3
The 1990s Generation is egoistic.		2.6	1.5
The 1990s Generation is living at the expenses of the older generation.		2.7	1.5
The 1990s Generation worships foreign things.		2.7	1.5
The 1990s Generation is spoiled.	Male students	3.2**	1.5
	Female students	2.5**	1.5
The 1990s Generation spends too much time online and playing games.	Male students	3.7**	1.4
	Female students	3.2**	1.6
The 1990s Generation spends too much time online and playing games.	Shanghainese students	3.8*	1.4
	Migrant students	3.4*	1.5
The 1990s Generation is superficial.	Male students	3.1**	1.4
	Female students	2.6**	1.5
The 1990s Generation has more chances than the 1980s and 1970s Generations.	Shanghainese students	4.0*	1.2
	Migrant students	3.7*	1.3
The 1990s Generation is spoiled.		3.0	1.5

Notes: * = sign .05, ** = sign .01; Likert Scale 1 = 'Do not agree at all' – 5 = 'Totally agree'

Source: Author's own survey 2014, 2015

For other students, being normal, being just like everybody else, was understood as something neutral but positive, in the sense of 'being good enough'. Students did not believe that they would have a chance to be outstanding either in a moral or in a professional sense. Therefore, 'normal' became the new goal. Han Feng (1_M/F3), for example, explained that he could not call himself noble-minded but he also would not do anything bad, such as committing a crime. He concluded that he was just normal, which eased the pressure on him to strive for higher standards and communicated a feeling of content. Li An (1_F/F2) also considered herself average and was content with it: "I do not have hopes for the future, just ordinary [...]. Being an ordinary person, I read a book about being an ordinary person. I think this is not bad." (LA1_88). When asked about her interests, Li An also saw herself as similar to everybody else: "I think we are all pretty much the same [laughs], we read books, listen to music or sometimes chat." (LA1_68).

When asked directly about their generation, students were aware of the bad traits it had been associated with in public discourses but instead of defending their generation or arguing against the notion of a decade-based generation, they distanced themselves from the rest of the *90 hou*. After listing examples of the 1990s Generation's bad behavior which Li Miao (1_F/Q2) observed among her peers, such as smoking, fighting with their parents and too much vanity, she no longer wanted to be associated with them. Li Miao said that she could not understand them and preferred to do her own thing. In her future, too, she wanted to do things slightly differently, e.g. by buying her own apartment, and with that gaining more independence from her husband. Da Ming's account (1_M/Q1) was very similar to Li Miao's. He first listed bad traits of his own generation such as picking fights with parents, being rebellious and playing computer games instead of studying, and then he admitted that he used to be similar but changed for the better. According to him, he started to become more reasonable towards the end of lower middle school, and focused on studying so that he could enter his current vocational school, one of the better ones in Shanghai. With his statement, he distanced himself from the 1990s Generation in a similar way to Li Miao.

Students' way of dealing with the bad reputation of their own generation has a striking resemblance to the discourse of urban recipients of welfare aid for a minimal living standard (*dibao* 低保), as was found by Alpermann (2016). The interviewed recipients were aware of the bad reputation they as a group have, such as being lazy or obtaining welfare by fraud. Yet, instead of using themselves as an example to argue against these accusations, they accepted the bad reputation and the stigmatization of *dibao* recipients and portrayed themselves as exceptions. The students in the present sample not only used this same method in relation to their generation but also in relation to the bad reputation vocational education students have in society (see Chapter 9.7.1).

9.7 Students' Identities

This chapter concentrates on how students constructed their identity in relation to their social identity 'vocational education student', and the following subsection will go into further detail by analyzing how students managed the stigma that society attributes to the identity 'vocational education student'.

There are numerous ways to define identity. The present analysis draws on Erving Goffman's understanding and his distinction between self-identity, social and personal identities. Goffman refers to Erik Erikson, one of the most well-known identity experts, when he defines self-identity as the self-perception of the individual. It is the reflexive result of different social experiences and, therefore, subjective. In addition to self-identity, Goffman uses the concepts of social and personal identities, which include an outer perspective. The social identities are the roles the individual has in society, e.g. student, son, skater-boy/girl. The personal identity refers to how the individual is seen by others. Personal identity can exist even before the individual is born and continues to exist after their death (Goffman 2003: 132–133). Without using the same terms, Stryker and Burke (2000) further explain the idea of social identity: according to them, the self consists of identities linked to different social roles, and their internalization forms the overall identity of the individual. The social roles are hierarchical according to how important they are for the individual. The more committed the individual is to a specific role, the more likely they will choose to behave according to this role. When the individual fails to behave according to their social role, they fail to verify their identity, which produces negative emotions. A verification of identity due to matching role and behavior, on the other hand, produces positive emotions. (Stryker, Burke 2000: 288). The importance of accommodating self-identity with personal and social identities goes so far that studies have shown that positive life events have negative health consequences for people with low self-esteem, but not for people with high self-esteem (Burke 1991: 839). Erik Erikson, as well, mentions the importance of approval of an identity by the social environment. Individuals need to balance their own ideas about themselves with the social attributions from others (Förster 2003: 312–313). As a result, identity changes and develops throughout life (Erikson 1998: 20).

Several scholars pointed out that changes in society, with a transformation from a traditional to modern society, makes it more difficult for the individual to create their own, coherent identity. In traditional society, social identities were usually defined according to social class and profession, both stable categories throughout the individual's life (Erikson 1998: 130; Renn 2008: 205; Keupp 2014: 180). In modern society, though, individuals have to choose and work on their identities since they are not a given anymore (Renn 2008: 213; Keupp 2014: 173). A coherent identity is a "reflexive achievement" (Giddens 1991: 215) of the individual.

Erikson defined different stages of identity formation, with adolescence being an important phase where youth find their place in society and adjust their self-perceptions by how they are perceived by others. The aim is to create an identity which is accepted by the individual but also by their social environment (Förster 2003: 307–309). Due to the development of technology, society and economy, more years are spent in school, which heightens the relevance of adolescence as a time of identity formation and personal maturation (Erikson 1998: 131). Young adults want to find their role(s) and try to define themselves. They must start looking for other role models outside of their families (Erikson 1998: 87). In the process, youth form closely knit groups and exclude others in order to achieve a sense of belonging (Erikson 1998: 135–136). Technically talented students have a rather easy job when it comes to forming an identity, according to Erikson. They are able to identify with roles as technical experts (Erikson 1998: 132) but Erikson was referring to highly skilled young adults, and it remains to be seen whether students with fewer technical skills still use these as basis for their identity.

Since adolescence is usually spent in school, this institution and related experiences, such as failure, success and belonging, have a long-lasting influence on students' identities (Ecarius et al. 2011: 94; Hagedorn 2014: 18; Kramer 2014: 428). The most salient role in school is the student role, while other roles, for example related to family and upbringing, are still relevant. This student identity can be negative or positive in students' perceptions, depending on how they experience life in school (Engelhardt 2014: 99–103). As mentioned before, students need to accommodate their student identity with their self-identity and their other roles in life (Kramer 2014: 424). When Chinese students enter a vocational school, they are confronted with a negative identity which includes being dumb, lazy and difficult (Renmin Ribao 2013: 1; Hansen, Woronov 2013: 249).

Thinking about themselves in the context of vocational education, students had a sense of self-worth. They did not consider themselves book smart but they saw themselves as skilled communicators who would be useful in society.

Their contribution would be as valuable as any other. Overall, they saw them-selves as average people. In school, most students did not think they performed outstandingly well, but they also did not perform particularly poorly. They did not have what they considered high goals in life; instead, they aimed for what they perceived as an average life: having a job, a place to live and a family. The absence of socialist ideas, such as self-sacrifice for the collective, appears to be a commonality among young people in China despite party campaigns to rein-stall these ideals among the population (Liu 2008a: 204). Overall, students shared a sense of optimism, with most of them believing that they would reach their goals in the future. This positive outlook was also found in other studies conducted by Nelson and Chen, and the Shanghai Committee among Shang-hainese youth (Nelson, Chen 2007: 89). It is noteworthy that it applied to voca-tional education students and migrant students alike.

Students were still rooted in their nuclear family. Thinking about the future, it was not their future wife and child that played a major role, but their parents – for whom they would have to provide. Future-related goals and wishes always related to their parents, either becoming independent from them or, more often, having the ability to take care of them financially.

When it came to their professional lives, students were convinced that the laziness society attributed to their generation did not apply to them. They would be able to work hard, yet they hoped they would find an easy job after school. Only very few students related their identity to being a technician. Erik-son's idea that technically skilled youth can default to a 'technical expert' identi-ty did not apply to these students, which made it more difficult for them to find their place in society. The female students especially did not know what their future profession could be and basically faced a void (see Chapter 9.4). Lei Qiang was one of the very few students who embraced the idea of becoming a technician and although he failed the higher vocational education entrance exam the first time, he tried it a second time and successfully entered a voca-tional education school on the tertiary level. His self-worth was much more closely tied to the fact that skilled workers were needed in China and that many people did not understand how necessary they were for development. Streng-thening students' identifications with their training course and related profes-sions would help them form a positive identity and maybe also lead more stu-dents to jobs which match their education.

In her publication on vocational education students in Nanjing, Woronov (2016) dedicated a whole chapter on students' identities – though without de-fining or clarifying her understanding of the notion identity. Her conclusion – that students' identities were not fixed – seems to be redundant since it is gen-erally considered a given that identities are changeable and the formation is an ongoing, situation specific process. Woronov pointed out that students' identities were not defined by *hukou*, native place or dialect. Again, this appears to be stating the obvious when the focus is on the vocational education specific identity, in which other roles such as being a brother or sister, being a local or migrant, temporarily lose their relevance. Apart from these points of criticism, the traits Woronov attributed to her students' identities can also be found among the students of the present study. Both groups were deeply connected to their families and thought of themselves as filial. They did not consider themselves failures despite their bad reputation in society, and the students had common, leisure-related interests in sports, fashion and music (Woronov 2016: 111–112).

9.7.1 Managing Stigma

'Vocational education student' is a stigmatized identity in China. Referring to Erwin Goffman, stigma can be understood as a mismatch between virtual and actual social identity. The actual social identity does not match the norms of the virtual identity. There are different norms in different cultures or for different kinds of people, and these norms are subject to change. Goffman (2003: 11–13) uses the example of a cashier in a supermarket: this job might be a stigma for someone with higher education, but not for someone who never went to university. He distinguishes physical, genetic and personal stigma, with physical referring to disabilities as an example, genetic referring to race and color, and personal referring to mental illness or homosexuality, among others. If a stigma is not commonly known, the stigmatized person will usually try to pass as 'normal' – fulfilling expectations – by hiding the stigma. If a stigma is known, the stigmatized person will apply different techniques to manage it.

Vocational education is a personal stigma which is not innate and which is almost impossible to hide. The present section looks at the psychological and social consequences for the stigmatized individual – what Bos et al. (2013: 2–3) called 'self-stigma'. Stigma can have three consequences: bad treatment by others, altered experiences and expectations in social situations, and psychological difficulties such as loss of self-esteem. In order to manage their stigma, individuals can focus on their environment and compensate for the stigma, seek other stigmatized individuals and retreat from the 'normal', hide the stigma, advocate the normalization of the stigma; or they can focus on their emotions and compare themselves with other individuals who are worse off, focus on other strengths, deny or detach themselves from the stigma, and so forth. (Engelhardt 2008: 135–137).

During the interviews, the students could not hide their vocational education identity since they were recruited through their schools, but they could not
be certain if the interviewer, being a foreigner, would consider this identity a
stigma. This gave students the option to not talk about their education in relation to its bad reputation and stigma, and most students did focus solely on
positive aspects of vocational education until the interview became more in-
depth and they became more accustomed to the interviewer. When asked to
compare vocational education to academic education, it became clear that all
students were aware of their stigma and did not deny it. They realized that they
had not reached the 'normal' standard of entering an academic higher middle
school in order to go to university. Therefore, the stigma management began.
Goffman described this as a learning process. Individuals have to understand
how they differ from 'normal', and in a second step, they have to learn how to
deal with being different in social situations (Goffman 2003: 103). Horst Stenger (1985: 32) realized during his study on criminal youth that most people
apply several stigma management techniques at the same time, especially when
they cannot be certain how much is known about their stigma, or what others'
opinions are in a social situation. Therefore, it was to be expected that the students of the present study would also employ a variety of techniques.

It turned out that the most common method was to focus on other strengths
in order to neutralize the stigma. Students accepted vocational education as
inferior compared to an academic higher middle school, but they stressed positive aspects about their education and themselves to lessen the importance of
the stigma. They admitted that they failed in lower middle school, but they
spoke about the value of skilled workers for the economy. They did not reject
the idea that vocational education students are lazy and difficult, but they
pointed out how savvy they were with new social situations, e.g. during the
internship. Finally, they were convinced that they would be able to find jobs
and make a career or enter a higher vocational school, and with that they might
be able to leave their stigma behind.

Another common form of stigma management was the retreat from the
'normal': the stigmatized individuals stay amongst themselves and the stigma
stops mattering. In fact, especially in the beginning of their education, the stigma seemed to be less relevant for the students. They were amongst themselves
and the vocational schools told them about the value of their education and
future opportunities. Zhao Jing (1_M/F1) appeared to be thrilled after he had
entered his new school: "After I had just entered this school, everything was
unfamiliar, everything was new. I had left my parents and my grand-parents
because I wanted to be in a new place to break away from my old self." (ZJ1_2)
He explained that he chose Fengxian School because he would be able to board

during the week. Zhao Jing immersed himself in the new school and two years later he was one of the few students who preferred vocational over academic education:

> I personally think that vocational education is better than university because in university many students do not study but fudge through it. There are many university students but not a lot of vocational education students. Nowadays blue collar workers are missing, not white collar workers. (ZJ3_42)

Zhao Jing was arguing against the stigmatization of vocational education, which he considered better than university education. At the beginning of their education, other students shared his standpoint but close to graduation almost none of the interviewed students advocated for a de-stigmatization of vocational education. The conclusion must be that if students from key vocational schools in Shanghai still could not accept that vocational and academic education are of equal value, then the stigmatization of vocational education has been passed on to them and will likely be passed on to following generations as well (Harbrecht 2018).

9.7.2 Winners or Losers?

We have seen that vocational education students accepted and lived with their stigma but we have also seen that they experienced self-worth and were aware of strengths they have. One of the initial questions for this study had been: Will vocational education students consider themselves to be losers in Chinese society? Or will they look at the lack of skilled workers, and the fact that they went to key schools in Shanghai, and consider themselves hidden winners? This question has not been answered so far, and since the focus of this study is always the perception of students themselves, the logical consequence was to ask the students directly. This was done in 2015, during the last interviews. All students were either in the last year of their vocational education or had already graduated. Their answers can be seen as the result of the stigma management described above.

Generally, opinions on vocational education had become more realistic and differentiated. Students who had, in the beginning, stressed the chances they would have with vocational education realized that the jobs on offer to them were mostly poorly paid and simple, and students who felt that they had lost out by entering vocational education realized that there were development opportunities which were not linked to a higher education degree.

Asked to label themselves as winners or losers, most students were careful and pointed out that there was no finality in their lives yet. In the close future, there could still be good or bad development waiting for them. Their fate was not yet set in stone. This state of mind is already a change from the general opinions in society, in which vocational education is considered a dead-end, and a professional career is considered to be solely for university graduates. This reminds one of Chapter 8.2 where students' belief in being able to control their own fates had been brought to the fore. Although objectively their chances for careers had certainly been reduced by leaving the academic education system, students did not acknowledge, or rather did not want to acknowledge, that not everything depended solely on their own efforts.

Nonetheless, society's negative opinions of vocational education and vocational education students were still relevant for the students and influenced their points of view. Wang Ming (3_M/FG), for example, said that other people would consider him a loser but in his opinion, he was a winner who chose another road: vocational instead of academic education. De Hua (3_M/Q3) explained that it depended on oneself. If one has no respect for technical knowledge then one must consider oneself a loser – but he considered himself a winner: "I can look at the positive sides. I came here to a vocational middle school and I found this company [where I do my internship] where I can learn more. With this knowledge I can further impress people." (DH3_128). Students wanted to see themselves as winners. They received their degree after three years of studying, and with that they had a profession. They knew the value and the importance of skilled workers in China but at the same time they were aware of the bad reputation vocational education and they themselves, as vocational education students, had. Students tried to remove themselves from the prejudices and, as a result, had to endure the contradiction of accepting the bad reputation of vocational education, but not being affected by it personally.

Contrasting this, Qian Qin (3_M/Q3) did not separate himself from vocational education's bad reputation. He considered himself a loser and regretted going to a vocational school which was "a waste of time" (QQ3_148). Li Tao (3_F/F3) also used to think of herself as loser because her parents expected her to enter an academic higher middle school but while she was thinking about the question she appeared to change her mind: "[…] but now I'm thinking that you can also learn a lot in vocational education. When you're finished you can find work. You only need to think, learn a lot of things and then you can find work. Therefore, it is ok." (LT3_120). Li Tao managed to stop considering herself a loser because she suddenly thought of a different standard she could apply. An individual who would be able to find work could not be considered a loser –

whereas: an individual who does not fulfill their parents' expectations must be considered a loser.

Lei Qiang (3_M/FG), the student who identified most strongly with being a technician, considered himself mostly a winner. He believed in being able to achieve development through learning. After failing the lower middle school exam he chose electrical engineering because he always liked physics and chemistry in school. He was genuinely interested in his training course and focused on his studies. In his third year he prepared for the *gaofu* exam and after failing it the first time, he did not give up and passed the second time. He knew how hard he worked for his success in school:

> I was never discouraged and I never gave up. Instead, I kept learning diligently. That other people went to an academic middle school and I went to a vocational middle school does not mean that I'm weaker than they are. (LQ3_82)

He also cautioned that he is not ultimately a winner because he has not started to work yet. Lei Qiang recognized his achievement while being aware that society implied he must be "weaker" than students in academic education. He defended himself against this prejudice and, at the same time, refused to call his self-assessment final, being well-aware of the lack of job security in modern China. There was no guarantee that he would find the kind of job he wanted, in a foreign-owned company with an income that would allow him to be independent from his parents and accumulate some savings.

While the majority of students had a cautious attitude, Li Qing (3_M/QG) was able to see himself as a winner because he distanced himself from vocational education altogether. He never had a job related to his training. "In life, I'm a winner. [...] I never worked in electrical engineering; therefore, I cannot judge it [my training]. [...] The graduation certificate I received from school was useless to me." (LQ3_138) Li Qing related his professional success to his personality. He claimed that his training had been irrelevant in his life and, thereby, prejudices about vocational education students were also irrelevant for him.

When looking further into the future, students had down-to-earth ideas about where they would be in five years. Most of the male students were planning to have a family of their own, whereas female students did not mention family plans. Most migrant students were considering returning to their hometowns at some point within those five years. In relation to their working lives, students saw themselves employed and they also saw a continuous improvement in their situation, e.g. getting a higher salary in five years or even being able to climb up the hierarchy to a white collar position. None of the students expressed concern that they might have financial or other difficulties;

they generally still held on to the belief that with diligence they would be able to better their lives. Lei Qiang (3_M/FG), who was doing his higher vocational education degree, imagined his future: "I will find a good company and struggle hard. With diligence, I will improve my knowledge and climb the ladder step by step towards management level [...] and have a stable life." (LQ3_80) By the time they had come of age, the students had already dealt with setbacks and disappointments, having to enter a vocational education school and realizing that their training course qualified them for unattractive factory positions being two very common ones. Yet, students managed to refocus each time on positive aspects, new chances and the general openness of the course of life in modern China. As a result, there was no final answer to the question of being a winner or loser. Han Feng (2_M/FG) explained:

> Maybe my current life is already my ideal life; I have to see the end. [...] When I'm old, I might think that my life as it is now is ideal or not; but right now I cannot decide this yet. Maybe this is only a phase in my ideal life. (HF2_100)

These results are an important addition to Chen's study (2016) on academic middle school students' attitudes towards higher education. In her sample, students in key schools stressed the necessity to enter a key university; students in average schools said that they must enroll in higher education without specifying any university rank. Both groups shared the strong belief that entering tertiary education would be the only way to prove their value in society and to satisfy their parents, while failing would make them losers. Also, both groups agreed that success and failure in this regard was connected solely to their individual efforts – although, as Chen pointed out, socio-economic and other factors strongly influenced students' chances. The vocational education students in the present study did agree that by leaving the academic education system they had failed, but they did not accept that their value as a person would be affected. Instead they held on to the belief that success and social status depends on personal effort and hard work. Yet, while Chen's students figured their future chances depended solely on their efforts within the education system and their educational achievement, the vocational students assumed that efforts made in the labour market could still lead to progress and success.

9.8 Conclusion

The focuses of this chapter were students' personalities and the question of how they felt about themselves. During their self-assessments, students generally described their characters in a positive way while also pointing out deficits. During their second and third interviews, students were able to detect improvements in their personalities and their attitudes, such as becoming more considerate and more understanding. They saw themselves as having become more mature over the years. Students also tried to work on their perceived deficits by following their teachers' advice to find the golden middle path between being too extrovert and too introvert – a relatively new ideal in China where introvert personalities used to be the most desirable ones. Overall, male students had higher professional confidence but also more depressive tendencies than their female peers. While female students entered vocational education with slightly less professional confidence, they had gained confidence by their second year of study. Close to their graduation, students had a higher score for depressive tendencies. Although this year group was not part of the Panel Data and, therefore might have had equally high depressive tendencies when they entered their vocational school, the conclusion that students lose at least some of their positive attitudes during their last year in vocational school is still valid when additionally taking interview results into consideration.

In regard to students' motivations, it became clear that students studied to improve their own and their parents' lives. This is an extrinsic but stable motivation and it is remarkable that a majority of students developed in this way despite not studying well in lower middle school. Students had higher motivation levels if the three universal psychological needs – competence, relatedness and autonomy, as defined by Deci and Ryan – were satisfied. In fact, motivated students had a good relationship with their parents and made positive experiences in their schools. This triangular relationship showed that in order to motivate students, parents and schools need to work together to create conditions supporting students. Still, motivation was not solely correlated to experiences in school and families; it also had significant correlations with students' reasons for choosing vocational education and their training course. Students who chose a course according to their interest were much more likely to be part of a future-oriented motivated group in their second year of study, whereas students who could not make their own choice were more likely to belong to a listless group. This seems obvious but it proves the fact that Chinese students' lack of choice when it comes to their major – be it in vocational school or university – has a very bad long-term influence on their motivation.

The majority of the students enrolled in electrical engineering or mechatronics were male, and during the interviews very strong gender stereotypes came to the fore. Female students struggled with being trained in a field considered unsuitable for women. None of the students questioned stereotypes, even if they themselves did not fit in. It was widely accepted that women needed to do the housework, and it was also considered normal that they, in addition, would have fulltime jobs. Men, on the other hand, were responsible for providing an apartment when they got married and, therefore, faced the pressure of finding a well-paid job to save money. Traditionalist gender assumptions prevail in Chinese society despite the fact that some gender roles, such as taking care of parents in old-age being an obligation only for sons, are no longer valid.

Although students thought of themselves as having become more mature with vocational education, only a few of them considered themselves to be grown up by the end of their education. The most common criteria for being grown-up was being able to take care of one's parents financially. Again, parents played a decisive role in how students saw themselves.

The term 90 *hou* (90 后 = 1990s Generation) was not used by the students but they still thought of themselves as one generation. When they explained their own opinions they either placed them within this perceived mainstream or distanced themselves from it. When asked about 90 *hou* students were able to name several stereotypes about their generation. Again, they did not question the stereotypes but usually distanced themselves from negative ones, sometimes admitting that these had been true for them in the past but did not apply anymore.

Overall, students considered themselves to be average people with average goals such as having a job, a family and a place to live. Professionally they thought of themselves as being able to work hard while still hoping to find an easy job after finishing vocational education. Most importantly, students were rooted in their nuclear families and filial piety had a big influence on their values, their self-perception and their vision of their future. Facing the stigmatized identity of a vocational education student, most students tried to neutralize their stigma by pointing out their positive traits, such as their strong communication skills or future chances they still had. Others retreated from the 'normal' by banning the stigma from their minds and focusing on their surroundings in school, where the value of skilled workers was stressed.

The final part of this chapter let students answer the question whether they, after all, are losers or winners. Their answers showed the outcome of their stigma management. Very few students simply accepted the bad opinions society has of vocational education. In this, they became losers but also did not have to defend an individual standpoint. Other students, also a minority, saw themselves as winners, either because they considered education irrelevant for this question or because their goal was to become a technician and they were doing well during their vocational education. The majority of the students were not able to answer this question, pointing out that their future was still open. With this they distanced themselves from the general opinion. They were convinced that vocational education, while being an important part in their lives, was not the ultimate factor deciding their fate. They still saw enough opportunities which could render the stigma of vocational education irrelevant. These students shared ambivalent attitudes, meaning that they simultaneously experienced positive and negative feelings. According to Morrissey (2016: 9), ambivalent attitudes are prone to change and it depends on the situation whether positive or negative feelings prevail. During the interviews, students displayed pragmatic attitudes and a generally optimistic outlook. The majority were leaning towards positive feelings in this situation, unless they were confronted with the concepts of 'academic education' and 'vocational education as failure'.

10 Discussion and Conclusion

The present study focused on vocational education students' identities and attitudes throughout their education. It specifically asked what kinds of individuals key vocational schools in Shanghai produce, what values and motivations these individuals have and how they manage their education-related stigma. Drawing on Beck's individualization thesis, the present study examined how students make decisions and what opportunities and risks they perceive, thereby locating the group of students within the bigger spectrum of Chinese society. Chinese vocational education is rarely focused on in sociological or anthropological studies, and by zooming in specifically on students in key vocational schools in Shanghai, the present study has shed light on a group which has likely never been the focus of profound research before.

Not only the subject of the present study was unique, but also the data set. A mixed-method approach which combined interviews and questionnaires, as well as a panel design, allowed the tracking of changes and developments through students' training and after graduation. Students were interviewed up to three times over three years, and two sets of questionnaires were administered to the same cohort with one year in between. This research design gave an unprecedented insight into students' lives, personalities, opinions and values.

This final chapter lays out the findings of this study – the most important results of this research – starting with general insights into the student resources of key vocational schools in Shanghai, students' opinions on vocational education, and the resulting implications. The discussion will then turn to identities and stigma management, before lastly summarizing how the students of the present sample fit with Beck's individualization thesis.

General insights into student resources of key vocational schools in Shanghai

Finding A: Students have similar family backgrounds.
It turned out that 70% of students' parents had nine years of schooling or fewer and most of them worked in factories or peddled goods. Shanghainese parents tended to have higher education levels compared to migrants, but the majority of children will still surpass parents' education levels with a vocational education degree. Yet, due to diploma inflation it is to be expected that such students will not be able to better their status in society. They are becoming qualified for jobs similar to those their parents were already doing. This situation highlights

two facts. First, schools reproduce society and sustain social inequalities. This phenomenon has already been pointed out by researchers in Europe (e.g. Bourdieu and Passeron in France and Furlong and Cartmel (1997: 19) in the UK), and we can now also see it in China. Students' relative status in society does not change. Their parents can mostly be considered low skilled or unqualified workers and the children will also enter companies at the low end of the hierarchy. Additionally, many parents peddled goods. This way of making a living, as well as other precarious employment forms such as commission-based sales jobs, became relevant for students who wanted to avoid factory work. White collar workers were a minority among the parents and will also be a minority among the children. The second phenomenon is what Beck labelled the 'elevator effect' in society. While the relative status of the students does not change from their parents' status, there is still improvement in their lives compared to earlier generations. They have more years of schooling and are trained for a specific field of work. Also, given the overall development in China, the students will have assets their parents did not have and they will probably endure less hardship in their lives (Beck 1986: 122). With these insights the present study proved that important trends in Western society are also relevant in China: the development and improvement of living standards reaches lower levels of society as well, but those workers nonetheless stay on the lower end of the hierarchy.

Finding B: Differences between Shanghainese and migrant students are less significant than expected.

Shanghainese students ended up in vocational education mostly because they failed the lower middle school exam, whereas migrant students went to a vocational school because they could not, or did not want to, enter an academic middle school in their home province, while the regulations in Shanghai did not allow migrant students to enter academic higher middle schools in the city. Logically, Shanghainese students experienced more pressure and were more likely to feel that they had disappointed their parents. Therefore, the assumption that what might be failure for one student group can be considered a success for another is valid to some degree.

During interviews with teachers and students it became clear that there were differences between the Shanghainese and migrant students, but open stigmatization by teachers, classmates and parents as Lan (2014: 255–256) described it for academic middle schools in Shanghai could not be detected. This is in line with Woronov (2016: 62) who found that there was no segregation between locals and non-locals in her Nanjing vocational schools and therefore concluded that *hukou* was not an important part of students' identity.

Differences in attitude and development were mostly correlated with other aspects such as having a good relationship with parents or having been able to choose a training course. The origin of students did have an influence, but it was secondary to other factors. This result is important for future studies: socio-demographic variables are not sufficient to form attitude-based groups; other influential aspects must be taken into account instead.

Finding C: Most students are not interested in their training course and do not have a free choice.

The vast majority of students (79.2%) ended up in vocational education because they were migrant students or because they failed in lower middle school. This means that not even key vocational schools in Shanghai can attract students who are genuinely interested in technical education and it shows that the belief that vocational education is a substandard education is actually deeply rooted.

Additionally, a third of the students reported that parents had decided in which school to enroll, and for a quarter of students, parents also chose the training course. The analysis of motivation and attitudes towards vocational education in the second year showed that students who chose their course out of interest had a significantly more positive attitude later on. Taking into account the fact that students in China entering tertiary education also rarely have a choice when it comes to their subject, as had been reported by Hansen (2015: 81–82), the conclusion must be that there is a high number of unmotivated students who end up in courses they are not interested in at all. The present study left no doubt about how profound the differences are between students who were active agents making their own rational choice and students who were signed up for a course by others. Therefore, schools and policy makers need to explore options for giving students more agency.

Finding D: Different schools encounter different students.

It turned out that Fengxian School students in the alternating system gained professional confidence between the first and second year,[45] and they were happier in school and more motivated than their peers in Qingpu School by the time they reached the second year of training. Although the conclusion that the

---

[45] Fengxian School first year 3.4, second year 3.8; Qingpu School first year 3.6, second year 3.5 (1 = no professional confidence, 5 = very high professional confidence).

alternating system is superior to the 2+1 system seems to suggest itself, it cannot be drawn this easily. Contrary to my expectations, students never mentioned the Fengxian School's connections to Germany, and with few exceptions talked about the alternating system in mostly negative ways. Since the present study focused solely on students' perspectives and did not include any assessment of education quality, it therefore cannot explain the differences between the schools. Future studies would have to focus on how school profiles and the different teaching methods employed, influence students, while also accounting for other factors such as class size and differences in student resources. The results of the present study indicate that the alternating system could potentially have a positive influence on how students perceive their education.

Opinions on vocational education

Finding E: There is a typical pattern in how students' opinions change throughout their education.
The panel study allowed for the tracking of students' changing opinions. Just after entering a vocational school, students mostly felt positively about themselves and vocational education. This was a surprising result considering that they 'failed' academic education, yet it is a result which is in line with Schaupp (2014: 748–750), who pointed out the positive developments of German students after they had entered an undesired school form. These initially high opinions and positive attitudes entered a downward trend later on. Interviews showed how students lost their illusions and became disappointed during the internship. As a result, their opinions on vocational education became more negative and future plans changed, with more students aspiring to work in the service sector in order to avoid tiring factory work.

Certainly, there are multiple variations of this trajectory, e.g. female students scored significantly lower on the factor 'Likes Vocational Education' compared to their male peers in the first year, but by the second year this difference had leveled out and roughly 40% of female and male students fell into the cluster 'Happy in School' – suggesting that the trajectory would be less pronounced for female students. Also, students who had a chance to choose their training course were more positive overall, meaning that their opinions were still likely to follow the pattern but on an overall more positive level or with a steeper drop later on. Finally, there were students who entered the school with negative feelings and did not experience any change.

In summary, the trajectory applies, to different degrees, to a majority of students. This has three implications: first, positive development after a negative school selection happens in China as well as in Western countries such as Germany and might therefore be valid across cultures. Second, schools need to seize the opportunity to support and strengthen these positive feelings from the beginning. Third, improving the organization and content of internships is a prior condition towards a better reputation for vocational education and a more efficient supply of skilled workers.

Finding F: Vocational education fails (at least to some degree) in its purpose to provide skilled workers.

Only very few students were planning to work as electrical engineers after their graduation and among the graduated interviewees a vast majority had jobs unrelated to their training. Clearly, among every graduated cohort a significant proportion does not work in the field for which they are qualified. Taking students' negative experiences during the internships into account, it is evident that job conditions for skilled workers in technical fields are not attractive enough. Hence, the government's measures for expanding vocational education by forcing students to leave the academic education system will not be able to quench the industry's thirst for skilled workers.

Finding G: Vocational education succeeds (at least to some degree) in its purpose to prepare students for the Chinese market economy.

Vocational education students regained self-esteem during their education. They shared positive outlooks and strong beliefs in their ability to better their lives. Close to graduation and afterwards, students were confident that they have the skills needed for survival in today's society. Clearly, vocational education shapes individuals who have sense of responsibility and are prepared to make their own living. Graduates do not expect that the state or any other institution will take care of them, and they are positive enough to take on this (in Chinese society relatively new) challenge of independence and self-reliance in a competition-based labour market.

Stigma and Identity

Finding H: Both schools produced students with largely positive identities.

Students' personalities and identities turned out to be much more positive and healthy than what the prejudice towards vocational education students would suggest. Students were confident and aware of their strengths without being arrogant. They recognized their weaknesses but mostly took them as challenges to work on. Certainly, these conclusions are only based on self-reports, but the interviews with teachers also suggest that both schools do indeed succeed in mostly producing psychologically healthy subjects.[46]

Finding I: Most students are negatively affected by the stigma of 'vocational education'.

Although most students formed largely positive identities and looked into their future with confidence, they were nonetheless affected by the stigma of 'vocational education'. Students' narratives, when asked directly, suggests that the stigma was accepted as such and students protect themselves by focusing on the openness of their future and other positive aspects about themselves. Although it seems that most students were successful with this kind of stigma management, it nonetheless means that they are a group with a high risk of developing psychological problems or encountering discrimination by others.

Finding J: Vocational education is considered a stigma even in the best vocational schools.

Even students from key vocational schools in Shanghai did not argue that vocational education should be considered equally valuable as academic education. This shows once more how deeply rooted prejudices against vocational education are in Chinese society. It turns out that not only under-qualified teachers and a general lack of company investment (as described in Chapter 3.2.2) contribute to the bad reputation of vocational education, but also the stigmatized individuals themselves make no effort to argue for a de-stigmatization. With that in mind, it seems highly unlikely that the opinions in society will change anytime soon.[47]

Motivation

Finding K: Deci and Ryan's Self-Determination Theory (2000) is valid in the case of vocational education students in Shanghai.

Students formed stable extrinsic motivations which came close to intrinsic motivation if the three basic needs – autonomy, relatedness and competence – were satisfied.

---

[46] This is a general trend. In the sample were multiple varieties of personalities present.

[47] This is again a general trend. There were few students who argued, at least to some extent, that academic and vocational education are equal.

The analysis demonstrated that stable motivations develop if:

- students had a chance to choose their training course (autonomy)
- students had positive relationships with their parents (relatedness)
- students made positive experiences and (re-)gained self-esteem (competence)

Overall, roughly half of the students formed stable motivations. This, of course, is an idealized statistical group. Even so it suggests that a majority of students is likely to have some motivation which does not rely on tangible reward or punishment. Differences between the students came down to the factors of autonomy, relatedness and competence, and were not related to sociodemographic variables. This result further proves the inter-cultural transferability of Deci and Ryan's theory. It also shows the chances and limitations schools face when trying to motivate their students. Students need to be given some choice; school and family – as the two most important environments – need to work together, and schools need to give their students a chance to experience success.

Individualization in China

Finding L: Students share a strong sense of responsibility.
Students felt responsible for having to enter a vocational school without recognizing external factors which might have diminished their chances to enter an academic higher middle school in the first place. In the same manner, they felt responsible for their future, and they felt that reaching goals depended on personal efforts. These perceptions of reality are congruent with Beck's descriptions (1994) of individuals under the influence of individualization.

Also in line with Beck's theories is a perceived openness, meaning existing inequalities in society were not recognized by the students. Everything seemed possible to them and biography was created in a do-it-yourself fashion. Closely connected to this sense of responsibility is self-reliance. As had been pointed out before, students were prepared to take on the challenge of building their own lives. There were also risks which students sensed, such as the risk of not finding a good job or a spouse and, most prominently, the risk of failing to provide for their parents. All of these results confirm that the theories of second modernity are applicable in China – if adjusted appropriately – and that vocational education students in Shanghai strongly feel the defining traits of individualization in their lives.

Finding M: Traditional Chinese values prevail.

Despite the ongoing individualization – and with that the spread of new values such as independence – the present study concluded that traditional Chinese values prevail or, more precisely, make a comeback after the tumultuous years of the Cultural Revolution. Students did aspire to independence while materialism was also represented in the sample. Yet, a more in-depth analysis revealed that these values supported the overarching collectivistic value of 'family'. Students closely identified with their parents and showed a strong sense of filial piety. The interviews brought to the fore the fact that students wanted to be independent and have material assets in order to be able to support their parents and start their own families. Thus, students' value systems consisted of 'collectivistic values with individualistic characteristics'. This is an important addition to the ongoing debate of whether traditional Chinese collective-based values, such as filial piety, will lose their relevance with the onset of second modernity. The answer here is that in China, new values are neither contradicting nor replacing traditional values – a situation different from within Western society.

The retreat of the welfare state in the West and the abolition of the 'iron rice bowl' system in China have led to similar developments in both societies. Individuals perceive chances and risks and feel the necessity to become self-reliant and create their biographies. The present study has revealed how these trends manifest themselves in the lives of vocational education students in Shanghai, while it also demonstrated how China's modernity differs from the West.

Individualization in China is a forced development under tight government control. The goal for the CCP is to foster economic growth while restraining individual rights in order to stay in power (Beck, Beck-Gernsheim 2010a: 203–205). It therefore aims to shape the Chinese people into productive, independent, enterprising individuals who adhere to traditional collectivistic values such as the obligation to take care of one's parents and support the nation. While Liu (2008) found that enterprising traits have become dominant among young Chinese, and collectivistic values seem to disappear, Hoffman (2008) argued that there exists a blend where young professionals combine individual goals such as career and development with socialist values such as contributing to the state and society. Hansen (2015) described with which methods an academic higher middle school prepared students for the state controlled individualization, and concluded that the combination of teaching socialist ideals and practicing what the economy requires of individuals was an adequate preparation for Chinese realities. While these previous studies mainly focused on students and graduates from academic education, the present study brought the individuals in vocational schools to light.

To conclude, the state is indeed successful with forcing individualization in specific desired areas while preserving traditional values and orientations. The students in the sample were convinced that success and failure depended on themselves and that they would work on their career to become independent and stand on their own feet. In addition to that though, they firmly agreed that it is their responsibility to take care of their parents and any individualistic aspirations were secondary to this most important task. In essence, vocational education turned out to be unsuccessful in producing skilled workers for specific industries, while the stigma of this education is unchallenged for the time being and likely to remain in the future as well. On the other hand though, vocational education, as it is carried out in Shanghainese key schools, produces individuals which the state desires and who are likely to adapt well to the realities of modern China.

11 Bibliography

21 Shiji Jiaoyu Yanjiuyuan (21 世纪教育研究院) (Ed.) (2016): Shanghai Shi: Tansuo Zhiye Jiaoyu Guantong Peiyang Tixi (上海市：探索职业教育贯通培养体系). Available online at http://learning.sohu.com/20161220/n476386778.shtml, checked on 5/25/2017.

All-China Women's Federation (Ed.) (2013): Wo Guo Nongcun Liushou Ertong, Chengxiang Liudong Ertong Zhuangkuang Yanjiu Baogao (我国农村留守儿童，城乡流动儿童状况研究报告). Available online at http://acwf.people.com.cn/n/2013/0510/c99013-21437965.html, checked on 5/29/2017.

Alpermann, Björn (2011): Class, Citizenship and Individualization in China's Modernization. In ProtoSociology (28), pp. 7–24.

Alpermann, Björn (2012): Status Change and Social Identities in Contemporary Urban China. Paper to be presented at the Joint International Conference of the "Governance in China" Research Network and the Association of Social Science Research on China (ASC). Tübingen.

Alpermann, Björn (2013): Soziale Schichtung und Klassenbewusstsein in Chinas autoritärer Modernisierung. In Zeithistorische Forschungen/Studies in Contemporary History (10), pp. 283–296.

Alpermann, Björn (2016): Prekarisierung am Beispiel der städtischen dibao-Empfänger in China: Politik, Diskurs, Subjektivierung. In Stephan Köhn, Monika Unkel (Eds.): Prekarisierungsgesellschaften in Ostasien? Aspekte der sozialen Ungleichheit in China und Japan. Wiesbaden: Harrassowitz, pp. 177–208.

Anders, Benjamin; Pinkelman, Rebecca J.; Hampe, Manfred; Kelava, Augustin (2014): Development, Assessment, and Comparison of Social, Technical, and General (Professional) Competencies in a University Engineering Advanced Design Project - A Case Study. TU Darmstadt, Universität Tübingen.

Anderson, Craig A. (1999): Attributional Style, Depression, and Loneliness: A Cross-Cultural Comparison of American and Chinese Students. In Society for Personality and Social Psychology 25 (4), pp. 482–499.

Badger, Sarah; Nelson, Larry J.; Barry, Carolyn McNamara (2016): Perceptions of the Transition to Adulthood among Chinese and American Emerging Adults. In International Journal of Behavioral 30 (1), pp. 84–93. DOI: 10.1177/0165025406062128.

Barbalet, Jack (2016): Chinese Individualization, Revisited. In Journal of Sociology 52 (1), pp. 9–23. DOI: 10.1177/1440783315587413.

Beck, Ulrich (1986): Risikogesellschaft. Auf dem Weg in eine andere Moderne. 1. Aufl., Erstausg. Frankfurt am Main: Suhrkamp (Edition Suhrkamp, 1365 = n.F., Bd. 365).

Beck, Ulrich (Ed.) (1994): Riskante Freiheiten. Individualisierung in modernen Gesellschaften. Frankfurt am Main: Suhrkamp (Edition Suhrkamp, 1816 = N.F., 816).

Beck, Ulrich (1994): Jenseits von Stand und Klasse? In Ulrich Beck (Ed.): Riskante Freiheiten. Individualisierung in modernen Gesellschaften. Frankfurt am Main: Suhrkamp (Edition Suhrkamp, 1816 = N.F., 816), pp. 43–60.

Beck, Ulrich; Beck-Gernsheim, Elisabeth (1993): Nicht Autonomie, sondern Bastelbiographie. Anmerkungen zur Individualisierungsdiskussion am Beispiel des Aufsatzes von Günter Burkart. In Zeitschrift für Soziologie 22 (3), pp. 178–187.

Beck, Ulrich; Beck-Gernsheim, Elisabeth (1994): Individualisierung in modernen Gesellschaften - Perspektiven und Kontroversen einer subjektorientierten Soziologie. In Ulrich Beck (Ed.): Riskante Freiheiten. Individualisierung in modernen Gesellschaften. Frankfurt am Main: Suhrkamp (Edition Suhrkamp, 1816 = N.F., 816), pp. 10–39.

Beck, Ulrich; Beck-Gernsheim, Elisabeth (2002): Individualization. Institutionalized Individualism and Its Social and Political Consequences. London, Thousand Oaks, Calif: SAGE (Theory, Culture & Society).

Beck, Ulrich; Beck-Gernsheim, Elisabeth (2010a): Chinesische Bastelbiographie? Variationen der Individualisierung in kosmopolitischer Perspektive. In Anne Honer, Michael Meuser, Michaela Pfadenhauer (Eds.): Fragile Sozialität. Wiesbaden: VS Verlag für Sozialwissenschaften, pp. 199–206.

Beck, Ulrich; Beck-Gernsheim, Elisabeth (2010b): Foreword: Varieties of Indi-
vidualization. In Mette Halskov Hansen, Rune Svarverud (Eds.): iChina.
The Rise of the Individual in Modern Chinese Society. Copenhagen:
NIAS (NIAS Studies in Asian Topics, 45), xiii–xx.

Beck, Ulrich; Grande, Edgar (2010): Variations of Second Modernity: The
Cosmopolitan Turn in Social and Political Theory and Research. In The
British Journal of Sociology 61 (3), pp. 409–443.

Beck-Gernsheim, Elisabeth (1994): Auf dem Weg in die postfamiliale Familie.
In Ulrich Beck (Ed.): Riskante Freiheiten. Individualisierung in modernen Gesellschaften. Frankfurt am Main: Suhrkamp (Edition Suhrkamp,
1816 = N.F., 816), pp. 115–138.

Bian, Yanjie (2002): Institutional Holes and Job Mobility Processes: Guanxi
Mechanisms in China's Emergent Labor Market. In Thomas Gold,
Doug Guthrie, David L. Wank (Eds.): Social Networks in China. Institu-
tions, Culture, and the Changing Nature of Guanxi. Cambridge, UK:
Cambridge University Press (Structural analysis in the social sciences,
21), pp. 117–135.

Bian, Yanjie; Huang, Xianbi (2015): The Guanxi Influence on Occupational
Attainment in Urban China. In Chinese Journal of Sociology 1 (3),
pp. 307–332. DOI: 10.1177/2057150X15593709.

Blair, Sampson Lee; Madigan, Timothy J. (2016): Dating Attitudes and Expectations among Young Chinese Adults: an Examination of Gender Differences. In Chinese Journal of Sociology 3 (1), pp. 1–19. DOI:
10.1186/s40711-016-0034-1.

Boer, Heike de (2014): Bildung sozialer, emotionaler und kommunikativer
Kompetenzen – ein komplexer Prozess. In Carsten Rohlfs, Marius Harring, Christian Palentien (Eds.): Kompetenz-Bildung. Wiesbaden: Springer Fachmedien Wiesbaden, pp. 23–38.

Bos, Arjan E. R.; Pryor, John B.; Reeder, Glenn D.; Stutterheim, Sarah E. (2013):
Stigma: Advances in Theory and Research. In Basic and Applied Social
Psychology 35 (1), pp. 1–9. DOI: 10.1080/01973533.2012.746147.

Bradsher, Keith (2013): In China, Families Bet it all on College for their Children. Edited by The New York Times. Available online at http://www.nytimes.com/2013/02/17/business/in-china-families-bet-it-all-on-a-child-in-college.html, checked on 4/21/2017.

Buff, Alex (1991): Schulische Selektion und Selbstkonzeptentwicklung. In Reinhard Pekrun, Helmut Fend (Eds.): Schule und Persönlichkeitsentwicklung. Ein Resümee der Längsschnittforschung. Stuttgart: F. Enke Verlag (Der Mensch als soziales und personales Wesen, Bd. 11), pp. 100–114.

Burke, Peter J. (1991): Identity Processes and Social Stress. In American Sociological Review 86 (6), pp. 836–849. Available online at http://www.jstor.org/stable/2096259, checked on 8/18/2015.

Cai, Heping (2008): Berufliche Bildung im internationalen Vergleich unter Einbeziehung von Erfahrungen mit der deutschen dualen Berufsbildung in China. In Hans-Seidel-Stiftung (Ed.): Bildungspolitik und Arbeitsmarkt in der Volksrepublik China. Peking (KOORD Schriftenreihe, 2), pp. 48–65.

Cameron, Judy; Pierce, David; Banko, Katherine M. (2001): Pervasive Negative Effects of Rewards on Intrinsic Motivation: The Myth Continues. In The Behavior Analyst 24 (1), pp. 1–40.

Chan, Aris (2009): Paying the Price for Economic Development: The Children of Mirgant Workers in China. Edited by China Labour Bulletin. Available online at http://www.clb.org.hk/sites/default/files/archive/en/share/File/research_reports/Children_of_Migrant_Workers.pdf, checked on 6/29/2016.

Chen, Xinyin; Yang, Fan; Wang, Li (2013): Relations between Shyness-Sensitivity and Internalizing Problems in Chinese Children. Moderating Effects of Academic Achievement. In J Abnorm Child Psychol 41 (5), pp. 825–836. DOI: 10.1007/s10802-012-9708-6.

Chen, Xinyin; Zappulla, Carla; Lo Coco, Alida; Schneider, Barry; Kaspar, Violet; Oliveira, Ana Maria de et al. (2004): Self-Perceptions of Competence in Brazilian, Canadian, Chinese and Italian Children: Relations with Social and School Adjustment. In International Journal of Behavioral 28 (2), pp. 129–138. DOI: 10.1080/01650250344000334.

Chen, Yu (2016): Beliefs and Behaviours. Accessing Higher Education in Contemporary China. In Yu Chen (Ed.): Social Attitudes in Contemporary China. 1st Edition. London, New York, NY: Routledge, Taylor & Francis Group (Routledge contemporary China series, 143), pp. 153–185.

Chen, Yuanyuan; Feng, Shuaizhang (2013): Access to Public Schools and the Education of Migrant Children in China. In China Economic Review 26, pp. 75–88. DOI: 10.1016/j.chieco.2013.04.007.

Cheung, Millissa F. Y.; Wu, Wei-Ping; Chan, Allan K. K.; Wong, May M. L. (2009): Supervisor–Subordinate Guanxi and Employee Work Outcomes: The Mediating Role of Job Satisfaction. In J Bus Ethics 88 (S1), pp. 77–89. DOI: 10.1007/s10551-008-9830-0.

Cheung, Chau-Kiu; Kwan, Alex Yui-Huen (2009): The Erosion of Filial Piety by Modernisation in Chinese Cities. In Ageing and Society 29 (02), pp. 179–198. DOI: 10.1017/S0144686X08007836.

China Daily (Ed.) (2007): China's Children too Busy for Playtime. Available online at http://www.chinadaily.com.cn/china/2007-05/13/content_871182.htm.

China Daily (Ed.) (2012): China to Spend 4% of GDP on Education. Available online at http://www.chinadaily.com.cn/business/2012-10/04/content _15796868.htm, checked on 4/21/2017.

Cliff, Tom (2015): Post-Socialist Aspirations in a Neo-Danwei. In The China Journal 73 (1), pp. 132–157.

Cockain, Alex (2011): Students' Ambivalence toward their Experiences in Secondary Education. Views from a Group of Young Chinese Studying in an International Foundation Program in Beijing. In Chicago Journals (65), pp. 101–118.

Da, Tundong (大屯东)(2013): Zhiye Jiaoyu Shi Wo Guo Jiaoyu Shiye de Zhongyao Zucheng Bufen (职业教育是我国教育事业的重要组成部分). Zhongguo Jiaoyu Bao (中国教育报) (5). Available online at http://www.chinazy.org/models/adefault/news_detail.aspx?artid=50382&cateid=1539, checked on 4/25/2014.

Deci, Edward L.; Koestner, Richard; Ryan, Richard M. (2001a): Extrinsic Rewards and Intrinsic Motivation in Education: Reconsidered Once Again. In Review of Educational Research 71 (1), pp. 1–27.

Deci, Edward L.; Ryan, Richard M.; Gagné, Marylène; Leone, Dean R.; Usunov, Julian; Kornazheva, Boyanka P. (2001b): Need Satisfaction, Motivation, and Well-Being in the Work Organization of a Former Eastern Bloc Country: A Cross-Cultural Study of Self-Determination. In PSPB 27 (8), pp. 930–942.

Deci, Edward L.; Ryan, Richard M.; Koestner, Richard (2001c): The Pervasive Negative Effects of Rewards on Intrinsic Motivation: Response to Cameron (2001). In Review of Educational Research 71 (1), pp. 43–51.

Dettmer, Isabel (2017): HRM, Qualifizierung und Rekrutierung in China. Das Mismatch Problem dargestellt am Beispiel der Hotellerie. Würzburg: Würzburg University Press.

Deutscher Bundestag (7/5/2013): Strategiepapier der Bundesregierung zur internationalen Berufsbildungszusammenarbeit aus einer Hand. Unterrichtung durch die Bundesregierung. Available online at https://www.bibb.de/dokumente/pdf/Bundesanzeiger_Strategiepapier_der_Bundesregierung_zur_internationalen_Berufsbildungszusammenar beit.pdf, checked on 11/05/2017.

Dong, Junya (董骏亚) (2015): Wenhua Yu Jineng Bingzhong - Zhongzhisheng Jiang Geng Ju Jingzhengli (文化与技能并重 - 中职生将更具竞争力). In Shanghai Morning Post, 10/13/2015, C2.

Ecarius, Jutta; Eulenbach, Marcel; Fuchs, Thorsten; Walgenbach, Katharina (2011): Jugend und Sozialisation. 1. Aufl. Wiesbaden: VS Verlag für Sozialwissenschaften / Springer Fachmedien Wiesbaden GmbH Wiesbaden (Basiswissen Sozialisation, Bd. 3). DOI: 10.1007/978-3-531-92654-4.

Eigenmann, Philipp; Rieger-Ladich, Markus (2008): Michel Foucault: Überwachen und Strafen. Die Geburt des Gefängnisses. In Benjamin Jörissen, Jörg Zirfas (Eds.): Schlüsselwerke der Identitätsforschung. 1. Aufl. Wiesbaden: VS Verlag für Sozialwissenschaften, pp. 223–239.

Engelhardt, Michael von (2008): Erving Goffman: Stigma. Über Techniken der Bewältigung beschädigter Identität. In Benjamin Jörissen, Jörg Zirfas (Eds.): Schlüsselwerke der Identitätsforschung. 1. Aufl. Wiesbaden: VS Verlag für Sozialwissenschaften, pp. 123–140.

Engelhardt, Michael von (2014): Interaktion und Identität in der Schule. Zur Anwendung und Weiterentwicklung der Theorie von Erving Goffman. In Jörg Hagedorn (Ed.): Jugend, Schule und Identität. Wiesbaden: Springer Fachmedien Wiesbaden, pp. 81–107.

Erikson, Erik H. (1998): Jugend und Krise. Die Psychodynamik im sozialen Wandel. 4. Aufl. Stuttgart: Klett-Cotta.

Field, Andy P. (2013): Discovering Statistics Using IBM SPSS Statistics. And Sex and Drugs and Rock 'n' Roll. 4th Edition. London: Sage Publications.

Fong, Vanessa L. (2004): Only Hope. Coming of Age under China's One-Child Policy. Stanford, Calif: Stanford University Press.

Fong, Vanessa L. (2007): Parent-Child Communication Problems and the Perceived Inadequacies of Chinese Only Children. In ETHOS 35 (1), pp. 85–127.

Fong, Vanessa L.; Zhang, Cong; Kim, Sungwon; Yoshikawa, Hirokazu; Way, Niobe; Chen, Xinyin et al. (2012): Gender Role Expectations and Chinese Mothers' Aspirations for their Toddler Daughters' Future Independence and Excellence. In Andrew B. Kipnis (Ed.): Chinese Modernity and the Individual Psyche. New York: Palgrave Macmillan (Culture, Mind and Society), pp. 89–117.

Förster, Johanne (2003): Identität von Personen. Universität Mannheim, Mannheim.

Franke, Renata Fu-Sheng (2003): Wirtschaftstätigkeit von chinesischen Schulen. Ökonomie oder Pädagogik. In Renata Fu-Sheng Franke, Wolfgang Mitter (Eds.): Das Bildungswesen in China. Reform und Transformation. Köln: Böhlau Verlag (Bildung und Erziehung. Beiheft, 12), pp. 72–90.

Fuligni, Andrew J.; Zhang, Wenxin (2004): Attitudes toward Family Obligation among Adolescents in Contemporary Urban and Rural China. In Child Development 75 (1), pp. 180–192. Available online at http://www.jstor.org/stable/3696574.

Furlong, Andy; Cartmel, Fred (1997): Young People and Social Change. Individualization and Risk in Late Modernity. Buckingham [u.a.]: Open Univ. Press (Sociology and social change).

Garz, Detlef (2006): Sozialpsychologische Entwicklungstheorien. Von Mead, Piaget und Kohlberg bis zur Gegenwart. 3., erw. Aufl. Wiesbaden: VS Verlag für Sozialwissenschaften (Lehrbuch).

Giddens, Anthony (1991): Modernity and Self-Identity. Self and Society in the Late Modern Age. Cambridge, U.K: Polity Press in association with Basil Blackwell.

Goffman, Erving (2003): Stigma. Über Techniken der Bewältigung beschädigter Identität. Sonderausg. zum 30jährigen Bestehen der Reihe Suhrkamp-Taschenbuch Wissenschaft. Frankfurt am Main: Suhrkamp (Suhrkamp-Taschenbuch Wissenschaft, 140).

Goodburn, Charlotte (2015): Migrant Girls in Shenzhen: Gender, Education and the Urbanization of Aspiration. In The China Quarterly 222, pp. 320–338. DOI: 10.1017/S0305741015000429.

Grabowski, Ute (2007): Berufliche Bildung und Persönlichkeitsentwicklung. Forschungsstand und Forschungsaktivitäten der Berufspsychologie. 1. Aufl. Wiesbaden: Dt. Univ.-Verl.

Griffiths, Michael B. (2010): Lamb Buddha's Migrant Workers: Self-Assertion on China's Urban Fringe. In Journal of Current Chinese Affairs 39 (2), pp. 3–37.

Griffiths, Michael B. (2013): None for All and All for None: Moral Dynamics in China's Consumer Society. In International Journal of China Marketing 14 (1), pp. 65–81.

Griffiths, Michael B.; Zeuthen, Jesper (2014): Bittersweet China: New Discourses of Hardship and Social Organisation. In Journal of Current Chinese Affairs 43 (4), pp. 143–174.

Hagedorn, Jörg (2014): Jugend, Schule und Identität. Eine Einführung in das Themenfeld. In Jörg Hagedorn (Ed.): Jugend, Schule und Identität. Wiesbaden: Springer Fachmedien Wiesbaden, pp. 17–26.

Halpin, David (2014): Teaching and Learning in Chinese Schools: Core Values and Pedagogic Philosophy. In Chinese Studies 3 (1). DOI: 10.4236/chnstd.2014.31001.

Han, Sang-Jin; Shim, Young-Hee (2010): Redefining Second Modernity for East Asia. A Critical Assessment. In The British Journal of Sociology 61 (3), pp. 465–488. DOI: 10.1111/j.1468-4446.2010.01322.x.

Hansen, Anders Sybrandt (2012a): Learning the Knacks of Actual Existing Capitalism: Young Beijing Migrants and the Problem of Value. In Critique of Anthropology.

Hansen, Mette Halskov (2012b): Learning to Organize and to be Organized: Student Cadres in a Chinese Rural Boarding School. In Ane Bislev, Stig Thøgersen (Eds.): Organizing Rural China, Rural China Organizing. Lanham, Md: Lexington Books, pp. 125–139.

Hansen, Mette Halskov (2013a): Learning Individualism. Hesse, Confucius, and Pep-Rallies in a Chinese Rural High School. In The China Quaterly, pp. 60–77.

Hansen, Mette Halskov (2013b): Recent Trends in Chinese Rural Education. The Disturbing Rural-Urban Disparities and the Measures to Meet Them. In Éric Florence, Pierre Defraigne (Eds.): Towards a New Development Paradigm in Twenty-First Century China. Economy, Society and Politics. New York: Routledge, pp. 165–178.

Hansen, Mette Halskov (2015): Educating the Chinese Individual. Life in a Rural Boarding School. Seattle, London: University of Washington press.

Hansen, Mette Halskov; Pang, Cuiming (2008): Me and My Family: Perceptions of Individual and Collective among Young Rural Chinese. In European Journal of East Asian Studies 7 (1), pp. 75–99. DOI: 10.1163/156805808X333929.

Hansen, Mette Halskov; Pang, Cuiming (2010): Idealizing Individual Choice: Work, Love and Family in the Eyes of Young, Rural Chinese. In Mette Halskov Hansen, Rune Svarverud (Eds.): iChina. The Rise of the Individual in Modern Chinese Society. Copenhagen: NIAS (NIAS Studies in Asian Topics, 45), pp. 39–64.

Hansen, Mette Halskov; Svarverud, Rune (Eds.) (2010): iChina. The Rise of the Individual in Modern Chinese Society. Copenhagen: NIAS (NIAS Studies in Asian Topics, 45).

Hansen, Mette Halskov; Woronov, T. E. (2013): Demanding and Resisting Vocational Education: a Comparative Study of Schools in Rural and Urban China. In Comparative Education 49 (2), pp. 242–259. DOI: 10.1080/03050068.2012.733848.

Hanser, Amy (2002a): The Chinese Enterprising Self: Young, Educated Urbanites and the Search for Work. In E. Perry Link, Richard Madsen, Paul Pickowicz (Eds.): Popular China. Unofficial Culture in a Globalizing Society. Lanham, Md: Rowman & Littlefield Publishers, pp. 189–206.

Hanser, Amy (2002b): Youth Job Searches in Urban China: The Use of Social Connections in a Changing Labor Market. In Thomas Gold, Doug Guthrie, David L. Wank (Eds.): Social Networks in China. Institutions, Culture, and the Changing Nature of Guanxi. Cambridge, UK: Cambridge University Press (Structural analysis in the social sciences, 21), pp. 137–161.

Harbrecht, Isabelle (2018): Verlierer im Bildungswettbewerb? Einstellungen von Berufsschülern in Shanghai zu ihrer Ausbildung. In Björn Alpermann, Birgit Herrmann, Eva Wieland (Eds.): Aspekte des sozialen Wandels in China: Familie, Bildung, Arbeit, Identität. Wiesbaden: Springer VS, pp. 99–132

Hasmath, Reza (2011): From Job Search to Hiring and Promotion: The Labour Market Experiences of Ethnic Minorities in Beijing. In International Labour Review 150 (1–2), pp. 189–201.

Hepp, Rolf-Dieter (2009): Das Feld der Bildung in der Soziologie Pierre Bourdieus: Systematische Vorüberlegungen. In Barbara Friebertshäuser (Ed.): Reflexive Erziehungswissenschaft. Forschungsperspektiven im Anschluss an Pierre Bourdieu. 2., durchges. und erw. Aufl. Wiesbaden: VS, Verl. für Sozialwiss, pp. 21–39.

Hitzler, Ronald; Honer, Anne (1994): Bastelexistenz. Über subjektive Konsequenzen der Individualisierung. In Ulrich Beck (Ed.): Riskante Freiheiten. Individualisierung in modernen Gesellschaften. Frankfurt am Main: Suhrkamp (Edition Suhrkamp, 1816 = N.F., 816), pp. 307–315.

Hoffman, Lisa (2006): Autonomous Choices and Patriotic Professionalism: On Governmentality in Late-Socialist China. In Economy and Society 35 (4), pp. 550–570. DOI: 10.1080/03085140600960815.

Hoffman, Lisa (2008): Post-Mao Professionalism. Self-Enterprise and Patriotism. In Li Zhang, Aihwa Ong (Eds.): Privatizing China. Socialism from Afar. Ithaca: Cornell University Press, pp. 168–181.

Hu, Yang; Scott, Jacqueline (2016): Family and Gender Values in China. In Journal of Family Issues 37 (9), pp. 1267–1293. DOI: 10.1177/0192513X 14528710.

Huang, Renzhi; Yao, Shuqiao; Abela, John R. Z.; Leibovitch, Fallyn; Mingfan, Liu (2013): Key Dimensions and Validity of the Chinese Version of the Individualism-Collectivism Scale. In ChnStd 02 (01), pp. 1–7. DOI: 10.4236/chnstd.2013.21001.

Hurrelmann, Klaus; Harring, Marius; Rohlfs, Carsten (2014): Veränderte Bedingungen des Aufwachsens - Jugendliche zwischen Moratorien, Belastungen und Bewältigungsstrategien. In Jörg Hagedorn (Ed.): Jugend, Schule und Identität. Wiesbaden: Springer Fachmedien Wiesbaden, pp. 61–81.

Hurrelmann, Klaus; Neubauer, Georg (1986): Sozialisationstheoretische Subjektmodelle in der Jugendforschung. In Wilhelm Heitmeyer (Ed.): Interdisziplinäre Jugendforschung. Fragestellungen, Problemlagen, Neuorientierungen. Weinheim: Juventa (Jugendforschung), pp. 157–172.

International Maritime Information Website (Ed.) (2017): Shanghai Port's News. Available online at http://www.simic.net.cn/news_list.php?lan= en&id=368&flag=cnports&pname=shanghai, checked on 5/17/2017.

Ipsos (Ed.) (2017): Americans Too Preoccupied with Their Problems to Worry About Others. Ipsos. Available online at https://www.ipsos.com/sites/ default/files/2017-04/GTS%20Materialism-Press%20Release-2017-04-24 .pdf, checked on 10/2/2017.

Jiang, Dayuan (姜大源) (2011): Zhongguo Zhiye Jiaoyu Fazhan yu Gaige: Jingyan yu Guilv (中国职业教育发展与改革：经验与规律). In Zhiye Jishu Jiaoyu (职业技术教育) 32 (19), pp. 5–10.

Jiang, Xia (姜峡); Tang, Peng (唐鹏) (2007): Xiandai Xiaodao Lunli Shifan Tansuo (现代孝道伦理失范探索). In Gui Hai Tribune (桂海论丛) 23 (4), pp. 25–27.

Jörissen, Benjamin (2008): George Herbert Mead: Geist, Identiät und Gesellschaft aus der Perspektive des Sozialbehaviorismus. In Benjamin Jörissen, Jörg Zirfas (Eds.): Schlüsselwerke der Identitätsforschung. 1. Aufl. Wiesbaden: VS Verlag für Sozialwissenschaften, pp. 87–108.

Kaiman, Jonathan (2014): Nine-Hour Tests and Lots of Pressure: Welcome to the Chinese School System. The Guardian. Available online at https://www.theguardian.com/world/2014/feb/22/china-education-exams-parents-rebel.

Keupp, Heiner (2014): Eigenarbeit gefordert. Identitätsarbeit in spätmodernen Gesellschaften. In Jörg Hagedorn (Ed.): Jugend, Schule und Identität. Wiesbaden: Springer Fachmedien Wiesbaden, pp. 167–186.

Keupp, Heiner; Höfer, Renate; John, René; Knothe, Holger; Kraus, Wolfgang; Straus, Florian (2004): Selbstverortung im bürgerschaftlichen Engagement. Zur Ambivalenz subjektiver Konstruktionen von Gemeinschaft. In Ulrich Beck, Christoph Lau (Eds.): Entgrenzung und Entscheidung. Was ist neu an der Theorie reflexiver Modernisierung? 1. Aufl., Originalausg. Frankfurt am Main: Suhrkamp (Edition zweite Moderne), pp. 234–257.

Kipnis, Andrew B. (1997): Producing Guanxi. Sentiment, Self, and Subculture in a North China Village. Durham, NC: Duke University Press.

Kipnis, Andrew B. (2001): The Disturbing Educational Discipline of "Peasants". In The China Journal (46), pp. 1–24. Available online at http://www.jstor.org/stable/3182305, checked on 4/1/2016.

Kipnis, Andrew B. (2002): Practices of Guanxi Production and Practices of Ganqing Avoidance. In Thomas Gold, Doug Guthrie, David L. Wank (Eds.): Social Networks in China. Institutions, Culture, and the Changing Nature of Guanxi. Cambridge, UK: Cambridge University Press (Structural Analysis in the Social Sciences, 21), pp. 21–34.

Kipnis, Andrew B. (2011a): Governing Educational Desire. Culture, Politics, and Schooling in China. Available online at http://site.ebrary.com/lib/alltitles/docDetail.action?docID=10462232.

Kipnis, Andrew B. (2011b): Subjectification and Education for Quality in China. In Economy and Society 40 (2), pp. 289–306. DOI: 10.1080/03085147.2011.548950.

Kipnis, Andrew B. (2012): Private Lessons and National Formations: National Hierachy and the Individual Psyche in the Marketing of Chinese Educational Programms. In Andrew B. Kipnis (Ed.): Chinese Modernity and the Individual Psyche. New York: Palgrave Macmillan (Culture, Mind and Society), pp. 187–202.

Kleinman, Arthur; Yan, Yunxiang; Jun, Jing; Lee, Sing; Zhang, Everett (Eds.) (2011): Deep China. The Moral Life of the Person. Berkeley: University of California Press. Available online at http://lib.myilibrary.com/detail.asp?id=329189.

Kong, Runnian (孔润年) (2012): Guanyu Zhongguo Chuantong Xiaodao de Yuan Yu Liu (关于中国传统孝道的源与流). In Journal of Baoji University of Arts and Sciences (Social Sciences) 32 (1), pp. 14–17.

Kramer, Rolf-Torsten (2014): Identität als Passungsverhältnis von Schüler-Selbst und Schulkultur. "Neue" biographieanalytische und rekonstruktive Perspektiven auf ein "altes" Problem. In Jörg Hagedorn (Ed.): Jugend, Schule und Identität. Wiesbaden: Springer Fachmedien Wiesbaden, pp. 423–437.

Krappmann, Lothar (1982): Soziologische Dimensionen der Identität. Strukturelle Bedingungen für die Teilnahme an Interaktionsprozessen. 6., unveränd. Aufl. Stuttgart: Klett-Cotta (Veröffentlichung des Max-Planck-Instituts für Bildungsforschung).

Krawczyk, Olaf; Legler, Harald; Gehrke, Birgit (2008): Asiatische Aufhol-Länder im globalen Technologiewettbewerb - Die FuE- und Bildungsanstrengungen von Korea, China und Indien im Vergleich. In Vierteljahreshefte zur Wirtschaftsforschung 77 (2), pp. 79–94.

Kuczera, Malgorzata; Field, Simon (2010): A Learning for Jobs Review of China 2010. Paris: OECD (OECD Reviews of Vocational Education and Training).

Kupfer, Antonia (2014): Schule als soziales System und die Entwicklung des Persönlichkeitssystems. In Jörg Hagedorn (Ed.): Jugend, Schule und Identität. Wiesbaden: Springer Fachmedien Wiesbaden, pp. 141–151.

Lan, Pei-chia (2014): Segmented Incorporation: The Second Generation of Rural Migrants in Shanghai. In The China Quarterly 217, pp. 243–265. DOI: 10.1017/S030574101300146X.

Lappe, Lothar (2006): Jugend in der Berufsbildung. In Rolf Arnold, Antonius Lipsmeier (Eds.): Handbuch der Berufsbildung. 2., überarb. und aktualisierte Aufl. Wiesbaden: VS Verl. für Sozialwiss., pp. 73–83.

Li, Dongxue (2010): Qualitätssicherung und nachhaltige Entwicklung der Berufsbildung in China am Beispiel der Provinz Guangxi. Paderborn (Darmstädter Beiträge zur Berufspädagogik, 30).

Li, He (2013): Rural Students' Experiences in a Chinese Elite University. Capital, Habitus and Practices. In British Journal of Sociology of Education 34 (5-6), pp. 829–847. DOI: 10.1080/01425692.2013.821940.

Li, Zhenxi (李镇西) (2016): Mingxiao Jiazhi He Mingshi Zunyan Jiujing Zai Na (名校价值和名师尊严究竟在哪). Available online at http://www.jyb. cn/opinion/gnjy/201605/t20160520_660398.html, checked on 1/3/2017.

Lin, Yi (2005): Muslim Narratives of Schooling, Social Mobility and Cultural Difference. A Case Study in Multi-Ethnic Northwest China. In Japanese Journal of Political Science 6 (1), pp. 1–28. DOI: 10.1017/ S1468109905001702.

Lin, Yi (2007): Ethnicization through Schooling. The Mainstream Discursive Repertoires of Ethnic Minorities. In The China Quarterly 192. DOI: 10.1017/S030574100700210X.

Lin, Yi (2011): Turning Rurality into Modernity: Suzhi Education in a Suburban Public School of Migrant Children in Xiamen. In The China Quarterly 206, pp. 313–330. DOI: 10.1017/S0305741011000282.

Ling, Minhua (2015): "Bad Students Go to Vocational Schools!": Education, Social Reproduction and Migrant Youth in Urban China. In The China Journal (73), pp. 108–131. Available online at http://www.jstor.org/ stable/10.1086/679271.

Liu, Fengshu (2006): Boys as Only-Children and Girls as Only-Children – Parental Gendered Expectations of the Only-Child in the Nuclear Chinese Family in Present-Day China. In Gender and Education 18 (5), pp. 491–505. DOI: 10.1080/09540250600881626.

Liu, Fengshu (2008a): Constructing the Autonomous Middle-Class Self in Today's China: The Case of Young-Adult Only-Children University Students. In Journal of Youth Studies 11 (2), pp. 193–212. DOI: 10.1080/13676260701800746.

Liu, Fengshu (2008b): Negotiating the Filial Self: Young-Adult Only-Children and Intergenerational Relationships in China. In Young 16 (4), pp. 409–430. DOI: 10.1177/110330880801600404.

Liu, Fengshu (2011): The Norm of the 'Good' Netizen and the Construction of the 'Proper' Wired Self: The Case of Chinese Urban Youth. In New Media & Society 13 (1), pp. 7–22. DOI: 10.1177/1461444809360701.

Liu, Jiantong (2008c): Die Reform der chinesischen Berufsbildung – neueste Entwicklungen, Trends und Perspektiven. In Hans-Seidel-Stiftung (Ed.): Bildungspolitik und Arbeitsmarkt in der Volksrepublik China. Peking (KOORD Schriftenreihe, 2), pp. 1–7.

Liu, Wenrong (2017a): Intergenerational Emotion and Solidarity in Transitional China. Comparisons of Two Kinds of "ken lao" Families in Shanghai. In J. Chin. Sociol. 4 (1), p. 243. DOI: 10.1186/s40711-017-0058-1.

Liu, Wenrong (2017b): Intergenerational Support. In Anqi Xu, John D. DeFrain, Wenrong Liu (Eds.): The Chinese Family Today. London, New York: Routledge (Routledge contemporary China series, 158), pp. 210–247.

Mayring, Philipp (2003): Qualitative Inhaltsanalyse. Grundlagen und Techniken. 8th ed. Weinheim: Beltz.

Mead, George Herbert (2013): Geist, Identität und Gesellschaft. Aus der Sicht des Sozialbehaviorismus. 17. Aufl. Frankfurt a.M: Suhrkamp (Suhrkamp-Taschenbuch Wissenschaft, 28).

Meng, Liyan (孟利艳); Liu, Jiaxing (刘加星) (2014): Qingshao Nian Shouji Shiyong Yu Richang Shenghuo Fangshi De Bianqian (青少年手机使用与日常生活方式的变迁). In Qingnian Tansuo (青年探索) (181), pp. 64–67.

Ministry of Education (1995): Education Law of the People's Republic of China. Education Law. Available online at http://www.china.org.cn/english/education/184669.htm, checked on 4/21/2017.

Ministry of Education (2007): Jiaoyubu Zhishu Shifan Daxue Shifansheng Mianfei Jiaoyu Shishi Banfa (Shixing) (教育部直属师范大学师范生免费教育实施办法（试行）). Available online at http://www.moe.edu.cn/jyb_xxgk/moe_1777/moe_1778/tnull_27694.html.

Ministry of Education (2014): Shanghai Shi Shidian Zhongzhisheng zhisheng yingyong benke (上海市试点中职生直升应用本科). Renmin Ribao. Available online at http:/www.moe.edu.cn/publicfiles/business/ htmlfiles/moe/s5147/201411/178203.html, checked on 11/3/2016.

Ministry of Education (2016): 2015 Quanguo Zhongdeng Zhiye Xuexiao Jiuyelv Da 96.3% (2015 全国中等职业学校就业率达 96.3%). Available online at http://www.jyb.cn/job/jysx/201602/t20160226_653070.html, checked on 6/2/2017.

Ministry of Education; Ministry of Development and Reform; Ministry of Finance; Ministry of Human Resources and Social Securities; Ministry of Agriculture; State Council Department for Aid-the-poor (2014): Xiandai Zhiye Jiaoyu Tixi Jianshe Guihua (2014-2020) (现代职业教育体系建设 规 划 (2014–2020)). Available online at http://wenku.baidu.com/ link?url=2tNzTKO7j_XuAuyWyQFIXdRkahJLEtKMm1lw1b5eedI9AV3 n8ZvKBN5GU5tGihlwHGvN9RBoM6S6iTLu0w1pSoqpm4fNAwMaC9 ZtM7s1BjO.

Ministry of Education of Taiwan (Ed.) (2016): International Comparison of Education Statistical Indicators. Available online at http://stats.moe.gov. tw/files/ebook/International_Comparison/2016/i2016.pdf, checked on 5/31/2017.

Ministry of Human Resources and Social Securities (Ed.) (2005): Zhiye Jineng Jianding De Zhuyao Neirong Shi Shenme? (职业技能鉴定的主要内容 是什么?) Available online at http://www.molss.gov.cn/gb/ywzn/2005- 12/05/content_96598.htm, checked on 8/10/2010.

Minjin Shanghai Shiwei (民进上海市委) (Ed.) (2011): 2009 Nian Diaoyan Keti: Shanghai Wailai Liudong Renkou Zinv Jiaoyu Wenti Yanjiu (2009 年调 研课题：上海外来流动人口子女教育问题研究). Available online at http://www.shmj.org.cn/node809/node827/node829/ userobject1ai1731844.html, checked on 5/29/2017.

Morrissey, Paul (2016): Introduction. In Yu Chen (Ed.): Social Attitudes in Contemporary China. 1 edition. London, New York, NY: Routledge, Taylor & Francis Group (Routledge contemporary China series, 143).

Mühlhahn, Klaus (2010): 'Friendly Pressure': Law and the Individual in Modern China. In Mette Halskov Hansen, Rune Svarverud (Eds.): iChina. The Rise of the Individual in Modern Chinese Society. Copenhagen: NIAS (NIAS Studies in Asian Topics, 45), pp. 226–249.

Murphy, Rachel (1999): Turning Peasants into Modern Chinese Citizens: "Population Quality" Discourse, Demographic Transition and Primary Education. In The China Quarterly 177, pp. 1–20. DOI: 10.1017/S0305741004000025.

Naftali, Orna (2010): Caged Golden Canaries. Childhood, Privacy and Subjectivity in Contemporary Urban China. In Childhood 17 (3), pp. 297–311. DOI: 10.1177/0907568209345612.

National Bureau of Statistics of China (Ed.) (2014): China Regional Economic Development 2013. Available online at http://data.stats.gov.cn/english/swf.htm?m=turnto&id=3, checked on 6/1/2016.

National Bureau of Statistics of China (2015): China Statistical Yearbook 2014. Beijing: Zhongguo Tongji Chubanshe (中国统计出版社). Available online at http://www.stats.gov.cn/tjsj/ndsj/2014/indexch.htm, checked on 11/25/2015.

National Bureau of Statistics of China (2017): China Statistical Yearbook 2016. Beijing: Zhongguo Tongji Chubanshe (中国统计出版社). Available online at http://www.stats.gov.cn/tjsj/ndsj/2016/indexch.htm, checked on 11/05/2017.

Nelson, Larry J.; Chen, Xinyin (2007): Emerging Adulthood in China: The Role of Social and Cultural Factors. In Child Development Perspectives 1 (2), pp. 86–91.

Nittel, Dieter (1992): Gymnasiale Schullaufbahn und Identitätsentwicklung. Eine biographieanalytische Studie. Dr. nach Typoskript. Weinheim: Dt. Studienverl. (Interaktion und Lebenslauf, Bd. 6).

Noack, Juliane (2008): Erik H. Erikson: Identität und Lebenszyklus. In Benjamin Jörissen, Jörg Zirfas (Eds.): Schlüsselwerke der Identitätsforschung. 1. Aufl. Wiesbaden: VS Verlag für Sozialwissenschaften, pp. 37–53.

OECD (2010): PISA 2009 Results: Executive Summary. Available online at http://www.oecd.org/pisa/pisaproducts/46619703.pdf, checked on 3/1/2018.

OECD (2011): Education at a Glance 2011: OECD Indicators. Paris: OECD Publishing. DOI: 10.1787/eag-2011-2n.

OECD (2016a): Education at a Glance 2016: OECD Indicators. Paris: OECD Publishing. DOI: 10.1787/eag-2016-en.

OECD (2016b): Education in China. A Snapshot. Available online at http://www.oecd.org/china/Education-in-China-a-snapshot.pdf, checked on 4/24/2017.

Ong, Aihwa; Zhang, Li (2008): Introduction: Privatizing China. Powers of the Self, Socialism from Afar. In Li Zhang, Aihwa Ong (Eds.): Privatizing China. Socialism from Afar. Ithaca: Cornell University Press, pp. 1–19.

Renmin Ribao (人民日报) (2013): Zhongzhi Jiaoyu, Weihe Bu Shou Daijian (中职教育，为何不受待见). Edited by Zhongguo Jiaoyu Xinwen Wang (中国教育新闻网). Available online at http://www.jyb.cn/zyjy/zjsd/201302/t20130228_529358.html, updated on 2/28/2013, checked on 7/2/2013.

Renn, Joachim (2008): Reflexive Moderne und ambivalente Existentialität - Anthony Giddens als Identitäts-Theoretiker. In Benjamin Jörissen, Jörg Zirfas (Eds.): Schlüsselwerke der Identitätsforschung. 1. Aufl. Wiesbaden: VS Verlag für Sozialwissenschaften, pp. 203–221.

Rohlfs, Carsten (2011): Bildungseinstellungen. Schule und formale Bildung aus der Perspektive von Schülerinnen und Schülern. 1. Aufl. Wiesbaden: Springer Fachmedien.

Rose, Nikolas (1992): Governing the Enterprising Self. In Paul Heelas, Paul Morris (Eds.): The Values of the Enterprise Culture. The Moral Debate. London, New York: Routledge, pp. 141–164.

Rose, Nikolas (1996): Identity, Genealogy, History. In Stuart Hall, Paul Du Gay (Eds.): Questions of Cultural Identity. London: Sage Publications, pp. 128–150.

Rosen, Stanley (2004): The Victory of Materialism: Aspirations to Join China's Urban Moneyed Classes and the Commercialization of Education. In The China Journal 1 (51), pp. 1–48.

Ryan, Richard M.; Deci, Edward L. (2000): Self-Determination Theory and the Facilitation of Intrinsic Motivation, Social Development, and Well-Being. In American Psychologist 55 (1), pp. 68–78. DOI: 10.1037//0003-066X.55.1.68.

Schaupp, Ulrike (2014): Identitätsprozesse im Zusammenhang schulischer Übergänge. In Jörg Hagedorn (Ed.): Jugend, Schule und Identität. Wiesbaden: Springer Fachmedien Wiesbaden, pp. 741–760.

Schnarr, Alexander; Sun, Yang; Gleißner, Kai (2008): Vocational Education and Training and the Labour Market. A Comparative Analysis of China and Germany. Bonn. Available online at http://www.unevoc.unesco.org/fileadmin/user_upload/pubs/VETandLabourMarket.pdf, checked on 11/29/2015.

Schulte, Barbara (2003): Social Hierarchy and Group Solidarity: The Meanings of Work and Vocation/Profession in the Chinese Context and their Implications for Vocational Education. In International Review of Education 49 (1/2), pp. 213–239. Available online at http://www.jstor.org/stable/3445482, checked on 8/1/2015.

Schulte, Barbara (2012): Joining Forces to Save the Nation: Corporate Educational Governance in Republican China. In Jennifer Y. J. Hsu, Reza Hasmath (Eds.): The Chinese Corporatist State: Adaption, Survival and Resistance, pp. 1–62. Available online at http://lup.lub.lu.se/record/3232322, checked on 5/27/2017.

Schulte, Barbara (2013): Unwelcome Stranger to the System: Vocational Education in Early Twentieth-Century China. In Comparative Education 49 (2), pp. 226–241.

Schulte, Barbara (2014): Chinas Bildungssystem im Wandel: Elitenbildung, Ungleichheiten, Reformversuche. In Doris Fischer, Christoph Müller-Hofstede (Eds.): Länderbericht China. Bonn: Bundeszentrale für politische Bildung (1501), pp. 499–541.

Shanghai Bureau of Statistics (2015): Shanghai Statistical Yearbook 2014. Shanghai. Available online at http://www.stats-sh.gov.cn/tjnj/tjnj2014.htm, checked on 11/25/2015.

Shanghai Bureau of Statistics (2017): Shanghai Statistical Yearbook 2016. Shanghai. Available online at http://www.stats-sh.gov.cn/html/sjfb/201701/1000339.html, checked on 11/06/2017.

Shanghai Education (Ed.) (2014): 2013 Nian Shanghai Shi Zhongdeng Zhiye Xuexiao Biyesheng Jiuye Qingkuang Fabu (2013 年上海市中等职业学校毕业生就业情况发布). Available online at http://mp.weixin.qq.com/s?__biz=MjM5Njg0ODc5NA==&mid=200360736&idx=1&sn=ad4241c14bb2e765e9a3596d85b508fe&scene=2&from=timeline&isappinstalled=0#rd, checked on 5/4/2014.

Shanghai Education Commission (Ed.) (2015): Shanghai Shi Zhongdeng Zhiye Xuexiao Xuesheng Zonghe Suzhi Pingjia Shishi Banfa (上海市中等职业学校学生综合素质评价实施办法). Available online at http://www.shmec.gov.cn/html/xxgk/201509/403032015005.php, checked on 4/17/2017.

Shanghai Education Commission (Ed.) (2015): Shi Jiaowei Fabu 2014 Shanghai Shi Zhongzhi Biyesheng Jiuye Zhuangkuang (市教委发布 2014 上海市中职毕业生就业状况). Available online at http://www.shmec.gov.cn/web/wsbs/webwork_article.php?article_id=80621, checked on 6/23/2015.

Shanghai Education Commission (Ed.) (2016): Shanghai Shi Jiaowei Yinfa 2016 Nian Shanghai Shi Zhiye Jiaoyu Gongzuo Yaodian (上海市教委引发 2016 年上海市职业教育工作要点). Available online at http://www.eol.cn/shanghai/shanghainews/201602/t20160222_1367651.shtml, checked on 9/16/2016.

Shanghai Fabu (上海发布) (Ed.) (2016): 2016 Nian Shanghai Gaozhong Zhongdeng Zhiye Xuexiao Xuefei Shoufei Biaozhun Yilan (2016 年上海高中中等职业学校学费收费标准一览). Available online at http://sh.bendibao.com/news/2016314/157195_2.shtm, checked on 3/1/2018.

Shanghai Population 2017 - World Population Review (2017). Available online at http://worldpopulationreview.com/world-cities/shanghai-population/, updated on 5/8/2017, checked on 5/25/2017.

Sharma, Yojana (2014): What to do with Millions of Extra Graduates. Edited by BBC News. Available online at http://www.bbc.com/news/business-28062071, checked on 6/5/2017.

Shi, Yaojiang; Zhang, Linxiu; Ma, Yue; Yi, Hongmei; Liu, Chengfang; Johnson, Natalie et al. (2015): Dropping Out of Rural China's Secondary Schools: A Mixed-Methods Analysis. In The China Quarterly 224, pp. 1048–1069.

Shieh, Chich-Jen; Wang, I-Ming; Yang, Yung-Sheng (2008): Study on Factors Impacting the Development of Vocational Education in China. National Social Science Association. Available online at http://www.nssa.us/journals/2008-31-1/2008-31-1-19.htm, updated on 10/6/2009, checked on 4/25/2014.

Standing Committee of the National People's Congress (1996): Zhonghua Renmin Gongheguo Zhiye Jiaoyufa (中华人民共和国职业教育法). Available online at http://www.gov.cn/banshi/2005-05/25/content_928.htm, checked on 11/29/2015.

Standing Committee of the National People's Congress (2012): Law of the People's Republic of China on Protection of the Rights and Interests of the Elderly (2012 Revision). Available online at http://www.lawinfochina.com/display.aspx?lib=law&id=12566&CGid=#menu1.

State Council (2014): Guowuyuan Guanyu Fazhan Xiandai Zhiye Jiaoyu De Jueding (国务院关于发展现代职业教育的决定). Available online at http://www.moe.edu.cn/publicfiles/business/htmlfiles/moe/moe_1778/201406/170691.html.

Stenger, Horst (1985): Stigma und Identität. Über den Umgang straffälliger Jugendlicher mit dem Etikett "kriminell". In Zeitschrift für Soziologie 14 (1), pp. 28–49.

Stryker, Sheldon; Burke, Peter J. (2000): The Past, Present, and Future of an Identity Theory. In Social Psychology Quaterly 63 (4), pp. 284–297. Available online at http://www.jstor.org/stable/2695840, checked on 8/12/2015.

Sun, Peijie (孙佩洁); Zhang, Shuhan (张淑晗) (2015): Wo Guo Zhiye Jiaoyu Gaige yu Fazhan de Zhengce Wenben Fenxi (我国职业教育改革与发展的政策文本分析). In Henan Keji Xueyuan Xuebao (河南科技学院学报) (2), pp. 1–3.

Sun, Wanning (2008): 'Just Looking': Domestic Workers' Consumption Practices and a Latent Geography of Beijing. In Gender, Place & Culture 15 (5), pp. 475–488. DOI: 10.1080/09663690802300829.

Tamis-LeMonda, Catherine S.; Way, Niobe; Hughes, Diane; Yoshikawa, Hirokazu; Kalman, Ronit Kahana; Niwa, Erika Y. (2007): Parents' Goals for Children: The Dynamic Coexistence of Individualism and Collectivism in Cultures and Individuals. In Social Development 17 (1), pp. 183–209. DOI: 10.1111/j.1467-9507.2007.00419.x.

Tan, Lilian (覃隶莲); Zhong, Jianming (钟健民); Chen, Qingbo (陈清波); Liang, Wuhua (梁武华); Li, Ying (李英) (2007): Zhongzhuansheng Buliang Renge Tezheng Xinli Ganyu Xiaoguo Yanjiu (中专生不良人格特征心理干预效果研究). In Weisheng Zhiye Jiaoyu (卫生职业教育) (23), pp. 118–120.

Tang, Tuhong (唐土红); Chen, Lan (陈兰) (2013): Jiazhi Duoyuan Shidai "90 Hou" Qingnian De Aiqingguan Ji Qi Yindao (价值多元时代"90 后"青年的爱情观及其引导). In Qingnian Tansuo (青年探索) (180), pp. 83–87.

The Economist (Ed.): Comparing Chinese Provinces with Countries: All the Parities in China. Available online at http://www.economist.com/content/chinese_equivalents, checked on 6/1/2017.

The Encyclopedia of Shanghai Editorial Committee (Ed.) (2010): The Encyclopedia of Shanghai. Available online at http://zhuanti.shanghai.gov.cn/newencyclopedia/en/Default2.aspx, checked on 5/25/2017.

UNESCO-UNEVOC (Ed.) (2011): World Data on Education. People's Republic of China. Available online at http://www.ibe.unesco.org/fileadmin/user_upload/Publications/WDE/2010/pdf-versions/China.pdf.

UNESCO-UNEVOC (Ed.) (2013): World TVET Database China. Available online at http://www.unevoc.unesco.org/wtdb/worldtvetdatabase_chn_en.pdf, checked on 7/31/2015.

UNICEF: Definitions Education. Available online at https://www.unicef.org/infobycountry/stats_popup5.html, checked on 2/28/2018.

Valtin, Renate; Wagner, Christine (2004): Der Übergang in die Sekundarstufe I: Psychische Kosten der externen Leistungsdifferenzierung. In Psychologie in Erziehung und Unterricht (51), pp. 52–68.

Veith, Hermann (2008): Das Konzept der balancierenden Identität von Lothar Krappmann. In Benjamin Jörissen, Jörg Zirfas (Eds.): Schlüsselwerke der Identitätsforschung. 1. Aufl. Wiesbaden: VS Verlag für Sozialwissenschaften, pp. 179–202.

Voß, Werner; Khlavna, Veronika; Schöneck, Nadine M. (2012): Einführung in die Datenanalyse und Datenmanagement mit SPSS. Bochum.

Wang, Fei-Ling (2010a): Renovating the Great Floodgate. The Reform of China's Hukou System. In Martin King Whyte (Ed.): One Country, Two Societies. Rural-Urban Inequality in Contemporary China. Cambridge, Mass: Harvard University Press (Harvard contemporary China series, 16), pp. 335–364.

Wang, Jianchu (2007): Lernfeldorientierte berufliche Curricula und deren Entwicklungspotenziale für die Modernisierung der Berufsbildung in der V.R. China. Darmstadt (Darmstädter Beiträge zur Berufspädagogik, 29).

Wang, Qiang (2013): China Needs Workers more than Academics. In Nature 499, p. 381. DOI: 10.1038/499381a.

Wang, Wenjin (2010b): Key Highlights of China's Approach to TVET/Skills Development. Background Note South-South Study Visit to China and India on Skills and Technical and Vocational Education and Training November 1-12, 2010. Available online at http://siteresources.worldbank. org/EDUCATION/Resources/278200-1121703274255/1439264-1242337 549970/6124382-1288297991092/ChinaNote-byWenjinWang.pdf, checked on 6/18/2015.

Wang, Xiaobing; Liu, Chengfang; Zhang, Linxiu; Luo, Renfu; Glauben, Thomas; Shi, Yaojiang et al. (2011): College Education and the Poor in China: Documenting the Hurdles to Educational Attainment and College Matriculation. In Asia Pacific Education Review 12 (4), pp. 533–546.

Wilson, Scott (2002): Face, Norms and Instrumentality. In Thomas Gold, Doug Guthrie, David L. Wank (Eds.): Social Networks in China. Institutions, Culture, and the Changing Nature of Guanxi. Cambridge, UK: Cambridge University Press (Structural analysis in the social sciences, 21), pp. 163–177.

Won, Jaeyoun (2004): Withering Away of the Iron Rice Bowl? The Reemployment Project of Post-Socialist China. In Studies in Comparative International Development 39 (2), pp. 71–93.

Worldbank (Ed.) (2015): Gross Domestic Product 2015. Available online at http://databank.worldbank.org/data/download/GDP.pdf, checked on 6/1/2017.

Woronov, T. E. (2016): Class Work. Vocational Schools and China's Urban Youth: Stanford University Press.

Woronov, T.E. (2011): Learning to Serve: Urban Youth, Vocational Schools and New Class Formations in China. In The China Journal (66), pp. 77–99.

Wu, Linfei (2012): China Releases Chinese Marriage Situation Survey Report 2011. Available online at http://www.womenofchina.cn/html/womenofchina/report/136873-1.htm, checked on 9/1/2016.

Wu, Weiping (1999): City Profile: Shanghai. In Cities 16 (3), pp. 207–216.

Xinhua News Agency (Ed.) (2007): Huge Investment to Further Improve Vocational Education. Available online at http://www.china.org.cn/english/education/197599.htm, updated on 5/21/2007, checked on 6/19/2015.

Xinhua News Agency (Ed.) (2015): China's Education Spending on the Rise. Available online at http://www.china.org.cn/china/2015-11/20/content_37120473.htm, checked on 4/21/2016.

Xu, Anqi (2017a): Gender Roles. In Anqi Xu, John D. DeFrain, Wenrong Liu (Eds.): The Chinese Family Today. London, New York: Routledge (Routledge contemporary China series, 158), pp. 169–209.

Xu, Anqi (2017c): The Establishment and Dissolution of Marriage. In Anqi Xu, John D. DeFrain, Wenrong Liu (Eds.): The Chinese Family Today. London, New York: Routledge (Routledge contemporary China series, 158), pp. 129–168.

Xu, Shuo (2003): Vom Buchwissen zur Handlungskompetenz. Ein Lernkonzept für die chinesische Berufsbildung am Beispiel der Zerspanungsfacharbeit. Aachen: Shaker (Berichte aus der Pädagogik).

Xu, Xiaozhou (徐小洲) (2009): Zhishi yu Jineng. Zhongguo Zhiye Jiaoyu 60 Nian (知识与技能。中国职业教育 60 年). Zhejiang: Zhejiang Daxue Chubanshe (浙江大学出版社).

Xu, Zhening (2017b): Child Care and Nurture. In Anqi Xu, John D. DeFrain, Wenrong Liu (Eds.): The Chinese Family Today. London, New York: Routledge (Routledge contemporary China series, 158), pp. 96–128.

Yan, Hairong (2003): Neoliberal Governmentality and Neohumanism: Organizing Suzhi/Value Flow through Labor Recruitment Networks. In Cultural Anthropology 18 (4), pp. 493–523.

Yan, Yunxiang (2006): Little Emperors or Frail Pragmatists? China`s '80s Generation. In Current History (692), pp. 255–262.

Yan, Yunxiang (2009): The Individualization of Chinese Society. Engl. ed. Oxford: Berg (Monographs on social anthropology, 77).

Yan, Yunxiang (2010a): Introduction: Conflicting Images of the Individual and Contested Process of Individualization. In Mette Halskov Hansen, Rune Svarverud (Eds.): iChina. The Rise of the Individual in Modern Chinese Society. Copenhagen: NIAS (NIAS Studies in Asian Topics, 45), pp. 1–38.

Yan, Yunxiang (2010b): The Chinese Path to Individualization. In The British Journal of Sociology 61 (3), pp. 489–512. DOI: 10.1111/j.1468-4446.2010.01323.x.

Yan, Yunxiang (2011): The Changing Moral Landscapes. In Arthur Kleinman, Yunxiang Yan, Jing Jun, Sing Lee, Everett Zhang (Eds.): Deep China. The Moral Life of the Person. Berkeley: University of California Press, pp. 36–77.

Yang, Jin (1998): General or Vocational? The Tough Choice in the Chinese Education Policy. In International Journal of Educational Development (4), pp. 289–304.

Yang, Weili (杨伟利) (2013): "90 Hou" Qingshaonian Yanjiu Shiye Tanxi ("90 后"青少年研究视野探索). In Qingnian Tansuo (青年探索) (179), pp. 91–96.

Yi, Hongmei; Zhang, Linxiu; Liu, Chengfang; Chu, James; Loyalka, Prashant; Maani, May; Wei, Jianguo (2013): How are Secondary Vocational Schools in China Measuring up to Government Benchmarks? In China & World Economy (21), pp. 98–120.

Yuan, Jingwei (袁静伟) (2015): Pandian 1977 Nian Yilai Lici Gaokao Gaige: Shijian Tiqian Huozan (盘点 1977 年以来历次高考改革：时间提前获赞). Education News Weibo. Available online at http://edu.qq.com/a/20150607/001939.htm.

Yue, Ai; Marsh, Lauren; Zhou, Huan; Medina, Alexis; Luo, Renfu; Shi, Yaojiang et al. (2016): Nutritional Deficiencies, the Absence of Information and Caregiver Shortcomings. A Qualitative Analysis of Infant Feeding Practices in Rural China. In PLoS one 11 (4), e0153385. DOI: 10.1371/journal.pone.0153385.

Zhan, H. J.; Xiaotian Feng; Baozhen Luo (2008): Placing Elderly Parents in Institutions in Urban China: A Reinterpretation of Filial Piety. In Research on Aging 30 (5), pp. 543–571. DOI: 10.1177/0164027508319471.

Zhang, Li (2002): Urban Experiences and Social Belonging among Chinese Rural Migrants. In E. Perry Link, Richard Madsen, Paul Pickowicz (Eds.): Popular China. Unofficial Culture in a Globalizing Society. Lanham, Md: Rowman & Littlefield Publishers, pp. 275–299.

Zhang, Qingxia (张清峡); Wang, Sainan (王赛男); Wang, Peng (王鹏); Gao, Fengqiang (高峰强) (2007): Zhongzhuansheng Renge Tezheng, Chengjiu Mubiao Yu Xinli Jiankang Zhijian De SEM Yanjiu (中专生人格特征，成就目标与心理健康质检的 SEM 研究). In Qingnian Tansuo (青年探索) (1), pp. 77–80.

Zhang, Rongming (张榕明) (2013b): Zhiye Jiaoyu Gaige Xu Qianghua Si Zhong Yishi (职业教育改革需强化四种意识). Zhongguo Jiaoyu Bao (中国教育报). Available online at http://www.chinazy.org/models/adefault/news_detail.aspx?artid=49967&cateid=1471.

Zhang, Shuo (张烁) (2013a): Jiuyelv Guo 95% Renkedu Zou Di Zhongzhi Jiaoyu Weihe Bu Shou Daijian (就业率过 95%认可度低中职教育为何不受待建). Xinhua News Agency. Available online at http://news.xinhuanet.com/edu/2013-02/28/c_124396185.htm, updated on 2/28/2013, checked on 4/25/2014.

Zhou, Kai (周凯); Mao, Chen (卯琛) (2013): Diaocha: Chongqing Bufen Jiuye Hao De Zhongzhixiao Weihe Fanyu Zhaosheng Nan (调查：重庆部分就业好的中职校为何反遇招生难). Edited by Zhongguo Jiaoyu Xinwen Wang （中国教育新闻网）. Available online at http://www.jyb.cn/zyjy/zyjyxw/201312/t20131208_562694.html, updated on 12/8/2013, checked on 4/24/2014.

Zhou, Yuhang (周宇航) (2016): 2015 Nian Quanguo Jiaoyu Jingfei Zongtouru Da 3.6 Wanyi Yuan Zhan GDP De 4.26% (2015 年全国教育经费总投入达 3.6 万亿 占 GDP 的 4.26%). Edited by Sina Finance. Available online at http://finance.sina.com.cn/roll/2016-11-11/doc-ifxxsmuu5371125.shtml, checked on 4/21/2017.

12 Appendix

12.1 Student Interviewees Overview

Student interviewees				
Name (anonymized)	School	Sex	Hukou	Age at the time of interview(s)
Ai Wu	Fengxian	M	Shanghai	38
Bai Wei	Qingpu	M	Migrant	18, 19
Da Ming	Qingpu	M	Shanghai	16, 17
Da Wei	Qingpu	M	Shanghai	15, 16, 17
De Hua	Qingpu	M	Migrant	15, 16, 17
Han Feng	Qingpu	M	Shanghai	19, 21
Huang Gui	Fengxian	M	Migrant	15, 16, 17
Lei Qiang	Fengxian	M	Shanghai	16, 18, 19
Li An	Fengxian	F	Migrant	18, 19, 20
Li Miao	Qingpu	F	Migrant	18
Li Qing	Qingpu	M	Migrant	20, 21, 22
Li Tao	Fengxian	F	Shanghai	16, 17, 18
Ming Ming	Fengxian	F	Shanghai	20
Qian Qin	Qingpu	M	Migrant	16, 17, 18
Shuang Shuang	Qingpu	F	Migrant	21
Wang Ming	Fengxian	M	Migrant	18, 19, 20
Wang Yuan	Qingpu	M	Shanghai	20
Wen Qing	Fengxian	F	Migrant	16, 17, 18
Xue Mei	Qingpu	F	Migrant	19
Zhang Hua	Fengxian	F	Migrant	21, 22
Zhao Jing	Fengxian	M	Migrant	16, 17, 18

12.2 Teacher/Tutor Interviewees Overview

Teacher/Tutor interviewees		
Name (anonymized)	Position	Sex
Guo Yanbo	Qingpu School teacher	M
Lin Keping	Fengxian School teacher	M
Xu Yingke	Company tutor	F
Zeng Weina	Company tutor	F
Zhang Yuzhou	Qingpu School teacher	M
Zheng Lina	Fengxian School teacher	F